# MENTORING LANGUAGES TEACHERS IN THE SECONDARY SCHOOL

*Mentoring Languages Teachers in the Secondary School* helps mentors of beginning languages teachers in both developing their own mentoring skills and providing the essential guidance beginning teachers need as they navigate the roller-coaster of the first years of teaching. Offering tried and tested strategies based on the best research and evidence, it covers the knowledge, skills and understanding every mentor needs and offers practical tools such as lesson plans, feedback guides, observation sheets and examples of dialogue with beginning languages teachers.

Research suggests that the role of the mentor is highly influential to the beginning teacher, and this book considers language-specific aspects as well as a focus on the holistic well-being of the beginning teacher. Together with analytical tools for self-evaluation, this book is a vital source of support and inspiration for all those involved in developing the next generation of outstanding languages teachers. Key topics explained include the following:

- Roles and responsibilities of mentors
- The subject knowledge and understanding required by beginning languages teachers
- The lesson planning process
- Guidance on teaching core skills of reading, writing, speaking and listening
- Development opportunities for languages teachers
- Observations and pre- and post-lesson discussions

Filled with the key tools needed for the mentor's individual development, this new text offers an accessible guide to mentoring languages teachers with ready-to-use strategies that support, inspire and elevate both mentors and beginning teachers alike.

**Laura Molway** is a Senior Lecturer at the University of Oxford Department of Education, specialising in second language teacher education.

**Anna Lise Gordon** was a Modern Languages Postgraduate Certificate of Education (PGCE) tutor, before taking on wider leadership and research roles at St Mary's University, Twickenham.

# MENTORING TRAINEE AND EARLY CAREER TEACHERS

Series edited by: Susan Capel, Julia Lawrence and Sarah Younie

The **Mentoring Trainee and Early Career Teachers** Series are subject (or age)-specific, practical books designed to reinforce and develop mentors' understanding of the different aspects of their role, as well as exploring issues that mentees encounter in the course of learning to teach. The books have two main foci: first, challenging mentors to reflect critically on theory, research and evidence, on their own knowledge, their approaches to mentoring and how they work with beginning teachers in order to move their practice forward; and second, supporting mentors to effectively facilitate the development of beginning teachers. Although the basic structure of all the books is similar, each book is different to reflect the needs of mentors in relation to the unique nature of each subject or age phase. Elements of appropriate theory, research and/or evidence introduce each topic or issue, with emphasis placed on the practical application of material. The chapter authors in each book have been engaged with mentoring over a long period of time and share research, evidence and their experience.

We hope that this series of books supports you in developing into an effective, reflective mentor as you support the development of the next generation of teachers.

For more information about this series, please visit: https://www.routledge.com/Mentoring-Trainee-and-Early-Career-Teachers/book-series/MTECT

## Titles in the series

*Mentoring Religious Education Teachers in the Secondary School: A Practical Guide*
Edited by Helen Sheehan

*Mentoring History Teachers in the Secondary School*
Terry Haydn, Victoria Crooks and Laura London

*Mentoring Mathematics Teachers in the Secondary School: A Practical Guide*
Edited by Rosa Archer, Sian Morgan, David Swanson, Claire Clemmet and Stef Sullivan

*Mentoring Languages Teachers in the Secondary School: A Practical Guide*
Edited by Laura Molway and Anna Lise Gordon

# MENTORING LANGUAGES TEACHERS IN THE SECONDARY SCHOOL

A Practical Guide

Edited by Laura Molway and
Anna Lise Gordon

LONDON AND NEW YORK

Designed cover image: © Getty Images

First edition published 2025
by Routledge
4 Park Square, Milton Park, Abingdon, Oxon, OX14 4RN

and by Routledge
605 Third Avenue, New York, NY 10158

*Routledge is an imprint of the Taylor & Francis Group, an informa business*

© 2025 selection and editorial matter, Laura Molway and Anna Lise Gordon; individual chapters, the contributors

The right of Laura Molway and Anna Lise Gordon to be identified as the authors of the editorial material, and of the authors for their individual chapters, has been asserted in accordance with sections 77 and 78 of the Copyright, Designs and Patents Act 1988.

All rights reserved. No part of this book may be reprinted or reproduced or utilised in any form or by any electronic, mechanical, or other means, now known or hereafter invented, including photocopying and recording, or in any information storage or retrieval system, without permission in writing from the publishers.

*Trademark notice*: Product or corporate names may be trademarks or registered trademarks, and are used only for identification and explanation without intent to infringe.

*British Library Cataloguing-in-Publication Data*
A catalogue record for this book is available from the British Library

ISBN: 978-1-032-80106-3 (hbk)
ISBN: 978-1-032-80103-2 (pbk)
ISBN: 978-1-003-49546-8 (ebk)

DOI: 10.4324/9781003495468

Typeset in Interstate
by KnowledgeWorks Global Ltd.

# CONTENTS

Contributors — viii
Acknowledgements — xii
An introduction to the series: mentoring trainee and early career teachers — xiii

**SECTION 1**
**Introduction to mentoring** — 1

    **Introduction** — 3
    Laura Molway and Anna Lise Gordon

1  **Models of mentoring** — 6
    Laura Molway and Anna Lise Gordon

2  **Understanding yourself and how your experiences influence your approach to mentoring** — 17
    Gillian Peiser

3  **What makes a good mentor in modern languages? How to help beginning teachers flourish** — 29
    Trevor Mutton and Robert Woore

**SECTION 2**
**Getting started as a mentor** — 43

4  **Setting your mentee up for success** — 45
    Kirsten Gregory

5  **Supporting emerging languages teachers: key principles to guide the journey** — 53
    Judith Rifeser, Bernadette Holmes, and Caroline Conlon

6 Supporting the integration of beginning languages teachers into the community of practice  64
*Crista Hazell*

## SECTION 3
## Developing beginning languages teachers' pedagogical knowledge, skills, and understanding  75

7 Supporting beginning languages teachers to analyse teaching that they observe  77
*Sandra Cohen*

8 Supporting the lesson planning process of beginning languages teachers  87
*Sophie Vauzour*

9 Helping beginning language teachers to analyse their own planning and teaching  101
*Trevor Mutton*

10 Observing your mentee's teaching and giving written feedback  114
*Francesca Knight*

11 Holding pre- and post-lesson discussions with beginning languages teachers  125
*Laura Dixon, Lynda Hamilton, and Lisa Madden*

12 Accelerating mentorship: coaching insights for empowering mentor meetings  137
*Candida Javaid*

## SECTION 4
## Providing effective support for beginning languages teachers' well-being  153

13 Managing well-being and workload with beginning languages teachers  155
*Juliette Claro and Anna Lise Gordon*

14 Supporting a beginning languages teacher who is struggling: a range of scenarios  167
*Kathryn Broom, Juliette Claro, Adam Lamb, Lisa Panford, Sallie Roberts-Crystal, and Maud Waret*

## SECTION 5
## Supporting languages teachers as they progress through later stages of their training and beyond  — 179

15  Engaging with and in research for classroom practice supporting the beginning languages teacher — 181
   *Suzanne Graham*

16  Developing the wider professional role of the beginning languages teacher — 196
   *Rob Bown*

17  Continuing to mentor beginning languages teachers beyond their initial teacher training — 208
   *Elizabeth Cundick, Anselm Fisher, and Emily Thornton*

18  Supporting expert languages teachers: educative mentoring for success — 225
   *Bernadette Holmes, Judith Rifeser, and Caroline Conlon*

*Appendix 1: Modern languages lesson observation schedules* — 239
*Appendix 2: Proforma structure for interactions* — 249
*Appendix 3: Possible responses to scenarios in Task 17.5* — 251
*Index* — 252

# CONTRIBUTORS

**Rob Bown** is Senior Lead for trainees and Early Career Teachers (ECTs) at Cheney School in Oxford. He oversees the mentoring of trainee and beginning teachers and leads the Personal, Social and Health Education (PSHE) curriculum. Rob teaches Spanish and German to pupils aged 11-18 and has been teaching in secondary schools for over 20 years.

**Kathryn Broom** is the course leader of the Modern Foreign Languages (MFL) Postgraduate Certificate of Education (PGCE) at the University of Southampton where she also leads mentor training and development across the secondary ITE programme.

**Juliette Claro** is Lecturer in Education at St Mary's University for the PGCE in MFL, where she supports the development of international trainee teachers. Juliette teaches French, Spanish and German to pupils aged 11-18 and has over 20 years' experience as a teacher in secondary education and 10 years as a school leader.

**Sandra Cohen** is Head of German at Didcot Girls' School, where she regularly mentors beginning languages teachers. Sandra teaches German, French and Spanish to pupils aged 11-18 and has seven years of experience of teaching in secondary schools.

**Caroline Conlon** is Honorary Associate Professor (Languages Education) at University College London Institute of Education (UCL IOE). After teaching in London schools, Caroline worked for CILT, the National Centre for Languages. She joined the PGCE team at UCL IOE in 2011, where she led the Languages PGCE for six years. She was a founding member of UCL IOE's National Consortium for Languages Education (NCLE).

**Elizabeth Cundick** is part of the Teach First team at Bath Spa University. Before this, she taught French, German and Spanish for over 30 years in various schools around the Bristol area and was Head of Languages in a secondary school in Bath and Northeast Somerset.

**Laura Dixon** is the Assistant Headteacher for Post 16 at Batley Girls' High School having had great success as Head of Department and Head of Faculty in varied settings across Yorkshire. She has enjoyed mentoring beginning teachers throughout her 12-year teaching career. Laura teaches Spanish and French to pupils aged 11-18 in KS3, 4 and 5.

**Anselm Fisher** is currently a Teaching Fellow on Bath Spa University's School-centred Initial Teacher Training (SCITT) PGCE and a Senior Fellow of the Higher Education Academy. He has a background in secondary Modern Languages teaching and Initial Teacher Education (ITE) course leadership, including a range of PGCEs and the Teach First Postgraduate Diploma in Education (PGDE). He has served as a Senior Lecturer at several higher education institutions in England and is deeply committed to lifelong learning. In addition to leading mentor development in Primary and Secondary schools, Anselm has also designed and taught Education Studies and Education Leadership degrees, from Foundation through to Masters level.

**Anna Lise Gordon** is Head of the School of Education at St Mary's University, Twickenham and Co-Director of the Centre for Wellbeing in Education, where her focus is on all aspects of teacher recruitment, retention and well-being. Previously, she taught French and German in London and Surrey before becoming a Modern Languages PGCE tutor. Anna Lise was President of the Association for Language Learning (ALL) from 2016 to 2018 and continues to serve as a trustee.

**Suzanne Graham** is Professor of Language and Education at the University of Reading. She led the University's PGCE MFL course from 2003 to 2023 and still teaches on it. She has researched and published widely on teacher development and the role of research in that process. Her latest research examines the impact of digital professional development on language teacher motivation.

**Kirsten Gregory** is Head of Languages at The Bicester School in Oxfordshire where she has been mentoring beginning languages teachers for more than ten years. Kirsten teaches French and Spanish to pupils aged 11-18 years and she also teaches on the Modern Languages PGCE course at the University of Oxford.

**Lynda Hamilton** has ten years' experience working as a languages teacher in Leeds where she gained vast experience of mentoring beginning languages teachers and other teaching colleagues. Lynda is qualified in instructional coaching and firmly believes that good quality mentoring is essential to support new entrants to the teaching profession.

**Crista Hazell** is Development Manager for the ALL in England. She has more than 20 years' experience at classroom, middle and senior leadership level across a number of schools and a particular passion for Modern Languages.

**Bernadette Holmes**, Member of the British Empire (MBE), is a distinguished linguist and languages expert, recognised for her contributions to language education and diversity. A passionate advocate for languages for all, she has worked extensively in promoting multilingualism and cultural understanding. She is currently Director of the NCLE and Honorary Professor at UCL IOE.

**Candida Javaid** is an independent coach, a member of the International Coaching Federation (ICF) and a former senior leader with over 20 years of experience in education across the United Kingdom and Germany. She supports teachers and educational leaders to build clarity and confidence through coaching. Candida holds two MAs and an advanced diploma in integrative coaching and teaches coaching skills to adult learners.

**Francesca Knight** is the lead curriculum tutor for the secondary PGCE in languages, as well as being the subject lead for primary languages at the University of Sussex. In both roles, she works closely with beginning languages teachers. Francesca has taught in both primary and secondary settings around East Sussex and Brighton and Hove and has 15 years of teaching experience.

**Adam Lamb** is Director of MFL at United Learning. Previously, Adam has overseen a Languages at Mossbourne Community Academy in Hackney, London. Adam also has been Lead Practitioner, during which time he looked after on-site Initial Teacher Training (ITT) provision and worked closely with a number of ITT providers. Adam has also mentored numerous newly qualified Teachers (NQTs) and ECTs during his career.

**Lisa Madden** is PGCE course tutor for MFL at Leeds Trinity University. After teaching French, German and Spanish for 18 years and having curriculum responsibility for languages in a range of schools, she wanted to pass on the skills she has developed and encourage others to become teachers of ML. She loves being able to research and share good practice in teaching with colleagues, beginning teachers and host teachers/mentors.

**Laura Molway** has a background in teaching French and German at Secondary School level. She is currently a Senior Lecturer at the University of Oxford Department of Education, where she specialises in second language teacher education.

**Trevor Mutton** is a Professor of Teacher Education at the University of Oxford. He led the PGCE modern languages programme for a number of years and was PGCE course director from 2009 to 2017. His research focuses on teachers' professional learning as well as wider aspects of teacher education policy. He is Deputy Editor of *Journal of Education for Teaching*.

**Lisa Panford** is Associate Professor and the Course Lead of PGCE Secondary Languages at St Mary's University, Twickenham. She is a former lead practitioner with over 14 years' experience of teaching languages in London secondary schools. Lisa is the founder and co-chair of the Decolonising Secondary Languages Special Interest Group of the ALL.

**Gillian Peiser** is the Modern Languages Co-ordinator for PGCE pupils at Liverpool John Moores University, working in partnership with mentors who support student teachers on placement. Prior to this, she worked for 11 years as a languages teacher and Head of Department in secondary schools. Gillian has carried out research on mentoring and the cultural dimension in languages education.

**Judith Rifeser**, formerly a teacher and teacher trainer, is now Associate Professor in Education at UCL IOE, Faculty of Education and Society. She is the Director of Strategic Learning Futures at the NCLE. Judith is the current president of the ALL.

**Sallie Roberts-Crystal** is a PGCE tutor at Goldsmiths University London. She also worked closely with UCL to develop her mentor skills and became an interim PGCE tutor there in 2023. At Norbury Manor High School, Croydon, she was Head of the Languages Faculty and PCM until 2022. Sallie taught MFL for over 30 years and mentored many student teachers and ECTs.

**Emily Thornton** currently teaches on ITT programmes at Bath Spa University. She taught French and German for 15 years to 11- to 18-year-olds in a variety of roles across the United Kingdom and abroad and has always really enjoyed mentoring beginning teachers towards QTS and in their ECT years.

**Sophie Vauzour** is a language-specialist teacher educator who leads the Secondary Modern Languages PGCE course at the University of East Anglia. Through her university teaching, the supervision of teaching practice and her role in mentoring development in partnership schools, she aims to support beginning teachers to develop their skills so they can inspire the next generation of linguists.

**Maud Waret** is a French citizen of mixed heritage living in the United Kingdom. A feminist and environmentalist, she believes in the right to education for all children. She teaches

Foreign Languages and Humanities in North London and works as a Senior Curriculum Developer at the NCLE, focusing on decolonising the curriculum and promoting diverse cultural identities.

**Robert Woore** is Associate Professor in Applied Linguistics at the University of Oxford Department of Education. Formerly a secondary school teacher of French and German, his research interests include the learning and teaching of second languages in instructed classroom settings, with a particular focus on reading. He has undertaken various projects aiming to strengthen links between research and classroom practice.

# ACKNOWLEDGEMENTS

The editors would like to express their sincere gratitude to the Association for Language Learning (ALL), which provides a network and hub for languages teachers to connect with and learn from each other. Thanks to the ALL through which we have been able to reach out to so many languages teachers and language teacher educators, who have contributed their time and expertise to this book.

# AN INTRODUCTION TO THE SERIES: MENTORING TRAINEE AND EARLY CAREER TEACHERS

Mentoring is a very important and exciting role. What could be better than supporting the development of the next generation of subject teachers? A mentor is almost certainly an effective teacher, but this doesn't automatically guarantee that he or she will be a good mentor, despite similarities in the two roles. This series of practical workbooks covers mentoring a range of subjects in the secondary curriculum and mentoring in primary schools. They are designed specifically to reinforce mentors' understanding of different aspects of their role, for mentors to learn about and reflect on their role, to provide support for mentors in aspects of their development and enable them to analyse their success in supporting the development of beginning teachers (defined as trainee, newly qualified and beginning teachers). This book has two main foci: first, the focus is on challenging mentors to reflect critically on theory, research, evidence, on their own knowledge, how they work with beginning teachers, how they work with more experienced teachers and on their approaches to mentoring in order to move their practice forward. Second, the focus is on supporting mentors to effectively facilitate the development of beginning teachers. Thus, some of the practical activities in the books are designed to encourage reflection, whilst others ask mentors to undertake activities with beginning teachers.

This book can be used alongside generic and subject books designed for student and newly qualified teachers (NQTs). These books include *Learning to Teach in the Secondary School: A Companion to School Experience*, 9th edition (Capel, Leask, Younie, Hidson and Lawrence, 2022) which deals with aspects of teaching and learning applicable to all subjects. Further, the generic books are complemented by two series: *Learning to Teach (subject) in the Secondary School: A Companion to School Experience* and *A Practical Guide to Teaching (subject) in the Secondary School*, as well as *Learning to Teach in the Primary School*. These books are designed for student teachers on different types of initial teacher education programmes (and indeed a beginning teacher you are working with may have used/currently be using them). However, these books are proving equally useful to tutors and mentors in their work with student teachers, both in relation to the knowledge, skills and understanding the student teacher is developing and some tasks which mentors might find useful to support a beginning teacher to do.

It is also supported by a book designed for NQTs, *Surviving and Thriving in the Secondary School: The NQT's Essential Companion* (Capel, Lawrence, Leask and Younie, 2019). These titles cover material not generally needed by student teachers on an initial teacher education course but which is needed by NQTs in their school work and early career.

The information in this book should link with the information in the generic text and relevant subject book in the series or book for primary student teachers in a number of ways. For example, mentors might want to refer a beginning teacher to read about specific knowledge, understanding and skills they are focusing on developing, or to undertake tasks in the book, either alone or with their support, then discus the tasks. It is recommended that you have copies of these books available so that you can cross-reference when needed.

In turn, the books complement a range of resources on which mentors can draw (including other mentors of beginning teachers in the same or other subjects or age phase, other teachers and a range of other resources including books, research articles and websites).

The positive feedback on *Learning to Teach* and the related books above, particularly the way they have supported the learning of student teachers in their development into effective, reflective teachers, encouraged us to retain the main features of that book in this series. Like teaching, mentoring should be informed by theory, research and evidence. Thus, this series of books introduce theoretical, research and evidence-based advice and guidance to support mentors as they develop their mentoring to support beginning teachers' development. The main focus is the practical application of material. Elements of appropriate theory, research and/or evidence introduce each topic or issue, and recent research into mentoring and/or teaching and learning is integral to the presentation. Tasks are provided to help mentors identify key features of the topic or issue and reflect on and/or apply them to their own practice as they mentor beginning teachers. Although the basic structure of all the books is similar, each book is different to reflect the needs of mentors in relation to the unique nature of each subject.

The chapter authors in the books have been engaged with mentoring over a long period of time and are aiming to share theory, research, evidence and their experience. We, as series editors, are pleased to extend the work in initial teacher education to the work of mentors of beginning teachers. We hope that this series of books supports you in developing into an effective, reflective mentor as you support the development of the next generation of subject teachers.

Susan Capel, Julia Lawrence and Sarah Younie,<br>December 2024

# SECTION 1
# Introduction to mentoring

# Introduction

*Laura Molway and Anna Lise Gordon*

## Languages teachers: the case for a subject-specific volume on mentoring

As you are reading this volume, we expect that you are either about to be, or already, involved in some way in the endeavour of supporting a languages teacher to develop their practice. We hope that the chapters of this book will offer you some food for thought and some practical advice about mentoring practices, their underpinning aims and philosophies, and what is known about their impact on teacher learning. The book is written by both school-based and university-based teacher educators in England, and most examples are taken from this context. However, we hope that the information and advice in this volume will be of value to any language teaching colleague who is tasked with supporting another languages teacher in their professional learning, whatever their context might be.

We have chosen to focus this book specifically on the mentoring of languages teachers for several reasons. Research suggests that teacher learning is most effective when it is directly focussed on enriching teachers' subject-specific content knowledge and pedagogical knowledge, or when it contextualises generic pedagogic strategies within a specific subject classroom (Cordingley et al., 2018). This is likely due to domain-specific differences in the nature of teaching. For example, in a language lesson, it is possible to introduce pupils to the vocabulary and structures of the target language using the target language itself as the medium of instruction, whilst in other disciplines the subject content (e.g. the concept of "evidence" in history) and the medium (e.g. in England, English) are usually clearly distinct. Teachers of a second or foreign language[1] (L2) are faced with decisions regarding when and how to communicate with their pupils in the L2 and/or their pupils' first language (L1). A decision to use the L2 requires considerable skill in manipulating the language forms to maximise opportunities for pupils to practise their TL listening skills, whilst ensuring pupils' comprehension and the efficient use of lesson time (Macaro, 2005).

We are also mindful that languages teachers are a distinct population within the school workforce in England: a significant minority of languages teachers may have themselves been educated within different national education systems (Block, 2002). Even "homegrown" languages teachers are likely to have lived and worked abroad in the process of developing their own language proficiency and, as a result, they typically enter Initial Teacher Education (ITE) programmes with rich and diverse experience of other education contexts that they are able to draw on in the process of becoming a teacher. This means that mentors of languages teachers need to be particularly mindful of the likely diversity of prior experiences and current learning needs that their mentee may bring with them.

## Languages teaching and the big challenges in mentoring beginning languages teachers

Beginning languages teachers in England face challenges in teaching a subject for which there is very little timetabled time within a crowded curriculum, and in which pupils have historically appeared to display consistently low achievement and motivation (British Academy, 2019). Most would agree that the essential function of a language is to communicate, and therefore that teachers should support their pupils to use their language as a communicative tool. However, the predominant model of language teaching in this country has been a "weak" version of communicative language teaching where key features of a language (e.g. vocabulary and grammar) are isolated, practiced and assessed within discrete topics, but pupils are rarely given opportunities to try to communicate ideas that are meaningful to them, making use of the language they have learned in communicative tasks (Woore et al., 2021).

There are several contested methodologies for language teaching, each of which have their proponents and their detractors in the language acquisition research and teaching field. For example, there is not currently any generally accepted consensus amongst teachers and researchers on key aspects of language teaching such as: the role that explicit grammar teaching should play in the classroom; the role of "chunks" in the learning process; the extent to which teachers should use the pupils' first language as a teaching tool; the value of authentic resources; or the prominence that should be given to the development of intercultural understanding (Molway, 2022).

It is within this context that mentors need to support beginning teachers to experiment with and make sense of contested ideas about what works best in language teaching, developing personal, practical, and research-informed theories to underpin their practice within a specific school context.

In this volume, we take the position that teaching is a complex endeavour that requires the development and continual updating of a range of professional skills, subject content, and pedagogical knowledge. Teachers need to be supported to draw on multiple strands of evidence and engage in *clinical reasoning*, which has been defined as "the analytical and intuitive cognitive processes that professionals use to arrive at a best judged ethical response in a specific practice-based context" (Kriewaldt & Turnidge, 2013, p. 106). As is explored in Chapter 1, the role of the languages mentor requires highly developed professional knowledge and skills both in language teaching and language teacher education.

Research suggests that the role of the mentor is highly influential to the beginning teacher, and this book considers language-specific aspects as well as a focus on the holistic well-being of the beginning teacher (Gordon, 2020, 2023). Section 1 (Chapters 1-3) provides an introduction to mentoring, prompting you to reflect on models of mentoring and your skills and experiences as a mentor to date. The importance of a good start in the mentor/beginning teacher relationship is the focus for Section 2 (Chapters 4-6), as you seek to integrate the new colleague into your department, school, and the wider languages community. In Section 3 (Chapters 7-12), attention focuses on language-specific pedagogy, particularly in the way a mentor supports the development of the beginning teacher with planning as well as effective feedback on their teaching. The shorter Section 4 (Chapters 13 and 14) highlights the importance of a supportive mentor for the well-being of the beginning teacher as they adjust to a new and sometimes challenging career. Section 5 (Chapters 15-18) considers the professional growth of beginning teachers of languages, including ways to make effective use of research, professional networks, and ongoing mentoring to inform development and practice.

## How to use this book

The following chapters have been designed to be used as a research-informed practical workbook. Each chapter includes reflective tasks for you to complete and signposts you to useful further reading. You can work through them in order, or you can use the book as a "just-in-time" reference guide, making use of the title headings and/or index to find issues that are currently of relevance to your practice.

## Note

1. We use "second language" or "L2" loosely in this volume to denote the learning of an additional language. We acknowledge that for multilingual learners, the language that is the object of study may be the third, fourth or nth language in which they are developing some linguistic skill.

## References

Block, D. (2002). Communicative language teaching revisited: Discourses in conflict and foreign national teachers. *The Language Learning Journal*, 26(1), 19-26.

Cordingley, P., Greany, T., Crisp, B., Seleznyov, S., Bradbury, M., & Perry, T. (2018). *Developing great subject teaching: Rapid evidence review of subject-specific continuing professional development in the UK*. Available at https://wellcome.org/sites/default/files/developing-great-subject-teaching.pdf

Gordon, A. L. (2020). Educate - Mentor - Nurture: Improving the transition from initial teacher training to qualified teacher status and beyond. *Journal of Education for Teachers*, 46(5), 664-675.

Gordon, A. L. (2023). Early career teaching and resilience. In R. J. Tierney, F. Rizvi, & K. Erikan (Eds.), *International encyclopedia of education* (vol. 5, pp. 153-160). Elsevier.

Kriewaldt, J., & Turnidge, D. (2013). Conceptualising an approach to clinical reasoning in the education profession. *Australian Journal of Teacher Education*, 38(6), 103-115.

Macaro, E. (2005). Codeswitching in the L2 classroom: A communication and learning strategy. In E. Llurda (Ed.), *Non-native language teachers. Perceptions, challenges and contributions to the profession*. Springer.

Molway, L. (2022). Which aspects of their practice do modern languages teachers in England's secondary schools say they want to develop? *The Language Learning Journal*, 50(5), 627-649. https://doi.org/10.1080/09571736.2020.1862897

The British Academy with the Academy of Medical Sciences, Royal Academy of Engineering and The Royal Society. (2019). Languages in the UK: a call for action. https://www.thebritishacademy.ac.uk/publications/languages-uk-academies-statement/.

Woore, R., Molway, L., & Macaro, E. (2021). Keeping sight of the big picture: A critical response to Ofsted's 2021 curriculum research review for languages. *The Language Learning Journal*, 50(2), 146-155.

# 1 Models of mentoring

*Laura Molway and Anna Lise Gordon*

## Introduction

There are many different conceptions of what it means to be a mentor, and this chapter aims to explore a range of these along with their underlying assumptions about the nature of teaching and learning. At the end of this chapter, you should be able to:

- Understand what is meant by the term 'mentor' within the field of education
- Have an awareness of the range of different models of practice associated with mentoring and coaching teachers at different stages of teacher development
- Understand the current rights and responsibilities of a mentor in England
- Articulate and defend your own personal goals for the development of mentoring practices to support beginning languages teachers

## What is a mentor?

Before reading further, consider Task 1.1.

---

### Task 1.1 Reflect on your own understanding and experience of mentoring

- How would you define the role of a mentor?
- What are your own experiences of mentoring in your teaching career so far?
- How do your definition of mentor and your personal experiences inform your practice as a mentor?
- Are there any other factors (personal or context-based) that influence your practice as a mentor?

---

The terms 'mentoring' and 'coaching' are often used interchangeably in the literature focussed on supporting teachers' professional learning. Rather than focussing on contested definitions, this chapter will focus on the underlying purposes that drive the work of a mentor (or coach), the nature of the mentoring relationship, and the practices that are subsequently undertaken in the mentoring role.

## Underlying purposes for mentoring and the associated roles of mentors

Why do we mentor beginning teachers? Kemmis et al. (2014) identify three distinct purposes for mentoring: support, supervision, and collaborative self-development, each of which is explored below:

## Support

One obvious purpose of mentoring is to help beginning teachers to learn how to be effective classroom practitioners. However, is there consensus amongst mentors about what counts as 'effective'? For example, some might define effective teaching as teaching that has a positive impact on pupil attainment. Others would want to include broader indicators such as teaching that supports pupils' well-being and sense of inclusion. Within our subject area, effective language teacher mentoring might depend on the specific aims, possibilities, and constraints that characterise the language programme within which a beginning teacher is working. For example, a language teacher in an immersion context may need to adopt different teaching strategies to one who is teaching in a mainstream classroom in England, where the time allocated to languages is more limited and the high-stakes examination system exerts a strong washback effect on the languages curriculum. It is also important to acknowledge that there are key issues in the teaching of languages that are subject to ongoing debate (for example, how best to teach grammar, or what the ideal balance might be between the use of the pupils' first language and the target language within the classroom (see Molway, 2021). In these instances, mentors need to support beginning languages teachers to explore the available evidence and reflect on the efficacy of their own teaching practices in relation to the desired pupil outcomes in a given context.

Another aspect of 'support' within mentoring relates to beginning teacher well-being: mentors often fulfil a pastoral role, providing emotional support, shielding their mentee from excessive workload, listening to their concerns, and helping them to find coping strategies to maintain a healthy work-life balance (Hobson et al., 2009). This crucial aspect of mentor support is understood to improve the likelihood of teachers remaining within the profession in the longer term, something that is a current concern worldwide (Gordon, 2020).

## Collaborative self-development

Mentoring may be broadly seen as part of career-long professional development (Lofthouse, 2018), of benefit to both the mentor and mentee. This involves the mentor working together with the mentee to identify aspects of teaching practice as targets for development. Both the mentor and mentee then adopt an inquiry-oriented, evidence-informed approach to exploring the impact of different teaching approaches, engaging in open, reflective learning conversations where the mentee is encouraged to articulate their own ideas and observations and where they are given space to develop their own theories and philosophies of teaching. This collaborative approach also features in models of 'facilitative' mentoring (Knight, 2017) and 'educative mentoring' (Trevethan, 2017). Each of these models align with a commitment to the process that McIntyre (1993, p. 375) termed 'practical theorising', which involves testing the 'feasibility, effectiveness-in-context and general practicality of ideas' through a process of classroom experimentation, discussion and observation of other teachers' practice (Task 1.2). There are clear benefits for both the mentor and mentee from the process of co-learning and co-inquiry (see Gallo-Fox & Scantlebury, 2016).

---

**Task 1.2 Considering 'Practical Theorising' within a collaborative model of mentoring**

Consider an instance of 'practical theorising' with a beginning languages teacher or a colleague.

- How did you select the issue that you were exploring together?
- Why was this important in the learning journey?
- How did you gather evidence of the impact of the teaching strategies with which you and your co-learner were experimenting?
- What role did you play in the discussion? You may like to revisit this question once you have read the next part of the chapter.

How did the discussion inform subsequent practice?

---

## Supervision

In some models of mentoring, particularly in initial teacher education (ITE), the mentor has a role to play in assessing the development of the beginning teacher and reporting judgements on the mentee's competence to a third party (i.e. to the ITE provider or to senior colleagues within the school). Where this is the case, tensions frequently arise between the competing aims of 'support' and 'supervision' in the mentor's work, which can make it challenging to maintain a sense of mentoring discussions as safe spaces within which the beginning teacher can take risks and explore the problems of practice that they are encountering.

Curtis et al. (2024) conducted a study exploring mentor's and beginning teachers' perceptions of the mentor's role and found clear evidence of a mismatch between the roles identified by the two. Beginning teachers identified four key roles that they felt their mentor fulfilled, which can be summarised as 'expert', 'gatekeeper', 'neighbour', and 'parent'. You may notice that these roles relate to the categories of 'support' and 'supervision' explored in the section above. Mentors, on the other hand, identified just two key roles for themselves: 'expert' and 'learning partner'. It is of note that mentors sometimes saw themselves as partners in the learning process but that mentees did not see their mentors in this way (see Figure 1.1). Curtis et al. (2024) argue that this is problematic as it suggests that mentees feel a strong sense of hierarchy in the relationship that may constrain their own sense of agency to contribute their

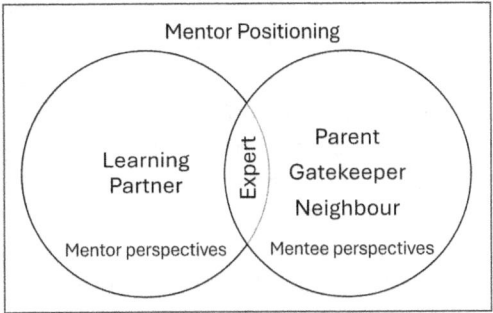

*Figure 1.1* Mentor positioning from the perspectives of mentors and mentees. (Adapted from Curtis et al., 2024, p.1339.)

ideas when engaging in collaborative learning activities with their mentor. They suggest that mentors who wish to engage in collaborative self-development may need to actively and repeatedly reject the automatic positioning of themselves as 'expert' during conversations with their mentee, thus creating space for an interrogation and reflection with their mentee of their own thoughts and values. This may help to avoid mentees falling into a pattern of unquestioningly replicating the teaching practices of their mentor, frustrating opportunities for deeper learning for both parties. Task 1.3 may help you to consider your own positioning as a mentor and whether this positioning creates optimal conditions for learning.

> **Task 1.3 Your different roles**
>
> Reflect on your most recent experience of mentoring a beginning languages teacher. Were you more of an expert, a neighbour, a gatekeeper, a learning partner, or a parent? Did you claim these roles actively or were you positioned in these roles by your mentee? Did your role change at different times? If yes, why?

## Instructional coaching as an influential model of mentoring

One issue in the mentoring of beginning teachers is that experienced teachers often find it difficult to explain to beginning teachers *how* and *why* they are doing things in the classroom. Over time, teachers' knowledge and skills become automatised to the point that the teacher may engage in behaviours in the classroom that they are not consciously directing. McIntyre and Hagger (1993) identify the difficulty of providing student teachers with access to this 'craft knowledge' and suggest that mentoring practices such as collaborative planning and teaching may provide ways to explore this. One popular model of mentoring with the potential to break down automatised teacher behaviours in a helpful way for beginning teachers is known as instructional coaching (IC) (Knight, 2017). IC centres on deliberate, repeated practice of recommended teaching behaviours via an observation, feedback, and practice cycle under the guidance of an expert mentor. Knight and van Nieuwerburgh (2012) assert that 'what distinguishes this model from other approaches is that instructional coaches teach others how to learn very specific, evidence-based teaching practices such as formative assessment' (p. 103). The IC approach to teacher development has been rigorously researched and has shown consistently positive correlations with pupil attainment (see Sims & Fletcher-Wood, 2021 for a discussion of this evidence). The current curriculum for beginning teachers in England (known as the 'ITTECF', DfE, 2024b) endorses an IC model of mentoring in the way that it offers a series of 188 statements specifying the knowledge and the skills that beginning teachers should learn, as a minimum entitlement during the first three years of teaching. Beginning teachers are informed that they 'should expect multiple opportunities to rehearse and refine particular approaches' and that they should receive 'structured feedback from expert colleagues' as they deconstruct 'what makes a particular approach successful or unsuccessful' (DfE, 2024b, p. 5).

Knight (2017) explains that IC can be implemented in various different ways, which can be mapped along a spectrum from more 'directive' to more 'facilitative'. In directive models, the mentor selects and sets out the key teaching behaviours that are to be practised and reviewed. In more facilitative models, the mentor and mentee co-design every aspect of the process, from the choice of teaching strategies to focus on, to the ways in which the success of those strategies will be evaluated. Mentors may make use of more directive and facilitative approaches at different stages of their mentee's development, but it is generally agreed that over time, mentors should aim to make room for ever-increasing levels of autonomy and agency for the mentee to take control of their professional learning (for a fuller discussion of this see the principles for mentoring outlined by Mutton & Woore in Chapter 3 of this volume).

Although IC is generally understood to be an effective approach to supporting teacher learning, a potential risk to this approach is that it emphasises a technical mastery of teaching approaches, which may have the unintended effect of de-centralising important discussions around *why* these approaches are recommended (Daly et al., 2023, p. 8) and how teachers may select between competing priorities in a classroom and arrive at a 'best judged ethical response in a specific practice-based context' (Kriewaldt & Turnidge, 2013, p. 106) (Task 1.4).

### Task 1.4 Instructional coaching

Take a look at the selection of 'Learn How To' statements below, which have been taken from the ITTECF (DfE, 2024b). Select one and consider how you might support a beginning teacher to master the targeted teaching approach through an IC cycle of structured rehearsal, discussion and analysis, observation, and focused feedback.

What might a more directive approach to this look like? And a more facilitative one?

- Discussing and analysing with expert colleagues how to teach different forms of writing by modelling, planning, drafting, and editing.
- Teaching unfamiliar vocabulary explicitly and planning for pupils to be repeatedly exposed to high-utility and high-frequency vocabulary in what is taught.
- Narrating thought processes when modelling to make explicit how experts think (e.g. asking questions aloud that pupils should consider when working independently and drawing pupils' attention to links with prior knowledge).

# What is known about how languages teachers learn at different stages?

It is recognised that the mentoring role may shift over time in accordance with different stages of teacher learning and it is therefore helpful for mentors to have some understanding of what is known about how languages teachers learn to teach and continue to develop their skills over time.

Beginning teachers often undergo a shift in their prioritisations over time, moving from a focus on their own teaching performance (What do I need to do? How am I being perceived by my pupils/my mentor?) towards an increasing awareness of and focus on their pupils' learning (What do the pupils need to do next? Have the pupils understood this concept?). Mentors play an important role in acknowledging beginning teachers' performativity concerns whilst also gently prompting them to shift their attention to the pupils' learning at all stages of the planning, teaching, reflection, and evaluation process (Mutton et al., 2011).

Teacher learning is known to be complex and non-linear. Clarke and Hollingsworth (2002) propose a multidirectional model of teacher learning (see Figure 1.2), which captures some of the complexity of teacher development, presenting it as a process mediated by teachers' reflection in and on their actions (they use the term 'enactment' to describe teacher actions). Teachers can be stimulated to grow and learn by change in any of the four domains. For example, a teacher may observe their mentor using a teaching strategy (external domain), try out the strategy for themselves (domain of practice), notice that this results in improved pupil engagement (the domain of consequence), change their beliefs about what pupils find engaging (the personal domain), and decide to continue their experimentation (domain of practice).

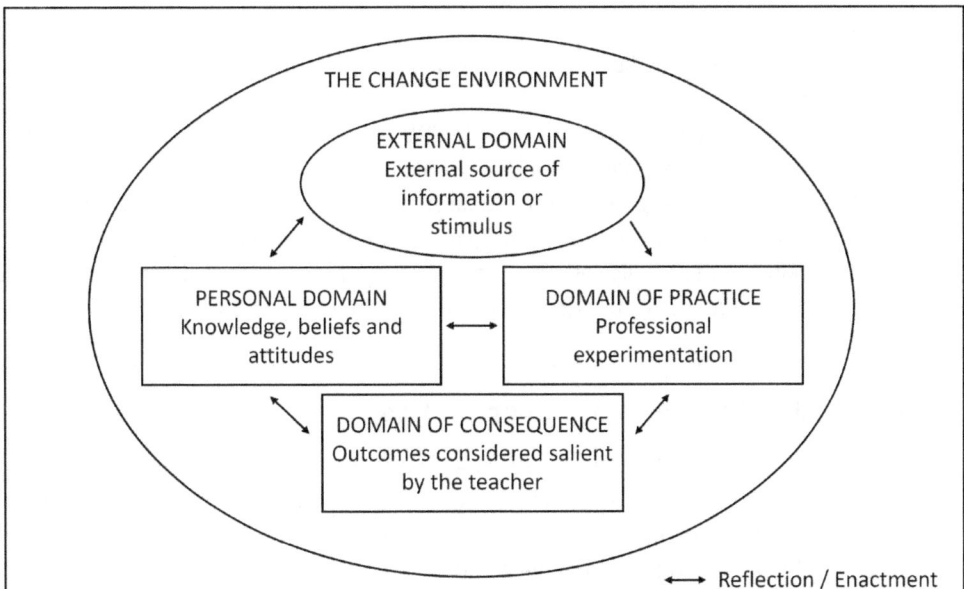

*Figure 1.2* (Adapted from Clarke and Hollingsworth's model of professional growth, 2002, p. 951.)

It is commonly understood that, although a beginning teacher may attempt to act on newly received ideas and advice, if these ideas do not align with their existing beliefs and attitudes (which may be deeply, and sometimes unconsciously held) then they are not likely to be adopted in the longer term (Opfer & Pedder, 2011). For this reason, it is helpful for mentors to maintain an ongoing dialogue about their mentee's beliefs and ideas and to encourage reflection on whether these ideas are supported by evidence in the form of pupils' learning.

Teachers' professional learning at all stages is known to be most effective when it is directly focussed on subject-specific knowledge and pedagogy (Fletcher-Wood & Zuccollo, 2020). Mentoring by language teaching specialists is therefore likely to yield greater benefits for beginning teachers than generic mentoring.

Lastly, in their review of teacher professional learning experiences, Cordingley et al. (2015) identify eight key teacher learning actions that are associated with measurable effects on pupil outcomes. Task 1.5 prompts you to consider these actions (listed below) both in the context of your own professional learning and also as prompts to shape your work with mentees.

1. Making use of specialist expertise, including expertise in the form of research evidence; using evidence and expertise to support planning in particular
2. Giving and receiving structured peer support using collaboration, especially reciprocal risk taking and professional dialogue, as core learning strategies
3. Undertaking sustained, enquiry-oriented learning over (usually) two terms or more supported by use of tools and protocols to discipline learning and secure coherence and progression
4. Learning to learn from looking through exploration of evidence about pupil outcomes and from observing teaching and learning exchanges especially those involving experiments with new approaches
5. Using aspirations for specific pupils and evidence about their learning as a driver for development
6. Focusing on why things do and don't work in different contexts to develop an underpinning rationale or practical theory alongside practice
7. Seeking out leadership support – time/encouragement/modelling – including specialist coaching and engaging in enquiry-oriented approaches to development
8. Actively seeking out specialist and peer support and taking responsibility for creating and taking opportunities for professional learning within day to day school life

### Task 1.5 Effective learning opportunities

Consider your own school context for professional learning. What structures exist within the school to support you in developing your teaching? How many of the eight teacher actions do you feel regularly empowered to enact? How might you support your mentee to engage in these teacher actions?

## Current policies for mentoring in England

In many nations around the world, school-based mentors are recognised as key to the induction and retention of beginning teachers, which has led to much policy development focussed on defining the mentoring role. Mentors should make sure they are aware of these policies, which may require a certain model of mentoring aligned with different teacher development curricula in different jurisdictions. Here in England, there are several policies that set out the rights and responsibilities of mentors. Firstly, there is a set of non-statutory National Standards for school-based initial teacher training mentors (DfE, 2016), outlining some of the mentor's key roles in their work with beginning teachers across four domains (see Table 1.1).

*Table 1.1* A summary of the National Standards for school-based initial teacher training mentors (DfE, 2016)

**Standard 1: Personal qualities**
**Establish trusting relationships, modelling high standards of practice, and understand how to support a trainee through initial teacher training.**
Be approachable, make time for the trainee, and prioritise meetings and discussions with them.
Use a range of effective interpersonal skills to respond to the needs of the trainee.
Offer support with integrity, honesty, and respect.
Use appropriate challenge to encourage the trainee to reflect on their practice.
Support the improvement of a trainee's teaching by modelling exemplary practice in planning, teaching, and assessment.

**Standard 2: Teaching**
**Support trainees to develop their teaching practice in order to set high expectations of all pupils and to meet their needs.**
Support the trainee in forming good relationships with pupils, and in developing effective behaviour and classroom management strategies.
Support the trainee in developing effective approaches to planning, teaching, and assessment.
Support the trainee with marking and assessment of pupil work through moderation or double marking.
Give constructive, clear, and timely feedback on lesson observations.
Broker opportunities to observe best practice.
Support the trainee in accessing expert subject and pedagogical knowledge.
Resolve in-school issues on the trainee's behalf where they lack the confidence or experience to do so themselves.
Enable and encourage the trainee to evaluate and improve their teaching.
Enable the trainee to access, utilise, and interpret robust educational research to inform their teaching.

**Standard 3: Professionalism**
**Set high expectations and induct the trainee to understand their role and responsibilities as a teacher.**
Encourage the trainee to participate in the life of the school and understand its role within the wider community.
Support the trainee in developing the highest standards of professional and personal conduct.
Support the trainee in promoting equality and diversity.
Ensure the trainee understands and complies with relevant legislation, including that related to the safeguarding of children.
Support the trainee to develop skills to manage time effectively.

**Standard 4: Self-development and working in partnership**
**Continue to develop their own professional knowledge, skills and understanding and invest time in developing a good working relationship within relevant ITT partnerships.**
Ensure consistency by working with other mentors and partners to moderate judgements.
Continue to develop your own mentoring practice and subject and pedagogical expertise by accessing appropriate professional development and engaging with robust research.

In 2016, the first core content framework for initial teacher training was developed and a framework for beginning teacher development swiftly followed. These two documents have subsequently been combined and expanded into an Initial Teacher Training and Early Career Framework (ITTECF) (DfE, 2024b), creating a single 'curriculum' entitlement to cover the first three years of teaching in England's schools. The two-year induction process for qualified teachers in England recognises the complexity of teaching, and the need for ongoing professional development and support. The framework details an extensive list of practices that expert mentors must help beginning teachers learn how to enact (see Task 1.4 for some examples).

Mentors should also be aware of the Teacher Standards (DfE, 2011), which list the core competencies that teachers in England must demonstrate by the end of their initial teacher training programme in order to be awarded Qualified Teacher Status.

Lastly, mentors working within the ITTECF framework in England have been required to complete 20 hours of training, with each programme of mentor training being scrutinised and approved by the DfE (2024a). This requirement was suspended in November 2024, although teacher education providers are still expected to ensure mentors receive adequate training for their role.

## Conclusion

Mentoring is complex and requires high levels of subject knowledge, pedagogical knowledge, and relational expertise. Since beginning teachers bring with them a wealth of personal experience and knowledge, it is important for mentors to explore their mentee's initial conceptions of teaching and to take this as the starting point for building an honest, open relationship with each individual mentee. Collaborative self-development can occur when the mentee's personal theories of learning are brought into dialogue with the mentor's own, and both parties are willing to interrogate these theories through experimentation, observation, and debate during the course of the mentoring relationship.

## For discussion

- Which of the mentoring models discussed above most closely resembles your own sense of what a mentor should be?
- What are your own personal development goals as a mentor and what might be your first actions to take in order to work towards them?

## Further reading

Firstly, we recommend that you look at any national policies or frameworks for mentoring in your context to help you understand what model of mentoring is being suggested by these. The relevant frameworks for England can be found in the reference list below.

- Black, L., Gordon, A. L., Hughes, C., MacArthur, R. and Sandy, S. (n.d.). *Effective mentoring of trainee teachers.* Association for Language Learning e-book publication. https://www.all-languages.org.uk/product/effective-mentoring-trainee-teachers-e-book/

The main subject association for languages teachers in England has produced the above guide for mentors. It offers an excellent starting point for thinking about the subject-specific elements of the mentoring role.
- Curtis, E., Nguyen, H. T. M., Larsen, E. and Loughland, T. (2024). The positioning tensions between early career teachers' and mentors' perceptions of the mentor role. *BERJ*, 50, 1327-1349. https://doi.org/10.1002/berj.3974

  This open-access article explores how the mentoring role is differently perceived by mentors and their mentees. It is a useful starting point for thinking about your own positionality – both in terms of how you personally see your role(s) and how you are variously positioned by your institutional policies, the national policy context, and the (often unvoiced) expectations of your mentee.

## References

Clarke, D., & Hollingsworth, H. (2002). Elaborating a model of teacher professional growth. *Teaching and Teaching Education, 18*, 947–967.

Cordingley, P., Higgins, S., Greany, T., Buckler, N., Coles-Jordan, D., Crisp, B., Saunders, L., & Coe, R. (2015). Developing Great Teaching: Lessons from the international reviews into effective professional development. Teacher Development Trust. https://tdtrust.org/wp-content/uploads/2015/10/DGT-Full-report.pdf

Curtis, E., Nguyen, H. T. M., Larsen, E., & Loughland, T. (2024). The positioning tensions between early career teachers' and mentors' perceptions of the mentor role. *BERJ, 50*, 1327-1349. https://doi.org/10.1002/berj.3974

Daly, C., Glegg, P., Stiasny, B., Hardman, M., Taylor, B., & Pillinger, C. (2023). Mentors as instructional coaches for new teachers: Lessons learned from the early career framework in England. *International Journal of Mentoring and Coaching in Education*. https://doi.org/10.1108/ijmce-10-2022-0090

Department for Education (DfE). (2011). *Teachers' Standards*. https://assets.publishing.service.gov.uk/media/61b73d6c8fa8f50384489c9a/Teachers__Standards_Dec_2021.pdf

Department for Education (DfE) (2016). National standards for school-based initial teacher training (ITT) mentors, DfE, London, https://assets.publishing.service.gov.uk/media/5a803fe4ed915d74e33f9541/Mentor_standards_report_Final.pdf

Department for Education (DfE). (2024a). *Initial teacher training (ITT): Criteria and supporting advice* https://assets.publishing.service.gov.uk/media/65ccac0ec96cf300126a3718/2024-25_ITT_criteria_and_supporting_advice.pdf.

Department for Education (DfE). (2024b). *Initial teacher training and early career framework*. https://www.gov.uk/government/publications/initial-teacher-training-and-early-career-framework.

Fletcher-Wood, H., & Zuccollo, J. (2020). *The effects of high-quality professional development on teachers and students: A rapid review and meta-analysis.* https://doi.org/10.1016/j.steroids.2006.05.001

Gallo-Fox, J., & Scantlebury, K. (2016). Coteaching as professional development for cooperating teachers. *Teaching and Teacher Education, 60*, 191-202. https://doi.org/10.1016/j.tate.2016.08.007

Gordon, A. L. (2020). Educate – Mentor – Nurture: Improving the transition from initial teacher education to qualified teacher status and beyond. *Journal of Education for Teaching, 46*(5), 664-675. https://doi.org/10.1080/02607476.2020.1807296

Hobson, A. J., Malderez, A., Tracey, L., Homer, M. S., Ashby, P., Mitchell, N., McIntyre, J., Cooper, D., Roper, T., Chambers, G. N., & Tomlinson, P. D. (2009). *Becoming a teacher: Teachers'* experiences of initial teacher training, Induction and early professional development. Final report, DCSF-RR115. https://dera.ioe.ac.uk/id/eprint/11168/1/DCSF-RR115.pdf

Kemmis, S., Heikkinen, H. L., Fransson, G., Aspfors, J., & Edwards-Groves, C. (2014). Mentoring of new teachers as a contested practice: Supervision, support and collaborative self-development. *Teaching and Teacher Education, 43*, 154-164.

Knight, J. (2017). *The impact cycle: What instructional coaches should do to foster powerful improvements in teaching*. Corwin Press.

Knight, J., & van Nieuwerburgh, C. (2012). Instructional coaching: A focus on practice. *Coaching, 5*(2), 1-13.

Kriewaldt, J., & Turnidge, D. (2013). Conceptualising an approach to clinical reasoning in the education profession. *Australian Journal of Teacher Education, 38*, 103-115.

Lofthouse, R. (2018). Mentoring as part of the foundation for career long professional development and learning. *CollectivED Working Papers, 5*, 28-36.

McIntyre, D. (1993). Theory, theorizing and reflection in initial teacher education. In J. Calderhead & P. Gates (Eds.), *Conceptualising reflection in teacher development* (pp. 39-52). Falmer.

McIntyre, D., & Hagger, H. (1993). Teachers' expertise and models of mentoring. In D. McIntyre, H. Hagger, & M. Wilkin (Eds.), *Mentoring: Perspectives on school-based teacher education* (pp. 86-102). Kogan.

Molway, L. (2022). Which aspects of their practice do modern languages teachers in England's secondary schools say they want to develop? *The Language Learning Journal, 50*(5), 627-649. https://doi.org/10.1080/09571736.2020.1862897

Molway, L. (2021). Key issues in pre-service language teacher education. In E. Macaro & R. Woore (Eds.), *Debates in second language education*. Routledge. https://doi.org/10.4324/9781003008361-9

Mutton, T., Hagger, H., & Burn, K. (2011). Learning to plan, planning to learn: The developing expertise of beginning teachers. *Teachers and Teaching: Theory and Practice, 17*(4), 399-416. https://doi.org/10.1080/13540602.2011.580516

Opfer, V. D., & Pedder, D. (2011). Conceptualizing teacher professional learning. *Review of Educational Research, 81*(3), 376-407. https://doi.org/10.3102/0034654311413609

Sims, S., & Fletcher-Wood, H. (2021). Identifying the characteristics of effective teacher professional development: A critical review. *School Effectiveness and School Improvement, 32*(1), 47-63. https://doi.org/10.1080/09243453.2020.1772841

Trevethan, H. (2017). Educative mentors? The role of classroom teachers in initial teacher education. A New Zealand study. *Journal of Education for Teaching : JET, 43*(2), 219-231. https://doi.org/10.1080/02607476.2017.1286784

Winch, C., Oancea, A., & Orchard, J. (2015). The contribution of educational research to teachers' professional learning: Philosophical understandings. *Oxford Review of Education, 41*(2), 202-216.

# 2 Understanding yourself and how your experiences influence your approach to mentoring

*Gillian Peiser*

## Introduction

Chapter 1 has illustrated that there are many models of teacher mentoring. These may be adopted individually, in combination, or interchangeably, depending on factors such as the mentee's needs, the mentor's personal preferences, or the context. Irrespective of mentoring style, however, the mentor's work will always be characterised by the 'mentor self'. The support mentors offer is informed by professional knowledge, garnered through personal experiences in particular contexts, individual beliefs about languages education, and education in general, and due to its inherently social nature, their personality.

The literature tells us that student teachers greatly value the lived experiences and contextual advice of mentors (Murray et al., 2019). Indeed, mentees often rate mentors' knowledge more highly than professional knowledge from other sources (e.g. university-based teacher educators or research knowledge), since they perceive it as more helpful in finding practical, localised solutions in their classrooms (Peiser et al., 2022). Mentors provide *in situ* support, helping mentees to adapt to teaching norms, standards, and expectations (Hobson et al., 2009), in addition to playing an important role in developing beginning teachers' identities as subject specialists.

Mentor expertise and guidance based on 'personal practical knowledge' (Connelly & Clandinin, 1985), therefore, provide immensely valuable contributions for their mentee's professional learning. However, it is also possible, and despite very best intentions, that some aspects of the 'mentor self' can pose challenges for mentee development. Drawing on conceptual models from Borg (2009), Kelchtermans (2009), and Bhabha (1990), this chapter seeks to develop understanding of the role of the self in teaching practices and beliefs, and how these influence mentoring work.

## Borg's (2009) language teacher cognition model

In 2009, Borg published a model he referred to as language teacher cognition. This model is highly relevant in relation to the 'mentor self' since it refers to 'complex, practically-orientated, personalized, and context-sensitive networks of knowledge, thoughts and beliefs that language teachers draw on in their work' (p. 272). Borg (2019) explains that teacher cognition includes aspects that can be seen, i.e. teachers' behaviours, in addition to those which are less visible or explicit, such as thoughts, beliefs, theories, principles, feelings, knowledge, and attitudes. Teacher behaviours are pertinent in relation to the modelling of teaching practices in the mentoring role, whilst more implicit aspects of cognition are likely to influence the professional dialogue mentors have with mentees. However, Borg (2019) maintains that the less visible elements cannot be separated from behaviours and that the relationships between the implicit and explicit aspects of teacher cognition are interactive. Whilst practices may mirror beliefs or knowledge, this is not always the case, due to mitigating contextual factors in the classroom, school, or broader policy context. Furthermore, teachers' experiences in their professional practice can alter beliefs, feelings, and attitudes.

Borg (2009) conceptualises the interaction between visible and less visible elements in his framework for language teacher cognition with respect to three dimensions: 'schooling', 'professional coursework', and 'contextual factors'. 'Schooling' refers to individuals' experiences as learners in particular schools and classrooms, with specific histories of language learning, which were most likely influenced by teachers, significant adults (e.g. parents), and educational culture and policy. For example, a teacher who experienced, enjoyed, and benefitted from a strong grammar-translation teaching methodology may have reservations about a more naturalistic approach to language acquisition, where grammar is learnt implicitly. Or a teacher who was fascinated by the cultural elements of language learning, may be motivated to make this a strong feature in their teaching.

The thoughts, beliefs, and attitudes about language learning which are initially influenced by 'schooling' are then further impacted by and interact with the content and experiences of pre-service teacher education courses: 'professional coursework'. During initial teacher education, beginning teachers are presented with teaching methodologies and specialist subject pedagogies, based on research and theoretical knowledge. In many countries, teacher education providers are obligated to dovetail the pedagogies they promote with both national curricula for pupils in schools and statutory frameworks for qualifying to teach. Whilst many beginning teachers will respond favourably to pedagogies introduced in initial teacher education, consequently extending, developing, or altering cognition arising from their 'schooling', this is not always the case, especially if there is strong misalignment with prior beliefs (Task 2.1).

---

### Task 2.1 Personal influences on your beliefs and practice

- What are your experiences of 'schooling' (school, university, informal, other language learning experiences), and how have these impacted your language teacher cognition?
- Did your experience of 'professional coursework' influence your beliefs and practices in the early stages of your career?
- To what extend does your experience of 'professional coursework' influence your practices today? Can you provide reasons for this?

*Understanding yourself and your approach to mentoring* 19

Beginning languages teachers will draw on cognition from 'schooling' and 'professional coursework' in their practice. However, the relationship between schooling, professional coursework and pedagogical practice is complex and dynamic, due to the influence of 'contextual factors' in the practice environment. Often, the practice environment will have a positive influence, since beginning languages teachers learn how to apply more abstract elements of their cognition for the benefit of pupil learning. For example, they may learn about theoretical perspectives on motivation in second language learning and then discover practical ways to develop pupils' intrinsic motivation by teaching through topics, contexts, or media which directly resonate with young people's interests.

Contextual factors in the practice environment, however, can also create tensions in teacher cognition. For example, teachers may discover that the application of theory from professional coursework may not suit the needs or responses of their pupils, or, for instance, that the modern languages department's policy on target language usage does not mirror the teacher's own point of view. Similarly, a teacher's own beliefs may be challenged by assessment regimes. The mentor may believe in the role of modern languages education in promoting intercultural understanding, but if this is not assessed in official examinations, and owing to pressures of teacher accountability, it may receive little attention in practice. As Borg (2009, p. 275) explains, contextual factors in terms of 'social, institutional, instructional and physical settings' continue to have a major impact on teacher cognition and practices beyond pre-service preparation.

To assist you in considering contextual influences on your own language teacher cognition, you may find it helpful to engage with Reflection Task 2.2.

---

**Task 2.2 Contextual influences on your beliefs and practices**

- What are the main contextual influences that positively and negatively impact your language teaching practice?
- How may contextual factors filter (positively or negatively) into your mentoring role?
- In which ways have contextual experiences modified your cognition?
- How may contextual influences positively or negative impact advice you offer to your mentee?

---

## Kelchtermans' concepts of 'self-understanding', 'subjective educational theory', and the interference of 'systemic demands'

Kelchtermans' (2009) approach to explaining the teacher self can also be helpful for considering how individualised factors may influence teachers, and consequently mentors' work. Conscious that teaching is a social and public act, where the ideas the teacher has about the self are influenced by what others think, Kelchtermans (2009) presents the concepts of 'self-understanding', 'subjective educational theory', and 'systemic demands'.

Whilst there are five components of 'self-understanding', this chapter will deal with the three the author considers most pertinent to the mentor self, the first of which is 'self-image'. 'Self-image' is based on self-perception, which to large degree, is created by what others (mainly pupils) mirror back to teachers. Inevitably, pupils' responses will prompt all teachers at times to doubt or question the positive impact of their work, consequently affecting self-image. Critical reflective practice, however, is considered by teacher education to be a fundamental and positive aspect of professional development at all stages of a teacher's career, since it can result in intelligent and effective transformation of practice. Whilst newer teachers in the mentor role may still be in the process of creating and establishing their teacher 'self-image', mentors are often appointed or self-selected based on confidence in their pedagogical practice and ability to carry out the role. Accordingly, more experienced language teachers in the mentor role may view themselves as established subject specialists with strong 'pedagogical content knowledge' (Shulman, 1986), i.e. professional understanding and know-how regarding effective presentation and teaching and learning of subject matter. Indeed, the English Department for Education's (2024) framework for initial teacher training and early career development refers to the mentor as an 'expert practitioner', charged with the responsibility of demonstrating and teaching the mentee how to apply their own knowledge in practice.

Whilst the mentor's 'self-image' can greatly facilitate the role-modelling of effective practice, developing the mentee's language pedagogical content knowledge and subject identity, it may also have potential to result in bias about the merits of one's own practice. Indeed, Hobson and Malderez (2013) found that such bias could result in potentially damaging 'judgementoring', whereby mentors made value judgements of mentees' practice or thinking in relation to how they thought things should be done, rather than openly exploring possible courses of action (Task 2.3).

### Task 2.3 Attempting to avoid 'judgementoring'

- What do you see as your strengths in terms of your own language teaching practice?
- How may you create space for your mentee to question your practices and to experiment with other possible methodologies in the classroom?

A second element of Kelchtermans' (2009) self-understanding is 'job motivation', relating to the motives or drives for becoming and being a teacher. In their study investigating languages teachers' perceptions of the significance of intercultural understanding,

Peiser and Jones (2014) found that language teachers' job motivations varied greatly: some prioritised the promotion of academic knowledge; others wanted to open their pupils' eyes to a world and cultures beyond their own to promote alternative views and tolerance; some were more pastorally motivated, whilst there were also teachers who were uncertain in this regard.

The final element of self-understanding dealt with here is 'task perception'. This refers to how teachers conceptualise the necessary tasks and duties to do a good job. Task perception will be informed by language teachers' 'job motivation', their pedagogical content knowledge (Shulman, 1986), and personal and contextual experiences. It is highly likely that your job motivation and task perception influence your teaching philosophy and style, which, to greater or lesser explicit degrees, you are likely to convey to your mentee.

Like Borg (2009), Kelchtermans deals with relationships between teacher beliefs and practices, designating the interaction between these as 'subjective educational theory': a 'personal system of knowledge and beliefs about education that teachers use when performing their job' (p. 263) which develops during teacher education courses mixed with more personal experiences in applied situations. Here we note parallels with Borg's attention to the interaction between 'schooling', 'professional coursework', and 'contextual factors'. For example, an originally academic job motivation may be influenced by teacher education on the advantages of explicit vs. implicit grammar teaching, which in turn is modified because of professional experience.

Conscious, that subjective educational theory may be understood predominantly in terms of teacher enactment and agency, Kelchtermans also stresses that there is also a 'structural characteristic of the profession' (p. 265), over which teachers have little control. These include externally imposed regulations, quality control systems, and constantly changing policy demands. Teachers' job motivation and task perception, therefore, may be challenged by national curricula, official examination specifications, and school inspection regimes.

## Insights from Borg and Kelchtermans for mentoring practice

How are insights from Borg (2009) and Kelchtermans (2009) on language teacher cognition, self-understanding, subjective educational theory, or systemic demands relevant to the mentoring role? Firstly, mentors and mentees may have had similar or different experiences of schooling that influence thinking on how language should be taught or learnt. To develop an open and collaborative mentoring relationship, based on mutual understanding, it is therefore important for both parties to understand how each other's prior educational and autobiographical experiences influence cognition and task-perception.

Similarly, it is valuable to share understandings of each other's experiences of professional coursework, particularly when these are divergent. This sharing is significant since endorsement, popularity and knowledge of different pedagogies are susceptible to change, depending on the advancement of new research, and/or support in education policy and curriculum guidance.

To develop awareness of the 'mentee's self', and how this may differ to your own beliefs and practices, you may find it helpful to engage in Task 2.4.

---

**Task 2.4 Understanding your mentee's language teacher beliefs and (aspirational) practice**

With your mentee, discuss:

- how they think experiences of 'schooling' have impacted their views of language teaching and compare these with your own
- details about their 'professional coursework' and compare the extent to which these are reflected in your own or other colleagues' practices
- if appropriate, how their 'task perception' has been influenced by an alternative school placement
- how they may apply and experiment with different pedagogies encountered on their initial teacher education course on school placement.

---

Whilst the school placement experience provides student teachers with opportunities to enact, experiment with and critically reflect on the pedagogies they have learnt about in university, based on recent research and policy guidelines, the affordance to do so can be influenced by mentor 'permission'. This can be challenging when pedagogies are unfamiliar to the mentor, they are not part of their teaching repertoire, or the mentor considers them inappropriate.

In your dual role as mentor and class teacher responsible for pupil progress, it is only natural to sometimes be sceptical about mentees' experimentation with unfamiliar or alternative strategies. As Jaspers et al. (2014) established, many mentors identify themselves primarily as teachers of pupils rather than supporters of beginning teachers' learning. This may make mentors slightly uncomfortable with mentees taking perceived pedagogical risks. Due to policy measures of accountability, which place schools and teachers under increasing pressure to ensure pupils meet academic standards, mentors can therefore be more concerned with pupil progress than supporting beginning teachers' learning. Here we notice how contextual factors and systemic demands may create tensions with other aspects of teacher cognition or subjective educational theory, with potentially negative consequences for mentoring practices. Viewed from an alternative perspective, granting mentees with 'permission' or support for some trial and error can yield significant benefits.

The freedom to experiment with different pedagogies provides opportunities for rich collaborative reflection about reasons for or against their effectiveness. Together, mentors and mentees can discuss theoretical and practical reasons for teaching and learning strategies before they are trialled in the classroom. Following implementation, there are also opportunities to engage in reflective deliberation about their impact. In this way, mentors can assist mentees in developing autonomous pedagogical decision-making. This process contributes to the development of beginning teachers' professional identity, the creation of their personal philosophy of languages teaching, and sense of teacher agency.

Viewed from this standpoint, learning to teach is an intellectual endeavour, which draws on knowledge of research, theory, and context, rather than one that fits an apprenticeship model (Mutton et al., 2017). This naturally has implications for mentoring style that extend much further than role-modelling. Rather than expecting the mentee to mimic current modern languages practices within the school context, mentoring involves engaging with the mentee in collaborative inquiry, seeking the most appropriate ways to improve the educational experiences of young people.

We are noticing, therefore, how the mentoring of beginning teachers cannot rely solely only the mentor's own beliefs or knowledge, or 'first order' knowledge required for teaching in schools. Instead, it also demands what Murray (2002) termed 'second order knowledge'. Whilst this term was originally coined in relation to university teacher educators, it is now broadly accepted that school-based mentors, are also teacher educators (European Commission, 2012). Murray (2002) and McNamara et al. (2014) stress how mentors' second order knowledge should involve the development of pedagogical skills for mentoring. To inform these skills, this chapter has highlighted how part of this knowledge should include intrapersonal knowledge, i.e. awareness of the self and the dynamics of cognition, to assist mentors in working with adult learners as they enter the profession.

## Personalities, preferred mentoring styles, and third space

So far, we have dealt with the mentor self in terms of behaviours, knowledge, thoughts, and beliefs. We have learnt how particular experiences of mentors in specific contexts influence these. However, we also know from psychological research that personality has a key role to play in influencing behaviours, thoughts, and feelings (Ellingsen, 2016), which can also impact preferences for mentoring style (Leaver & Oxford, 2000).

Kemmis et al. (2014) referred to three broad mentoring styles: supervision (with a focus on achievement of statutory teacher competences, taking a behaviourist approach), support (provision of professional guidance with both reflective and humanistic emphases), and collaborative self-development to pedagogical practice from the perspectives of both mentor and mentee. To reflect on your preferred mentoring style and the influence of personality, you may wish to consider, for example, the extent to which you wish to control situations, with yourself more at the centre, or are happy to delegate responsibility to others. You may also ponder on your desire to nurture, whether you are intellectually curious and enjoy critical thinking, or the extent to which you are invested in their own professional learning.

Teachers favouring more authoritative approaches may be more at ease with behaviourist and supervisory mentoring styles. These contrast with those who prefer to entrust others with the paths that they forge. Teachers who value the affective and emotional elements of relationships and learning are likely to adopt a nurturing style, with an emphasis on the pastoral welfare of their mentee. Those who enjoy critical thinking and are invested in their professional development may be more secure with collaborative problem-solving and inquiry mentoring styles.

Although individuals' personalities and related preferences may mean that they sit more comfortably with particular styles (Leaver & Oxford, 2000), it is valuable to recognise the need for flexibility and to adopt these interchangeably, depending on your mentee's stage of development and needs. (That said, the time made available to you by school resources to carry out your mentoring work may positively or negatively impact your ability to adopt a range of styles.) Interestingly, research has established that mentees value multiple approaches, with Crutcher and Naseem (2016) discovering that mentees rated role-modelling behaviour, interpersonal skills, and the ability to promote reflective discussion.

Although mentees may find it a useful approach, an over-reliance on behaviourist approaches with an emphasis on role-modelling presents limitations. Role-modelling represents 'first order knowledge' (knowing how to teach). However, it falls short of the application of the necessary 'second order knowledge' (Murray, 2002) (mentoring pedagogy) to facilitate professional learning. As this chapter has already argued, an important part of second order knowledge should involve the respectful recognition and endorsement of the particular and individual experiences of both the mentor and mentee (McNamara et al., 2014), which will include a nurturing element.

Second order knowledge also involves the promotion of reflective practice through refined coaching skills, whereby the mentee is prompted to develop their own 'subjective educational theory' (Kelchtermans, 2009), as a basis for professional agency. This does not involve the rejection of mentor expertise, which is still crucial. Instead, mentors will draw on their professional craft and contextual knowledge as a premise for stimulating reflection, helping mentees to develop their professional voice and identity (Izadinia, 2015).

Mentors working within university-school initial teacher education partnerships act as a linchpin between higher education and the school. They are therefore ideally positioned for assisting mentees in 'knowledge transfer', involving appropriate application of more formal knowledge learnt in the university in particular practical situations (Eraut, 2014). With the support of the experienced and knowledgeable mentor, beginning teachers can test ideas from modern languages pedagogical research as well as their own preconceptions in practice with real-world criteria in schools (Hagger & McIntyre, 2006).

That said, the skilful and effective enactment of this process is no mean feat. Not only does it demand refined coaching skills, but also the mentor's courage and confidence to step away from the mentor self into a 'third space' (Bhabha, 1990), 'a metaphorical or material space, within which individuals can make sense of the (sometimes competing) discourses and systems which are prevalent in the other spaces they inhabit' (McIntyre & Hobson, 2016, p. 137). In mentoring third spaces, issues are analysed and interpreted drawing on multiple perspectives, including theoretical and practical knowledge, policy demands and the personal perspectives of the mentor and mentee in honest, and critically reflective discussions (McNamara et al., 2014).

Task 2.5 presents a language mentoring scenario where the mentor self may result in 'judgementoring' that constrains collaborative self-development. How could Amy move into a third space? What advice would you offer her?

---

**Task 2.5 Mentoring in a third space**

Eve (mentee) has been learning about contrasting theories of second language acquisition at university. The student teachers have spent considerable time learning about Conti and Smith's (2019) approach which favours a more implicit approach to grammar learning, based on Krashen's (1985) theory of comprehensible input. Eve is being encouraged by her university subject tutor to experiment with Conti and Smith's 'lexico-grammar' approach to explore its effectiveness. Eve is eager to try this out with her Year 8 class.

Amy's (Eve's mentor) modern languages departmental policy favours an explicit approach, which has recently been influenced by current curriculum policy guidance. Amy also favours an explicit approach in her practice, and in her view, has developed a strong repertoire for effective grammar teaching, which she has role-modelled for Eve.

*How could a conversation and learning in a 'third space' circumnavigate potential constraints on Eve's opportunity to experiment with and critically evaluate more implicit grammar teaching approaches in her practice?*

---

## Conclusion

This chapter has demonstrated how the 'mentor self' is intricately intertwined with mentoring work. The mentor's beliefs about modern languages education and their practical expertise can provide inspiration and precious guidance for beginning teachers. Mentors' strong pedagogical content knowledge, based on lived experiences of teaching languages, provide mentees with concrete models of how to teach. This applied and more tangible knowledge enables situated learning during the complex and potentially overwhelming experience of learning to teach.

However, we have learnt that despite best intentions, the 'mentor self' may also limit possibilities for professional learning. As Hodkinson and Hodkinson (2003) argue, each person learns in a context and is a reciprocal part of that context. The mentor's beliefs and practices are therefore products of experiences in particular contexts that, at times, may differ from, or stand in tension with, the experiences, vision, or aspirations of the mentee. Emotionally intelligent mentoring, with second-order knowledge, will acknowledge both the mentor and mentee selves and how these influence the process.

The chapter finally presented the concept of 'third space' mentoring to develop mutual understanding, and to provide a place for collaborative problem-solving drawing on multiple perspectives. In third spaces, mentoring shifts away from inculcating elements of the mentor self, and instead, focuses on enabling the mentee to develop their own language teacher self and identity.

## For discussion

- How could you inspire your mentee as an entrant to the profession with your task perception of modern languages education?
- How can you draw on the strongest elements of your professional craft knowledge in second language teaching to support your mentee?
- Do you think that there could be a link between aspects of your personality and your preferred mentoring style?
- What steps could you take to mitigate against 'judgementoring'?

## Further reading

- Birello, M. (2012). Teacher cognition and language teacher education: Beliefs and practice. A conversation with Simon Borg. *Bellaterra Journal of Teaching & Learning Language & Literature*, 5(2), 88-94. https://revistes.uab.cat/jtl3/article/view/v5-n2-birello/526

    This open access article is a helpful and concise way to learn about the work of Simon Borg who, in several seminal publications, has theorised the relationships between beliefs and practices of languages teachers, which he has called 'teacher cognition'. Borg stresses the importance of exploring and unpicking teacher beliefs in initial teacher education.

- Hobson, A.J. & Malderez, A. (2013). Judgementoring and other threats to realizing the potential of school-based mentoring in teacher education. *International Journal of Mentoring and Coaching in Education*, 2(2), 89-108.

    Whilst access to this journal article requires a library subscription, a copy of the originally deposited article also has open access here: https://shura.shu.ac.uk/7224/1/Hobson_and_Malderez_2013_Judgementoring_IJMCE_Post-print_draft.pdf

    This article explores how mentors' personal judgements or evaluations of a mentee's teaching, based on their own beliefs and practices, has potential to negatively impact mentoring relationships, mentees' self-esteem, motivation and professional learning.

## References

Bhabha, H. (1990). Interview with Homi Bhabha: The third space. In J. Rutherford (Ed.), *Identity: Community, culture, difference* (pp. 207-221). Lawrence and Wishart.

Borg, S. (2009). *Teacher cognition and language education: Research and practice*. Bloomsbury Publishing.

Borg, S. (2019). Language teacher cognition: Perspectives and debates. In X. Gao (Ed.), *Second handbook of English language teaching* (pp. 1149-1170). Springer.

Connelly, F. M., & Clandinin, D. J. (1985). Personal practical knowledge and the modes of knowing: Relevance for teaching and learning. In E. Eisner (Ed.), *Learning and teaching ways of knowing: The eighty-fourth yearbook of the National Society for the Study of Education* (pp. 174-198). University of Chicago Press.

Conti, G., & Smith, S. (2019). *Breaking the sound barrier: Teaching language learners how to listen*. Piefke Trading.

Crutcher, P. A., & Naseem, S. (2016). Cheerleading and cynicism of effective mentoring in current empirical research. *Educational Review*, 68(1), 40-55.

Department for Education. (2024). *Initial teacher training and early career framework*. https://www.gov.uk/government/publications/initial-teacher-training-and-early-career-framework.

Ellingsen, V. J. (2016). Personality and cognitive abilities. In V. Zeigler-Hill, & T. Shackelford (Eds.), *Encyclopaedia of personality and individual differences*. Springer. https://doi.org/10.1007/978-3-319-28099-8_990-1

Eraut, M. (2014). Developing knowledge for qualified professionals. In O. McNamara, J. Murray, & M. Jones (Eds.), *Workplace learning in teacher education. Professional learning and development in schools and higher education* (Vol. 10, pp. 47-72). Springer.

European, Commission (2012). *Supporting the teaching professions for better learning outcomes: Commission staff working document*. European Commission.

Hagger, H., & McIntyre, D. (2006). *Learning teaching from teachers: Realising the potential of school-based teacher education*. McGraw-Hill Education.

Hobson, A. J., Ashby, P., Malderez, A., & Tomlinson, P. D. (2009). Mentoring beginning teachers: What we know and What we don't. *Teaching and Teacher Education*, 25(1), 207-216.

Hobson, A. J., & Malderez, A. (2013). Judgementoring and other threats to realizing the potential of school-based mentoring in teacher education. *International Journal of Mentoring and Coaching in Education*, 2(2), 89-108.

Hodkinson, P., & Hodkinson, H. (2003). Individuals, communities of practice and the policy context: School teachers' learning in their workplace. *Continuing Education*, 25(1), 3-21.

Izadinia, M. (2015). A closer look at the role of mentor teachers in shaping preservice teachers' professional identity. *Teaching and Teacher Education*, 52, 1-10.

Jaspers, W. M., Meijer, P. C., Prins, F., & Wubbels, T. (2014). Mentor teachers: Their perceived possibilities and challenges as mentor and teacher. *Teaching and Teacher Education*, 44, 106-116.

Kelchtermans, G. (2009). Who I am in how I teach is the message: Self-Understanding, vulnerability and reflection. *Teachers and Teaching: Theory and Practice*, 15(2), 257-272.

Kemmis, S., Heikkinen, H. L., Fransson, G., Aspfors, J., & Edwards-Groves, C. (2014). Mentoring of new teachers as a contested practice: Supervision, support and collaborative self-development. *Teaching and Teacher Education*, 43, 154-164.

Krashen, S. (1985). *The input hypothesis: Issues and implications*. Longman.

Leaver, B. L., & Oxford, R. (2000). *Mentoring in style: Using style information to enhance mentoring of foreign language teachers*. Available from: https://files.eric.ed.gov/fulltext/ED481003.pdf

McIntyre, J., & Hobson, A. J. (2016). Supporting beginner teacher identity development: External mentors and the third space. *Research Papers in Education*, 31(2), 133-158.

McNamara, O., Murray, J., & Jones, M. (Eds.). (2014). *Workplace learning in teacher education: International practice and policy (Vol. 10)*. Springer.

Murray, J. (2002). Between the chalkface and the ivory towers?: A study of the professionalism of teacher educators working on primary initial teacher education courses in the English university sector (Doctoral dissertation) (Unpublished doctoral dissertation or master's thesis). Institute of Education, University of London, London.

Murray, J., Czerniawski, G., & Barber, P. (2019). Who is teaching me and what do they know? Student teachers' perceptions of their teacher educators and mentors. In J. Murray, A. Swennan, & C. Kosnik (Eds.), *International research, policy and practice in teacher education* (pp. 139-153). Springer International Publishing.

Mutton, T., Burn, K., & Menter, I. (2017). Deconstructing the Carter review: Competing conceptions of quality in England's 'school-led' system of initial teacher education. *Journal of Education Policy*, 32(1), 14-33.

Peiser, G., & Jones, M. (2014). The influence of teachers' interests, personalities and life experiences in intercultural languages teaching. *Teachers and Teaching, 20*(3), 375-390.

Peiser, G., Pratt, A., & Putwain, D. (2022). Student teachers' views about the university's research contribution to professional knowledge development. *Teaching and Teacher Education, 112*, 103647.

Shulman, L. (1986). Those who understand: Knowledge growth in teaching. *Educational Researcher, 15*(2), 4-14.

# 3 What makes a good mentor in modern languages? How to help beginning teachers flourish

*Trevor Mutton and Robert Woore*

## Objectives

At the end of this chapter, you should be able to:

- Understand what makes a good mentor in languages
- Consider the values and principles that underpin effective mentoring
- Be able to articulate how a strong, values-based approach informs the everyday, practical work of mentors in languages

## Introduction

This chapter explores how modern languages mentors can help beginning teachers to flourish. In asking the question 'What makes a good mentor?' our aim is not to produce a checklist of the qualities of the 'ideal' mentor or to provide 'recipes' for success. Nor do we want to encourage any approach that might rely on some kind of audit of mentor competences. Rather, our aim is to help you, as a mentor, to do the job as effectively as possible by thinking about the values and principles that might underpin effective mentoring. Some might worry that this will make our chapter 'abstract' or 'academic': on the contrary, we believe that it is supremely practical to think about underpinning values and principles, since these provide a strong, flexible foundation for decision-making across a range of everyday contexts and scenarios.

## The distinctiveness of languages teaching

Much of the guidance, training, and checklists that you encounter in relation to the mentoring of beginning teachers may be generic – intended to apply to all teachers, irrespective of their subject area. Why, then, are we asking what makes a good mentor in languages specifically? We do this because in our view, language learning and teaching differ from other subjects in at least four key respects (Mutton & Woore, 2014).

In languages classrooms, the target language may be both the object of learning, and (albeit to different extents) the medium of communication through which the learning is mediated. There is a close connection between the language(s) we speak and our identity – that is, how we see ourselves, and how we wish to be seen, in relation to different social and cultural groups. In the words of Gardner (2001, p. 6), to speak a 'foreign' language is to adopt 'the behavioural characteristics of another cultural group of people'. This is likely to make motivation a particularly complex issue for language learners, especially adolescent ones in a classroom context.

Various school subjects can be described as 'disciplines of inquiry' (Pring, 2013), in which pupils need to learn what kinds of questions are asked by, say, a historian or a biologist, and how those questions are investigated. However, whilst this may be true of 'learning about language' (linguistics), it does not apply to learning the language itself. In language classrooms, there are generally accepted 'correct forms'. These are not usually problematised or subject to 'inquiry' – they just have to be mastered.

Related to the previous point, languages teachers do not simply want their pupils to learn *about* the target language; rather, they want them to acquire the skill of *using* the language for communicative purposes. Various aspects of processing the language need to become automatised through extensive practice. It is a bit like the distinction between learning music theory and learning to play an instrument.

Additionally, compared to other subjects, pupils in the beginning stages of language learning are less able to work independently for extended periods of time. They are likely to need a great deal of support to help them attempt even basic communicative tasks in the language. As a result, there tend to be a greater number of shorter tasks in a modern languages lesson, necessitating more transitions between tasks. This can make the modern languages classroom particularly intensive and demanding for the teacher.

For all these reasons, language teaching does not fit neatly into the same boxes as other subjects – however much school-wide policies may wish it to. We believe that language teaching is distinctive; mentors of beginning languages teachers therefore need to understand this distinctiveness. They need to help their mentees develop the necessary subject-specific expertise, in addition to the generic expertise that all teachers must possess.

## Some mentoring scenarios

At this point, we would like to share with you some practical examples drawn from our own experience of working with beginning teachers. Some of the issues are specific to the languages context, while others are more generic (Task 3.1).

---

### Task 3.1 Considering scenarios

Think about the ways in which you might approach each of these scenarios. What seem to be the key issues? What might you do, to try to move each of the beginning teachers forward? What do you feel instinctively is the best approach? What are you weighing up when deciding what to do? What would you see as being the best outcome in each case?

---

**Kai** has good rapport with his classes and is highly creative in his lesson planning, coming up with original, engaging tasks and resources. However, his lessons often lack a logical progression in the sequence of tasks; they tend to be constructed around a collection of activities, rather than leading pupils through a series of steps in their learning to get to a particular end-objective. There has been some progress recently, but the stages of the lesson still sometimes come in the wrong order or have crucial steps missing. As a result, pupils are not sufficiently prepared to complete some tasks and behaviour starts to deteriorate.

**Paula** has strong classroom presence and uses her voice well to gain and hold pupils' attention. She is also very aware of what is going on in the classroom and quickly reminds pupils of her expectations. However, she has been reluctant to issue formal warnings and to follow up on poor behaviour, because she is worried about damaging her relationship with pupils. She has been advised to use the school's systems of rewards and sanctions, and to be more rigorous in following up on misdemeanours. This is starting to work with some classes but with others, things are more difficult. Patterns of poor behaviour, including widespread low-level chatter, are getting entrenched.

**Zara** plans lessons thoroughly and with careful thought to progression in the pupils' learning. However, she often misjudges the level at which to pitch the tasks she sets, particularly with Key Stage 3 classes. For example, her writing tasks are often completed quickly and effortlessly by high attaining pupils, whilst others find them a real challenge and barely manage to get started in the time available. As a result, pupils are getting restless or messing about.

**Noah** plans lessons logically and sets engaging tasks for the pupils. However, he tends to do everything in English, even though he is a native speaker of German. After reading some of the Second Language Acquisition literature, he has been trying to use more target language, particularly when giving basic instructions to the class. However, he has had more success with this in French (his second teaching language, which he teaches at Key Stage 3). In German, his language tends to be a bit too fast and complex for pupils to follow, causing them to get frustrated.

**Ada** has started to take on greater responsibility for her classes – planning and teaching all their lessons, marking work and recording progress. She is finding this challenging and is struggling to cope with the workload. She often leaves lesson planning till the night before, so there is no time for colleagues to give feedback on her plans. There are often problems with the tasks she sets for pupils or the sequencing of tasks – for example, pupils have not sufficiently practised the language they need in order to attempt a role play. Ada is resistant to the idea of handing in her lesson plans in advance and feels it is unreasonable for anybody to ask her to do so, but there is a feeling that she needs to be better organised.

## The role of the mentor

Before looking more closely at what makes a good mentor, we will begin by examining briefly what we understand to be the mentor's role. It is not difficult to find definitions of mentoring within the wealth of literature that focuses on both mentoring in general and that of beginning teachers more specifically. However, any attempt to define mentoring soon leads to an awareness of the complexity of what is involved and the multiple roles that you, as a mentor, may be required to fulfil.

Kemmis et al. (2014: p. 155) argue that mentoring can take different forms, in which it is 'understood and conceptualized in different ways (sayings), enacted in different ways (doings), and (...) people relate to one another differently (relatings)'. They go on to say that:

> ... there are contested purposes between (a) assisting newly qualified teachers to pass through the formal juridical requirements for probation, which we describe as mentoring as supervision, and/or (b) supporting new teachers in the development of their professional practices by more experienced teachers, which we describe as mentoring as support, and/or (c) assisting new teachers collectively to develop their professional identities, which we describe as mentoring as collaborative self-development.

Task 3.2 asks you to consider some of the different forms and purposes of mentoring.

---

### Task 3.2 Three aspects of mentoring – Supervision, support and collaborative self-development

Think about the three aspects identified by Kemmis et al. (2014) – see Table 3.1: mentoring as supervision, mentoring as support, and mentoring as collaborative self-development. What sort of things might you do as a mentor, working with beginning languages teachers, in relation to each of these? List as many different mentoring activities as you can that correspond to each of these types of mentoring. For example, you might: (a) in a mentor meeting, go through the teacher standards and help beginning teachers document how they have met each one (supervision); (b) arrange for them to observe colleagues in another subject area, to explore how questioning is used across the curriculum (support); and (c) set up a reading group to discuss a research article and its implications for practice (collaborative self-development).

---

In another attempt to define mentoring, Orland-Barak (2014, p. 180) describes it as a process that involves 'mediating between opposing yet complementing functions', which she labels 'matriarchal' and 'patriarchal'. Whilst we are somewhat hesitant about the use of this gendered terminology, we do feel that interesting questions are raised

*Table 3.1* Three types of mentoring (Kemmis et al., 2014)

| Types of mentoring | Possible mentoring activities |
|---|---|
| Mentoring as supervision | |
| Mentoring as support | |
| Mentoring as collaborative professional development | |

by the contrast between the two established approaches which Orland-Barak describes. The first approach 'entails establishing and sustaining relationships based on personal caring, emotional support and nurturing'; the second encapsulates the mentor's function as an expert, 'reflected in roles such as guiding, instructing, imparting knowledge, and challenging the novice protégé in the public sphere'. The process of mediating between these two different but complementary functions reflects the need for a particular pedagogical approach to mentoring which takes account of both the relational and instructional aspects of the role.

Also central to the mentoring relationship, we would argue, is an understanding of the ways in which beginning teachers might acquire the knowledge that will enable them to grow fully as professionals. Cochran-Smith and Lytle (1999, p. 250, original emphases) distinguish between three kinds of professional knowledge:

'Knowledge-*for*-practice': formal, codified knowledge about teaching which is passed down from expert to novice in a hierarchical relationship, albeit within a potentially supportive context.

'Knowledge-*in*-practice': the sort of practical knowledge that is embedded in the teacher's craft and comes from direct experience of being in the classroom, together with reflection on that experience.

'Knowledge-*of*-practice': the knowledge which is 'generated when teachers treat their own classrooms and schools as sites for intentional investigation at the same time that they treat the knowledge and theory produced by others as generative material for interrogation and interpretation'.

In other words, in such a model, neither 'knowledge-*for*-practice' nor 'knowledge-*in*-practice' is privileged: rather, teachers learn through opportunities to interrogate and critique the knowledge derived from both these sources. For example, teachers may question their own established practices in light of research findings and other evidence; and they may also question the strength of such evidence or its relevance to their own classroom contexts.

Your role, as mentor, is therefore to facilitate the way in which these different forms of knowledge are mediated through a process of what Kriewaldt and Turnidge (2013) call 'clinical reasoning' (p. 103): essentially 'bringing research-based understandings of teaching and learning into dialogue with the professional understandings of experienced classroom teachers' (Burn & Mutton, 2015, p. 219). In practice, this requires the mentor to adopt an open-minded, questioning and collaborative approach, rather than seeing themselves as the 'expert' who must pass on the 'correct' knowledge, and train beginning teachers to do things the 'right' way.

## Mentoring in different contexts

The other thing that needs to be acknowledged is that not all modern languages mentoring takes place in the same context. For example, there are different routes into teaching, including school-based models and university-school partnerships; and within each of these, there may be differences in both the practical arrangements and philosophical underpinnings of the programmes.

Trevethan (2017) usefully reminds us that the nature of the mentor's role depends very much on the particular model of initial teacher education (ITE) within which they are working.[1] She sees these models as falling into three broad categories (pp. 220-222):

The 'traditional model' (also referred to as the 'dominant' model): this reflects aspects of the more hierarchical relationship described in the previous section. It depends upon the notion of teaching as a craft, best learned from an expert.

The 'teaching as reflective practice model': this assumes an approach to mentoring which is characterised by informed conversations, in which the role of the mentor is to 'support student teachers to develop their own personal philosophy of teaching and to set and achieve personal goals rather than following the teacher model without question' (p. 221).

The 'learning in partnership model': Trevethan equates this to 'educative mentoring' (see Feiman-Nemser, 2012; Langdon & Ward, 2015): An educative mentor, she says, 'establishes the prior conceptions, skills and knowledge of the student teacher and provides learning opportunities through experiences and professional conversations, which support and challenge student teachers to ask questions and grow' (p. 221).

These three conceptualisations can be seen as lying on a continuum, in which beginning teachers have increasing agency over their own learning. In this way, they also broadly reflect McIntyre and Hagger's (1994, p. 86) 'levels of mentoring'. In their view, the form of mentoring which is most likely to support the development of beginning teachers effectively – which they call 'developed mentoring' (p.94) – requires mentors to have an enhanced understanding of the process of professional learning. Mentors can thus help beginning teachers 'to become aware of, and to question their preconceptions, in offering them new ideas from their own experience and practices, and in guiding the learner-teachers in the use and development of ideas acquired from different sources' (p. 94).

## Practical consequences of different contexts

Different models of ITE also have more immediate, practical consequences for the role of mentor. You may be working, for example, in a school that is part of a university PGCE partnership; this may include, among other things:

- a certain structure for the PGCE year, with designated times for extended periods of school experience (also known as the 'practicum');
- a particular framework for mentoring, such as a 'syllabus' of topics to be covered at particular times or in a particular way;
- specific resources that you are asked to use, such as 'mentor meeting record sheets';
- particular approaches to the assessment of beginning teachers' classroom-based competence – for example, forms to be filled in listing strengths and targets, which are to be completed collaboratively with the student teacher in advance of a meeting with their university tutor;
- partnership-wide agreements as to the specific roles and responsibilities of both mentors and university tutors.

Alternatively, you may be working within a school-led programme which has some or all of the above features, but where your mentee may be based with you for most of the school year, giving you a great deal of autonomy over the school-based programme.

Regardless of the context in which you work, there are likely to be many aspects of being a languages mentor that are common across a range of different contexts, since beginning teachers following an ITE programme will all be working towards fulfilling the requirements of the Teachers' Standards (DfE, 2011). It is these common aspects of mentoring which we will go on to explore next.

## Checklists and mentoring standards

A number of years ago, the government in England produced a set of *National Standards for School-Based Initial Teacher Training* (DfE, 2016). The introduction to these standards identifies the mentor's role primarily as a procedural one:

> A mentor should understand the course structure and the requirement of trainees to meet the Teachers' Standards. They should prioritise meetings and discussions with a trainee, monitor performance, and help develop their teaching practice and effective classroom management strategies. A mentor should also keep their subject knowledge up-to-date and have the awareness to signpost trainees to other expertise and knowledge, for example professional subject associations.
>
> (2016, p. 8)

The standards themselves (which are not statutory) set out guidance in relation to four key areas: personal qualities and relationships; supporting the trainee's teaching; inducting the trainee into the profession; and the mentor's own professional development. Although these standards are, by their very nature, somewhat general, the fact that they exist can be seen positively, in that they raise the status of school-based mentoring. For instance, Murtagh and Dawes (2021) found that mentors within one well-established ITE partnership saw the national mentoring standards as useful in terms of (a) developing consistency, recognition and support for their role; and (b) offering guidance, enhancing quality assurance, and leading to higher quality mentoring.

However, these authors also go on to identify some limitations of the standards. They argue that, in the way that the standards are presented, they tend not to acknowledge the wider complexity of the mentor's role (Peiser et al., 2018). Thus, it is likely that the standards will lead to a 'checklist' approach to mentoring which can never cover all eventualities, nor capture all aspects of being an effective mentor. It is ultimately a reductive approach which neglects the crucial part played by a mentor's professional judgement. Furthermore, there is the danger that a list of competences or standards, emphasising the procedural aspects of the role, could actually detract from effective mentoring by preventing you, as a mentor, from focussing on underlying values and principles.

In line with this concern, Murtagh and Dawes (2021) argue that the mentor standards, in their current format, 'prioritise mentoring to enable trainees to meet government standards and reinforce the role of the mentor as "assessor" of trainees' (p. 42) – which we would see as potentially inconsistent with the more educative aspects of the role. An over-emphasis on the mentor as 'assessor' – acting as a 'gatekeeper' to the profession – is likely to lead to what Hobson and Malderez (2013) call 'judgementoring'. They describe this as:

> a one-to-one relationship between a relatively inexperienced teacher (the mentee) and a relatively experienced one (the mentor) in which the latter, in revealing too readily and/or too often her/his own judgements on or evaluations of the mentee's planning and teaching (e.g. through 'comments', 'feedback', advice, praise or criticism), compromises the mentoring relationship and its potential benefits.
>
> (2013, p. 90)

The tendency to adopt such an approach may also arise when one of the aims of mentoring is seen as being to initiate beginning teachers into the practices of a particular school – where they are 'trained' to adopt such practices uncritically and expected to conform. For example, beginning teachers may be required to follow school-wide lesson formats with particular amounts of time devoted to silent, individual work, even if this does not always work well in languages: for example, pupils may be less able to access language independently, and so require more support; or the teacher may wish them to prepare, rehearse, and perform oral role-plays in small groups as a central strand of their learning.

Hobson and Malderez's (2013) research noted the prevalence of 'judgementoring' and expressed concern that this might be becoming 'the default understanding of mentoring in England' (p. 89). Yet, it does not equip new entrants to the profession to take responsibility for their own learning or to develop the adaptive expertise (Berliner, 2004; Hatano & Inagaki, 1986) that they will need once they are in post and working more independently. That is to say, how do we support beginning teachers to 'move beyond existing routines ... to rethink key ideas, practices, and even values in order to respond to novel situations' (Hammerness et al., 2005, pp. 358–359)?

## An alternative conceptualisation

Drawing on our own experiences of working with beginning teachers and their mentors, we would argue for a very different approach, one based not on checklists but on underpinning values and principles. The purpose of mentoring, we suggest, is to help beginning teachers to unfold and flourish; the mentor's expertise lies in discerning at any given moment what can best enable this to happen. In our view, effective mentoring – just like effective classroom teaching – is heavily context-dependent. It is founded on your ability to make well-informed, ethical judgements in response to the needs of the each of the beginning teachers with whom you are working. By 'ethical', we mean judgements that take into account the potential impact of your decisions not only on the learning, but also on the well-being of your mentee – and of their pupils and the wider social context.

Because of the complex, dynamic nature of the human relationships involved in classroom teaching, in learning to teach and in mentoring, this kind of ethical decision-making is something that no checklist can ever truly capture. We would therefore suggest that having a clear set of guiding principles is essential, to clarify and inform the myriad professional mentoring decisions that you will have to make on a day-to-day basis.

A few years ago – in response to our own observations of mentor-mentee relationships over many years, and to beginning teachers' feedback on what best supported their professional learning – we came up with a set of ten guiding principles to support mentors working within our own ITE programme. To emphasise the need for mentors to respond to beginning teachers first and foremost as individual human beings – who may not fit into the expected 'boxes' and may not respond predictably to the approaches listed in mentoring checklists – we called these the 'principles for human mentoring'.

Drawing on Ryan and Deci's (2000) *Self-Determination Theory*, and the idea that human beings are 'innately curious, interested creatures who possess a natural love of learning and who desire to internalize the knowledge, customs, and values that surround them' (Niemiec & Ryan, 2009, p. 133), our principles are founded on the belief that learning is most likely to flourish if three basic psychological needs are met:

- Autonomy: do people have a sense of agency and control over the learning process?
- Competence: do they feel they are meeting any challenges and making progress?
- Relatedness: do they feel liked, respected, and valued?

We believe that this holds true for all kinds of learners, whether they be pupils in our classrooms, beginning teachers or indeed ITE mentors and tutors themselves: we believe that the same needs for autonomy, competence, and relatedness help determine our own sense of professionalism (Hobson & Maxwell, 2017).

However, we may perhaps sometimes feel that the conditions in which we work are not ones in which these needs are being fully met. At times, it may be hard to feel that our own working environment allows us to grow and flourish as professionals – for example, if we work in a school culture dominated by 'targets' and performance management. What may then happen is that, for well-intentioned reasons, we are drawn – as teachers, tutors, mentors, and line managers – to adopt practices that go against people's basic psychological needs in our interactions with them. For example, we may ask them to comply with the school's prescribed lesson format, even though privately we may question how appropriate it really is for languages. As a result, in the words of Niemiec and Ryan (2009), we may find that those people's 'feelings of joy, enthusiasm, and interest that once accompanied learning are frequently replaced by experiences of anxiety, boredom, or alienation' (p. 134).

We would like to suggest that – whatever the constraints of our own context – we might at least aim to foster feelings of autonomy, competence, and relatedness amongst the beginning teachers with whom we work. In other words, we might strive to create a context or 'micro-climate' in which they feel safe and supported, and can flourish in their professional learning. In so doing, we can also model for them the sorts of practices that, we believe, will benefit their own pupils' learning. We offer the following ten guiding principles in pursuit of this aim, which we then suggest you consider in relation to your own practice in Task 3.3.

> **Task 3.3 Re-considering scenarios**
>
> Look back to the scenarios that we presented at the beginning of the chapter. What would a response to these look like, if you were to take an educative mentoring approach and if you were following the 'principles for human mentoring'?

## Principles for human mentoring

**Show generosity of spirit.** It is easy to find fault with beginning teachers. Look for the positives and help address any gaps.

**Establish a 'micro-climate' that supports professional learning** with your mentee, whatever might be happening in the school more widely.

**Treat your mentee as a learner.** Provide the conditions in which they can flourish, and help them to grow. Growth is organic, and cannot be forced. It will happen, given the right conditions. Remember the importance of fostering the skills and dispositions which will allow them to continue growing in the future, once they are in post.

**Don't think of yourself as a 'gatekeeper to the profession'.** The criterion-based assessment procedures of the ITE programme will take care of that.

**Assume that your mentee will succeed** and qualify successfully as a teacher. Most of them do!

**Remember that you are part of a team** within the ITE partnership. You do not need to feel that the responsibility is all yours.

**Keep reminding your mentee that teaching is an incredible profession.** It is a privilege and pleasure to induct beginning teachers. In spite of all the day-to-day stresses and strains, teaching – and mentoring – can be a wonderful and rewarding job.

**Allow your mentee to be imaginative and creative** so that they can determine what works for them and their pupils.

**Nurture and protect your mentee.** 'In at the deep end' might work for some people, but not for all. 'Sink or swim' is not a good approach for those who end up sinking. Provide a safety net if things go wrong. Keep an eye on your mentee's workload and help them to manage this if needed.

**Enjoy your work as a mentor and grow professionally yourself.** Mentoring provides so many opportunities to learn and develop. Your mentee's creativity, enthusiasm, and linguistic expertise can be both instructive and inspiring.

## Challenges of taking a principles-based approach

We have advocated an approach that fosters beginning teachers' autonomy, confidence, and relatedness, as part of the process of developing teachers who will engage with teaching as a 'professional endeavour'. Such an approach 'demands of teachers practical knowhow, conceptual understandings of education, teaching and learning, and the ability to interpret and form critical judgements on existing knowledge and its relevance to their particular situation (Winch et al., 2015, p. 202).

However, this is not without its challenges. In practice, it may be very difficult to realise, particularly in contexts where *what* is to be taught and *how* it should be taught are tightly prescribed, leaving the individual teacher very little opportunity to use critical judgement within their practice. Task 3.4 asks you to consider the challenges within your own context.

---

**Task 3.4 Challenges to consider**

It may be challenging to give your mentee the opportunity to be creative or to establish a 'professional learning micro-climate' when you and your colleagues are expected to adopt a particular approach, use 'scripted' lesson plans or follow tightly prescribed formulae. In such a context, how do you, for example, support beginning teachers who want to:

- Learn how to integrate more culture into their language teaching?
- Experiment with using songs or film clips over a sequence of lessons to improve listening comprehension?
- Focus on developing reading strategies through the use of authentic texts, which contain lots of low-frequency vocabulary outside the departmental Scheme of Work?

It could also be that your mentee wants to try something out that you would not normally consider yourself – or even that you think will be ineffective. How do you respond, given that you have to balance the learning needs of your own pupils on the one hand, and your mentee on the other, who has to learn through experimentation and subsequent evaluation of the outcomes? We do not underestimate the complexity of grappling with such questions, but we do not think they can be avoided within an educative approach to mentoring.

---

## Dealing with disagreement

There is huge variation in terms of pedagogical approaches in language classrooms, as well as in wider classroom practice in schools. Further, there is a vast body of research and theory in Second Language Acquisition, but this does not give a uniform account of how to do things. There remain many 'live' debates and conflicting recommendations in key areas of language pedagogy, such as how to teach grammar, the role of pupils' first language(s) in the classroom, and the kinds of texts to which pupils should be exposed in languages. It is therefore possible – indeed likely – that your mentee will develop different views or pedagogical interpretations to yourself, or your department, or the school, as a result of what they learn about language teaching, either from theory or from practice. Many of these different pedagogical approaches will be equally compliant with the requirements of the generically framed teachers' standards.

The key question then is to decide how best to support beginning teachers in working through these tensions themselves, rather than feeling that they have to comply with particular prescriptions in order to get past the 'gatekeeper', or placate their 'judgementor'. The fact that these challenges exist does not – in our view – mean that a principled approach is wrong *per se*. It is just that the tensions and challenges need be acknowledged and considered as part of the way in which you operate as a mentor. This acknowledgement is not, in itself, problematic: it simply reflects the complexity of learning to teach and of supporting those who engaged in this endeavour.

## Conclusion

In conclusion, we would like to emphasise that being a modern languages mentor is a complex and challenging activity – not just because mentoring is, in itself, complex, but also because of the complexity of classroom teaching generally, and of teaching languages in particular. In the face of such complexity, we have argued that taking a principled, values-based approach is an immensely practical thing to do, because it guides you in all your actions as a mentor, whatever the specific situations are that you encounter, and no matter how unpredictable these may be.

Working from your values and principles is, in turn, how you exercise your own ethical, professional judgement and make well informed, contextually appropriate decisions. We believe that it is not helpful to your own development as a mentor to follow prescriptions for mentoring, or to adhere to checklists enumerating what a mentor should be like, or what a mentor should do. Such an approach might make you superficially 'efficient', and compliant with external demands, but it does not necessarily make you effective in supporting beginning teachers' learning.

Of course, you do need to be efficient in terms of getting through some of what you are expected to do as a mentor – for example, meeting your mentee on a regular basis, observing them and giving feedback, setting targets, and so on. However, this is what McIntyre and Hagger (1994) refer to as 'minimal mentoring' (p. 90). Our hope is that mentors will aspire to a more 'educative' approach – what McIntyre and Hagger call 'developed mentoring' (p. 94). This means responding to your mentee as an individual, and using your professional judgement to establish conditions which will allow them to flourish in their learning – conditions which are consistent with the basic human needs of autonomy, competence, and relatedness (Ryan & Deci, 2000). It is only by taking a principled approach, we would argue, that this can be achieved and that you start to become fully effective as a languages mentor.

## For discussion

To what extent do you agree with our 'principles for human mentoring'? What principles of your own would you adopt in order to inform and guide your work as a mentor?

Think of an example of a challenging situation you have experienced in your own work as a mentor (or as a mentee). How might the 'principles of human mentoring' be applied to this situation?

What barriers exist in your own school context to the kind of mentoring approach we have advocated? To what extent, and how, could these barriers be overcome?

## Further reading

- Trevethan, H. (2017). Educative mentors? The role of classroom teachers in initial teacher education. A New Zealand study. *Journal of Education for Teaching*, 43(2), 219-231.

    Helen Trevethan's study was carried out with primary school mentor-teachers in New Zealand but usefully outlines different models of mentoring, and raises some interesting questions as to the way in which the concept of 'educative mentoring' was understood and interpreted by those working within a particular teacher education programme.
- Hobson, A. J., & Malderez, A. (2013). Judgementoring and other threats to realizing the potential of school-based mentoring in teacher education. *International Journal of Mentoring and Coaching in Education*, 2(2), 89-108.

    This chapter draws on data from a large, longitudinal study of beginning teachers in England and highlights both the prevalence and problematic nature of judgemental mentoring (which the authors refer to as 'judgementoring'). The authors provide examples of the way in which judgementoring is reflected in mentors' practice and discuss how it is more likely to occur within particular conceptualisations of the role.

## Note

1. The terms initial teacher training (ITT) and initial teacher education (ITE) are both used in England to describe the education of pre-service teachers. We generally use the term initial teacher education, which we feel better acknowledges the complexities of learning to teach. We refer to ITT where the term is used within any specific policy documentation.

## References

Berliner, D. C. (2004). Expert teachers: Their characteristics, development and accomplishments. *Bulletin of Science, Technology and Society*, 24(3), 200-212.

Burn, K., & Mutton, T. (2015). A review of 'research-informed clinical practice' in initial teacher education. *Oxford Review of Education*, 41(2), 217-233.

Cochran-Smith, M., & Lytle, S. L. (1999). Relationships of knowledge and practice: Teacher learning in communities. *Review of Research in Education*, 24(1), 249-305.

Department for Education (2011). *Teachers' Standards*. Accessed January 11, 2024, from https://assets.publishing.service.gov.uk/media/61b73d6c8fa8f50384489c9a/Teachers__Standards_Dec_2021.pdf.

Department for Education (2016). National standards for school-based initial teacher training (ITT) mentors, DfE, London. Accessed January 11, 2024, from https://assets.publishing.service.gov.uk/media/5a803fe4ed915d74e33f9541/Mentor_standards_report_Final.pdf.

Feiman-Nemser, S. (2012). *Teachers as learners*. Harvard Education Press.

Gardner, R. (2001). *Language learning motivation: The student, the teacher and the researcher*. Key-note address to the Texas Foreign Language Education Conference, University of Texas, Austin.

Hammerness, K., Darling-Hammond, L., Bransford, J., Berliner, D., Cochran-Smith, M., McDonald, M., & Zeichner, K. (2005). How teachers learn and develop. In L. Darling-Hammond, J. Bransford, P. LePage, K. Hammerness, & H. Duffy (Eds.), *Preparing teachers for a changing world: What teachers should learn and be able to do* (pp. 358-389). Jossey-Bass.

Hatano, G., & Inagaki, K. (1986). Two courses of expertise. In H. Stevenson, H. Azuma, & K. Hakuta (Eds.), *Child development and education in Japan* (pp. 262–272). Freeman.

Hobson, A. J., & Malderez, A. (2013). Judgementoring and other threats to realizing the potential of school-based mentoring in teacher education. *International Journal of Mentoring and Coaching in Education, 2*(2), 89–108.

Hobson, A. J., & Maxwell, B. (2017). Supporting and inhibiting the well-being of early career secondary school teachers: Extending self-determination theory. *British Educational Research Journal, 43*(1), 168–191. https://doi.org/10.1002/berj.3261

Kemmis, S., Heikkinen, H. L., Fransson, G., Aspfors, J., & Edwards-Groves, C. (2014). Mentoring of new teachers as a contested practice: Supervision, support and collaborative self-development. *Teaching and Teacher Education, 43*, 154–164.

Kriewaldt, J., & Turnidge, D. (2013). Conceptualising an approach to clinical reasoning in the education profession. *Australian Journal of Teacher Education, 38*, 103–115.

Langdon, F., & Ward, L. (2015). Educative mentoring: A way forward. *International Journal of Mentoring and Coaching in Education, 4*(4), 240–254.

McIntyre, D., & Hagger, H. (1994). Teachers' expertise and models of mentoring. In H. Hagger, D. McIntyre, & M. Wilkin (Eds.), *Mentoring: Perspectives on school-based teacher education* (pp. 86–102). Routledge.

Murtagh, L., & Dawes, L. (2021). National standards for school-based mentors: The potential to recognise the "Cinderella" role of mentoring? *International Journal of Mentoring and Coaching in Education, 10*(1), 31–45.

Mutton, T., & Woore, R. (2014). The language teacher's task: Promoting learning in the foreign language classroom. In I. Thompson (Ed.), *Designing tasks in secondary education: Enhancing subject understanding and student engagement*. Routledge.

Niemiec, C. P., & Ryan, R. M. (2009). Autonomy, competence, and relatedness in the classroom: Applying self-determination theory to educational practice. *Theory and Research in Education, 7*(2), 133–144.

Orland-Barak, L. (2014). Mediation in mentoring: A synthesis of studies in teaching and teacher education. *Teaching and Teacher Education, 44*, 180–188.

Peiser, G., Ambrose, J., Burke, B., & Davenport, J. (2018). The role of the mentor in professional knowledge development across four professions. *International Journal of Mentoring and Coaching in Education, 7*(1), 2–18.

Pring, R. (2013). *The life and death of secondary education for all*. Routledge.

Ryan, R. M., & Deci, E. L. (2000). Self-determination theory and the facilitation of intrinsic motivation, social development, and well-being. *American Psychologist, 55*(1), 68.

Trevethan, H. (2017). Educative mentors? The role of classroom teachers in initial teacher education. A New Zealand study. *Journal of Education for Teaching, 43*(2), 219–231.

Winch, C., Oancea, A., & Orchard, J. (2015). The contribution of educational research to teachers' professional learning: Philosophical understandings. *Oxford Review of Education, 41*(2), 202–216.

# SECTION 2
# Getting started as a mentor

# 4 Setting your mentee up for success

*Kirsten Gregory*

## Introduction

Arguably the most important factor in ensuring the success of a beginning teacher is the relationship with their mentor. The very first Initial Teacher Training (ITT) Mentor Standard (DfE, 2016) talks of "Establishing trusting relationships" and advises mentors to "Be approachable, make time for the trainee, and prioritise meetings and discussions with them." Therefore, the idea of taking on additional responsibilities by mentoring a beginning teacher, whether they are a training teacher or a beginning teacher, can be a daunting prospect. A teacher's life is a busy one and you are already responsible for the education of many young people. By taking on the Mentor role you are adding to that workload the support, guidance, and assessment of beginning teachers, which as the ITT Mentor Standards state is a "crucial role … in supporting teacher trainees during their ITT through to successful teacher accreditation and beyond the early stages of their careers." The compensatory benefits of this role have already been discussed in chapters two and three of this volume. The focus of this chapter is on practical suggestions which will help you prepare your mentee for success in their training and continued development, but which will also save you time in the long run, either by ensuring that the practicalities are all taken care of, or by empowering your mentee to take the initiative in their development.

The term "beginning teacher" is used in this chapter to encompass those beginning their training to become teachers, who will be temporary members of your team, and permanent members who have already completed their training and are in the first few years of practice. Their needs will on occasion be quite different, and I will refer to these differing needs as we work through the chapter.

The chapter has been written chronologically to identify the tasks which it will be necessary to complete at different points during the school year.

By the end of this chapter, you should be able to:

- Understand some of the key factors that can determine the success of a beginning teacher's initial entry into a mentoring partnership and socialisation into a languages department team
- Identify a range of actions that you can take before the arrival of a new mentee, and in the early stages of the mentor-mentee relationship to help ensure they make a good start

DOI: 10.4324/9781003495468-7

## The preparation period

Your mentoring role may begin before you have even met the beginning teacher. This period will inevitably be different in terms of timings for teachers in initial teacher education (ITE) and teachers in the early stages of their career (Early Career Teachers [ECTs]), as the latter will usually be starting on the first day of term whereas training teachers will join the school at various points in the year as dictated by their ITE provider.

Most schools designate one teacher to oversee all training and ECTs, and the Human Resources department will also be instrumental in facilitating the start of the beginning teacher. In order to identify a starting point for your preparation, it will be useful to know what will be provided by others in your setting. There may be induction programmes already in place which will cover the school-wide training such as safeguarding, the behaviour policy, and the teacher code of conduct (Task 4.1).

---

### Task 4.1 Exploring the existing provision in your school

Find out who in your school oversees training teachers and ECTs. Contact them and the HR department to find out what training they will provide to the beginning teacher.

---

There is a common saying that it takes a village to raise a child, I would also apply this to training a teacher! Although you are the mentor, the rest of your department will also be key to the development and support of the beginning teacher, especially if they are at the training stage. It is desirable to build a timetable for the training teacher which includes other experienced teachers' classes. Since you are not aiming to create a carbon copy of yourself, the opportunity to observe different teaching styles will be instrumental in allowing the mentee to experiment and try out different styles and techniques. As a trainee, the mentee may have observed other subjects in the early days, perhaps shadowing a pupil or in school visits before commencing their ITE, and when offered the opportunity at a later stage, many beginning teachers will say that they have already completed these observations having only spent a day or two observing experienced teachers. These extra-departmental visits can be of benefit throughout the training period and beyond. As their own practice develops, so too will their ability to notice elements of other teachers' practice, to think critically about it and to learn from it. It is unsurprising then that as areas for development are identified by ECTs they too will benefit from observing experienced teachers both within their own subject specialism and in other departments in the school. Whilst the time constraints of their timetables will limit the frequency of the opportunities for observation, these ECTs will be identifying areas of their own practice which they wish to develop and having a specific focus for the observation will enable the beginning teacher to get the most out of these opportunities. As a mentor you may be able to facilitate these observations by identifying colleagues who have a particular strength in the area for development. For example, observing a drama teacher may be useful for someone who is looking to develop their presence in the classroom or who would like to build in more roleplay opportunities for their pupils. Maths teachers are often skilled at explaining a process to pupils which may be transferable to explicit grammar teaching. If you have been teaching at your current school for a while, then you may know which teachers have a reputation for excellence in behaviour management or retrieval practice. This knowledge will enable you to facilitate the most effective use of the observation time. (See Chapter 7 in this volume for more on how to support your mentee in analysing the teaching that they observe.)

Keeping the rest of your department informed about the beginning teacher, when they will start, how often they will be in school, when they have assignments due etc., will help to make the training a team effort. If you have members of your team who have not been involved in ITE, then you may need to give them some training on how best to develop the beginning teacher.

## The first mentor meeting

The amount of information that a beginning teacher will need to acquire in the first few weeks at a new school may be overwhelming and it is not uncommon to have to remind the mentee of this information later in the school year.

In your first meeting you will want to convey the basic information that many experienced teachers take for granted, for example how the school day is organised, how homework is organised in the department, or what routines are standardised across the school such as where pupils assemble for their lessons. It is also a good idea to plan the calendar, at least for the first term. Having key dates such as meetings, whole school briefings, parents' evenings, and assessment deadlines mapped out in advance will help you avoid the need to chase your mentee and will encourage them to be independent from the start.

Next, you can move onto the specifics of how language teaching is organised in your setting, for example which languages are taught to each year group and over how many contact hours. This will vary greatly between schools and even more so for beginning teachers who were educated in non-UK systems. It will be useful to show the mentee how to access resources such as the schemes of work, platforms which are used for teaching or by the pupils for homework and where to find any other electronic resources which will be useful in their planning and teaching (Task 4.2).

---

### Task 4.2 Creating a portfolio of useful resources

Make a list of all the websites that the beginning teacher will need access to. Do you need to request access from the IT department for them or will all IT access be arranged by the HR department?

---

Finally, the first meeting is a good opportunity to allow the mentee to talk about their experiences. This is important for many reasons. Taking an interest in your mentee will help you to begin to build a strong relationship, whilst you will be in a position of giving advice and potentially assessing the mentee, the most productive mentor-mentee relationships are supportive and nurturing. There will inevitably be information that you need to obtain from the beginning teacher, such as their competency in the languages they are offering to teach and any areas of special interest, for example do they have a passion for film or music. This information will enable you to direct the beginning teacher towards additional opportunities, both departmental and school-wide, perhaps not in their first few weeks but as they gain confidence and experience in the new setting.

On a classroom practice level, understanding the prior experiences and preconceptions of the mentee is crucial in this process of getting to know them and introducing the beginning teacher to the concept of reflective practice. Borg (2004) explores the concept of the apprenticeship of observation, the idea that all beginning teachers will have spent many years in classrooms, being taught and so they may think that they know what it takes to be an effective teacher. However, as Borg (2004, p. 274) explains, "student teachers may fail to realize that the aspects of teaching which they perceived as students represented only a partial view of the teacher's job."

Explore with your mentee what they think good language teaching looks like. It is by doing this that you are able to challenge any notions of there being a right or wrong way to teach. Instead, what we should be encouraging the beginning teacher to do is take the needs of the pupils as the starting point and explore a variety of teaching methods to discover what works best, both for the class and the beginning teacher.

## Meeting needs and providing support

Becoming a teacher and starting your first teaching job can be challenging experiences and it is important to identify any needs or difficulties early on. Whilst, as teachers, we are adept at identifying the differing needs of the pupils we teach, we should also bear in mind that the adults we work with may also have needs which need to be catered for. Does your beginning teacher have any medical or physical needs which may necessitate a risk assessment? Do they work better with written instructions rather than verbal ones? Are there any adjustments which will need to be made for them in the classroom?

The optimal situation is for your mentor periods to be scheduled and part of your timetable loading, which will help you protect this time. In my experience I give a lot more time to the beginning teachers than the 1 hour per week which is on my timetable. Brief conversations at the end of a lesson, ad hoc training on projectors and photocopiers and debriefings at the end of the school day all add up. This is part and parcel of the role and will be instrumental in ensuring that your mentee feels welcomed and supported. However, there may be times when you are unable to give your time to your mentee, especially if you have additional responsibilities in the school, and you should not be afraid to tell them that you cannot talk with them right away but identify a time when you will be able to give them your full attention. In these cases, it is useful to have identified additional sources of support. As I have already mentioned, the other teachers in the department may be willing to give their time to the beginning teacher. As trainee teachers they will already be spending time talking about the lessons and observations with other teachers in the department and may start to develop a relationship which lends itself to some moral support. Any teacher at the start of their career may also feel more able to open up about any struggles with an experienced member of staff who is not also tasked with making a judgement about them, either for the ITE or the ECT period. Burn et al.'s (2007, p. 434) research into how student teachers acquire subject specific pedagogical knowledge highlights the importance of this collaborative approach. In observations of a science department they found that

> ... in terms of seeking help with knowledge for teaching science, there was an openness to request and offer support. Indeed all members, including student teachers, were seen as legitimate sources of different kinds of knowledge (Hodkinson & Hodkinson, 2005) and there was a recognition that this knowledge, held by members with widely differing levels of experience, ought to be distributed, shared and debated.

Therefore, in addition to the careful planning of the timetable it would be advantageous to explore ways in which this collaborative and supportive atmosphere can be curated.

Whilst it is true that we should be striving to create an environment where it is the norm to discuss matters of pedagogy and subject knowledge without the fear of judgement, in practice, teachers with full timetables and a heavy planning and assessment load might not always be the best resource. One of the most successful trainee teacher cohorts that I have known were a group who from the early days, identified themselves as a team, sought out a space in the staffroom where they would meet and support each other in their non-contact time and even gave themselves a group name to consolidate their identity. The fact that they were all teaching reduced timetables meant that it was likely they would find another trainee in the staffroom and there was usually someone there to discuss ideas with, even if they weren't teaching the same subject. This type of peer support can be easily encouraged at a school-level if the beginning teachers are meeting as a cohort for guided development sessions. Task 4.3 may help you to consider the various sources of support in your own context that a beginning teacher might access.

### Task 4.3 Directing your intern to support and resources beyond yourself

Consider the following scenario and identify the various resources to which you might signpost the beginning teacher:

Your mentee has identified that they are using the same activities to introduce vocabulary in each lesson. They are concerned that the pupils are becoming bored by the predictability of the lesson and that they are not motivating the pupils. Your mentee would like to explore ways of building variety into the presentation of new vocabulary, but they need some direction for ideas of how to do this.

### How to get the most out of the partnership

Working to ensure the success of your mentee will be a long-term project and while there are things that you can do to prepare your mentee well for starting their teaching experiences, as I stated in the introduction to this chapter, their success will to some extent be defined by the strength of your relationship. If the beginning teacher is open to reflecting on their practice and is willing to act upon the guidance they are given, they will be able to refine their teaching practice and pedagogical knowledge by means of their discussions with you, their observations, and opportunities to experiment with different strategies in the classroom. The conversations following the observation of the mentee and any written feedback need to be balanced between identifying the successes or areas of progress and the areas for development. Although as the experienced teacher you may have identified many improvements which could be made to the lesson, you should select a limited number of targets to include in your feedback, ensuring that the mentee is not overwhelmed and has a clear focus for their development. Hobson (2016) offers up a research-informed framework for mentoring which he calls ONSIDE mentoring. This framework has been developed in response to the phenomenon of "judgementoring," which Hobson and Malderez (2013, p. 6) consider to be "an inappropriate enactment of mentoring on the grounds that mentors were explicitly evaluative and judgemental and practised an unnecessarily directive form of mentoring." When mentors frequently provide directive feedback on mentees' lessons, this can be experienced as "unduly critical and negative" (Hobson & Malderez, 2013, p. 9).

By creating a "no blame" culture, whereby the feedback is constructive and takes on a coaching style you can facilitate this reflection and enable your mentee to take risks in their practice. This cyclical process of experimentation, reflection, feedback, and redesign is a valuable developmental tool which is dependent on the trust in the mentor-mentee relationship. Just as we encourage our pupils to step out of their comfort zones and use the language in the classroom, safe in the knowledge that our feedback will be formative and we will not allow them to feel a fool or failure, so we should endeavour to ensure that our mentees experience this same confidence in us, that we only want the best outcomes for them. This does not mean that we will prevent them from making mistakes but that we will support them in learning from these mistakes and becoming better teachers as a result. We will inevitably build resilience as a result of this practice. It has been my experience that beginning teachers and especially those who have started their training immediately after finishing their degree, have often been successful in all areas of their education to this point. They have inevitably worked hard for their success, but they may have limited experience of putting in the effort and the outcome not being what they envisaged. Throughout my own teaching career, I repeatedly experience times when I plan for a class and something unexpected happens which derails the learning. As long as we can reflect on why the lesson did not go as we had planned and adapt the lesson for the next time or take that knowledge with us for the next lesson we plan for that class, we become better teachers for these experiences. Working with this level of unpredictability requires resilience which we may need to build in the ITE and ECT careers years.

As a mentor it is important to model the values of lifelong learning and to embrace the learning opportunities that being a mentor presents. Pinnick (2020, p. 253) identifies that "the Mentor Standards do not currently consider the potential benefits to the mentor him/herself of being involved in mentoring." This is clearly seen as a considerable omission as she goes on to cite Freire (1972, p. 65) who suggested that teacher and learner 'become jointly responsible for a process in which all grow'. I have been privileged as a mentor to observe some innovative teaching by beginning teachers who, in the absence of a full teaching load, often have the capacity to be more creative with their planning. In these instances, I have made a point of discussing the things I have learnt with my mentee, perhaps the biggest compliment is when I ask them if they would share their resources with me. The topics covered in mentor meetings can also lead to some interesting discussions and discoveries. As part of their training the beginning teachers will be reading the latest research into language teaching and acquisition and so they are in a good position to identify and critique the latest trends. To get the most out of these conversations, and to support your own professional learning, you may want to keep up to date on the research that they are reading (Task 4.4).

### Task 4.4 Reading to support your own development

Ask your mentee or their ITE provider to share their reading list with you. Will any of these titles support your own developmental objectives?

The traditional model of teacher observations and judgements does not exploit all the benefits of this reciprocal relationship. Indeed Pinnick (2020, p. 251) tells us that "the way we view all teacher development, whatever the stage of the career – needs to be reconceptualised to be made far more dialogic and collaborative." Perhaps we will now see more educational settings changing their teacher development programmes to embrace the coaching model (see Chapter 12 in this volume for more information about coaching).

## Conclusion

Setting your mentee up for success is inextricably linked to the relationship that you cultivate with them. Becoming a teacher is a complex and challenging process which requires high levels of resilience and there will inevitably be times when your mentee may question whether this is the right career for them. By creating a nurturing environment, the beginning teacher can learn to accept that these challenges do not mean that they are failing. In anticipation of the times when difficulties occur, identify sources of support with your mentee and encourage them to take advantage of these resources. While we are not trying to create carbon copies of ourselves, we should model the behaviours that we are looking for in our mentees. If we are open to opportunities to develop our own practice, then the beginning teachers will see that we are not expecting them to be "perfect" but that we are expecting them to take responsibility for improving their practice as a long-term goal, not just for the first few years in the classroom.

## For discussion

1. To what extent has your own experience of being mentored shaped your approach to the role?
2. Do you agree that resilience is an essential characteristic in teachers and if so, have you had to develop resilience in yourself as a teacher?

## Further reading and resources

Alongside browsing the other chapters in this book, I recommend that new mentors prepare for their role by reading the DfE National Standards for school-based ITT (see references below).

The Association for Language Learning (ALL) hosts a Special Interest Group for any ALL members who are involved in language teacher education that you can subscribe to here: https://www.all-languages.org.uk/about/community/special-interest-groups/itet-sig/

There are many openly accessible summaries of research into language learning and teaching that can be searched by keyword on the OASIS database https://oasis-database.org/. At the time of writing, more than 100 summaries are tagged with "Teacher Education." For example, the following is an open access summary of research into the reciprocity of the mentor-mentee relationship:

Turan, P., & Yiğitoğlu Aptoula, N. (2023). How do mentors use (and retract) their professional knowledge when talking to language teacher trainees? *OASIS Summary* of Turan & Yiğitoğlu Aptoula (2023) in *The Modern Language Journal*. https://oasis-database.org

## References

Borg, M. (2004). The apprenticeship of observation. *ELT Journal*, 58(3), 274-276.

Burn, K., Childs, A., & McNicholl, J. (2007). The potential and challenges for student teachers' learning of subject-specific pedagogical knowledge within secondary school subject departments. *The Curriculum Journal*, 18(4), 429-445. https://doi.org/10.1080/09585170701687886

Department for Education. (2016). *National Standards for school-based initial teacher training mentors*. Retrieved from https://www.gov.uk/government/publications/initial-teacher-training-government-response-to-carter-review

Freire, P. (1972). *Pedagogy of the oppressed*. Penguin.

Hobson, A. J. (2016). Judgementoring and how to avert it: Introducing ONSIDE mentoring for beginning teachers. *International Journal of Mentoring and Coaching in Education*, 5(2), 87-110.

Hobson, A. J., & Malderez, A. (2013). Judgementoring and other threats to realizing the potential of school-based mentoring in teacher education. *International Journal of Mentoring and Coaching in Education*, 2(2), 89-108.

Pinnick, S. (2020). Mentoring secondary English trainee teachers: A case study. *English in Education*, 54(3), 251-264.

# 5 Supporting emerging languages teachers: key principles to guide the journey

*Judith Rifeser, Bernadette Holmes, and Caroline Conlon*

## Introduction

The exploration of the origins of the word "mentor" leads back in time to Greek mythology and brings us in contact with Homer's well-known story of Odysseus, King of Ithaca. As he leaves to fight in the Trojan war, he entrusts his son, Telemachus, to a close friend and counsellor. Mentor, so the name of the trusted friend, is tasked to guide, advise, and protect Telemachus. Here, in this brief story, we find a key element that sits at the heart of the endeavour of mentoring, namely trust. It is upon this pillar that a successful relationship between mentor and emerging mentee can be built. It is vital in supporting the process of an emerging teacher in "becoming" (Rogers, 1969), that is in developing and growing their knowledge(s), skills, and understanding as they build their confidence and agency as member of the (languages) teacher community. We have chosen the term "emerging" to emphasise the actual process, on the one hand, and on the other to acknowledge that these teachers are not a tabula rasa but rather come with a wealth of prior knowledge, skills, and experiences as they embark on their journey of growth and development, of "becoming."

As a mentor, then, this chapter aims to support you to:

- **Know that** mentors play a critical role in the development and growth of emerging teachers' knowledge(s) and related propositions (Shulman, 1987)
- **Know how to** critically explore epistemological beliefs and values with emerging teachers and support them on their journey of "becoming" through a relationship of trust and respect
- **Know why** it is critical for emerging teachers to engage in evidence-informed practice and high-quality subject-specific professional learning, beginning with principled practice

## The importance of teacher knowledge(s)

The way the chapter objectives are outlined might remind you of the "learn that ... /learn how to" model used in the key framework set out for emerging teachers in England, the ITTECF Framework (2025) – formerly known as the Initial Teacher Training Core Content Framework (Department for Education, 2019a) and Early Career Framework (Department for Education, 2019b) – which sets out the minimum entitlement of teachers in the first three years in the profession (1+2 years). In line with these frameworks, we have chosen to adopt this language familiar to mentors and mentees but have shifted the emphasis from "learning" to a focus on "knowing," hereby acknowledging the expertise of the mentor, whilst simultaneously drawing attention to ways in which our knowledge bases and we ourselves develop and grow. Hereby it is also important to draw attention to a third element in relation to "knowing that" and "knowing how to," that is the "why," the knowing not only that something is, and how to do/explain/question something but also, crucially, why it is so, why it works, why it is vital to whatever aims you might try to achieve to maximise opportunities for all learners. Similarly, it is possible to also support the emerging teacher in learning about the importance of understanding the "why." In other words:

> The teacher need not only understand *that* something is so; the teacher must further understand *why* it is so, on what grounds its warrant can be asserted, and under what circumstances our belief in its justification can be weakened and even denied. Moreover, we expect the teacher to understand why a given topic is particularly central to a discipline whereas another may be somewhat peripheral.
>
> (Shulman, 1987, p. 9)

The "knowing that" and "knowing why" necessitate then the "knowing how to" to enable teachers to develop these understandings to ultimately benefit their learners. These three elements are directly linked to the importance of teacher knowledge(s) (explored further in Task 5.1) and we will return to these different knowledges at the end of this chapter.

---

**Task 5.1 Reflecting on the knowledge that teachers need**

We invite you to explore what knowledge(s) and skills you consider, in your experience, to be vital for emerging languages teachers. Consider which of these are subject-specific and which are general. You might consider, for example, cognitive load theory and its implications on teaching and learning more generally, and then in relation to language learning. Write your thoughts down in Table 5.1.

---

*Table 5.1* What knowledge(s) and skills do emerging teachers need?

| What knowledge(s) do teachers needs generally? | What subject-specific knowledge(s) do teachers needs? | What general skills do teachers need? | What subject-specific skills do teachers need? |
|---|---|---|---|
| | | | |

In his paper entitled "Those Who Understand: Knowledge Growth in Teaching," Lee S. Shulman (1987: 12) sets out his taxonomy of what he calls "the knowledge base of teaching."

1. Content Knowledge
2. General Pedagogical Knowledge
3. Pedagogical Content Knowledge
4. Curricular Knowledge
5. Knowledge of Learners and their Characteristics
6. Knowledge of Educational Contexts
7. Knowledge of Educational Aims, Purposes, and Values

Shulman does not set them out to be specific to a certain subject, but it is useful to consider these both more broadly and in the specific context of our specialism. He highlights the importance of acknowledging both the differences as well as the interdependency of the different dimensions of knowledge, which will be revisited in Chapter 18, and can be summarised as follows:

1. **Content Knowledge**: Knowledge of subject matter and its organising structures.
2. **General Pedagogical Knowledge:** Knowledge of principles and strategies for supporting and fostering learning that go beyond subject matter.
3. **Curriculum Knowledge:** Knowledge and familiarity with the topics and issues that have been and will be taught in the same subject area during the preceding and later years in school.
4. **Pedagogical Content Knowledge:** A combination of content and pedagogical knowledge that is needed for teaching a subject.
5. **Knowledge of Learners and their Characteristics:** Including their linguistic and sociocultural background, their needs and interests.
6. **Knowledge of Educational Contexts:** Ranging from knowledge of the workings of the group or classroom to the governance of the school, to familiarity with the wider community.
7. **Knowledge of Educational Aims, Purposes, and Values:** Knowledge of their purposes and values, as well as their historical and philosophical foundations.

## The importance of exploring epistemological beliefs and values

One aspect that arises from an engagement with Shulman's taxonomy is ultimately the question: What is knowledge? And further: How do we know what we know? How do we learn what we know? These are critical questions for our emerging languages teachers. Our epistemological beliefs, that is the ways we think about the structure, source, and nature of knowledge, inform consciously and unconsciously the way we act and the way in which we develop our knowledge and understanding. Indeed, a prerequisite to providing emerging teachers with the support they need, is firstly, to acknowledge that "[p]rofessional growth requires novices to confront previously constructed images of teaching, acknowledge them and their sources and subsequently adapt them" (Calderhead & Elliot, 1995, p. 38).

Saying this, it is equally important for established teachers to engage in continual critical reflexive praxis – that is the entanglement between theory and practice (Nelson, 2013) – themselves – an aspect that will be introduced later in this chapter and re-visited in our work in Chapter 18, entitled: Supporting expert languages teachers. Our epistemological beliefs influence what and how we think about learning and teaching and help us justify why something is working (or not), and therefore have an impact on our teaching practice. It is critical to consider these different dimensions of subject knowledge both as mentor and emerging teacher as they provide a fruitful ground for the reflection of the interplay between the theoretical and practical knowledge that we hold and our actions that are informed by this knowledge. We will return to thinking about praxis, that is the interplay between theory and practice (Nelson, 2013) momentarily. Before doing so, we want to first briefly return to Shulman's (1987) work.

## Principled practice for emerging teachers

In addition to Shulman's (1987) classification of teacher knowledge, in the same article, he sets out three propositions:

1. Disciplined empirical or philosophical enquiry
2. Practical experience
3. Moral or ethical reasoning

The first one, **disciplined empirical or philosophical enquiry**, is nested in empirical knowledge. From it, we can derive principles for teaching and learning. These might be principles that are essential to teaching and learning more broadly such as the effects of metacognitive processes on the learning cycle, or the importance of a carefully sequenced curriculum. For example, we could explore Bruner's (1960) model of the Spiral Curriculum which, whilst developed for the natural sciences, is equally relevant for the context of languages. In Bruner's model, learning is envisioned as a spiral upwards, from basic to more advanced concepts, with them being revisited and reinforced as the level of complexity increase and additional learning objectives are presented. This then leads us to consider subject-specific principles that we need to keep in mind. For example, in relation to foundational knowledge and the teaching of phonology, vocabulary, and grammar, which relate back to curriculum knowledge and pedagogical content knowledge. It is critical for the emerging teacher to not only **know** these principles but also know **how to** and **why to** apply them to their classroom. It is here that the mentor plays a critical role in modelling good practice, showcasing how these principles are implemented short term, over a certain period and finally, over the long term. The mentor can explore with the emerging teacher the impact of the learning and teaching taking place in the classroom by using the idea of "thinking aloud" (White & Mackintosh, 2022). Furthermore, it is crucial for the mentor to showcase how **research evidence** is useful to inform practice, foregrounding the notion of **praxis**.

The Modern Foreign Languages Pedagogy Review (Bauckham, 2016) outlines the evidence-informed key recommendations for our subject area, which in turn link again to the above-mentioned knowledge areas. Under recommendation 14, we find a specific reference to the "systematic development of trainees' subject-specific knowledge and expertise in language teaching," with a special emphasis on the importance that a "clearly worked out curriculum is in place, which should include areas covered by this report, in particular the specific pedagogical knowledge and expertise required by languages teachers" (Bauckham, 2016, pp. 3-4). Out of these principles we can then derive and agree a shared language and common understanding of principled practice. Why is it important to have a set of clear definitions and principles out of which we can develop a shared language and common understanding? It is critical to identify, codify and systematise effective, research-informed teaching and learning to develop professional learning (Task 5.2).

---

**Task 5.2 Considering the principles that underpin your own practice**

How and why do you think definitions and principles are useful for you as mentor and for the emerging teacher you are supporting?

a. Which principles inform your own practice as a languages teacher?
b. Where do these principles come from?
c. How could you use these principles (and others from the literature) to support an emerging languages teacher in developing their practice?

---

In her work, bell hooks (2018) beautifully illustrates **the power of definitions** when she asserts:

> Definitions are vital starting points for the imagination. What we cannot imagine cannot come into being. A good definition marks our starting point and lets us know where we want to end up. As we move toward our desired destination we chart the journey, creating a map.
>
> (p. 4)

She uses these words in a slightly different context, in relation to relationships and love, though perhaps these can be useful also in our context here, for teaching and learning, in the relationship between mentor and mentee, and in what sits at the heart of this work overall: It is on the one hand, the love and passion for supporting our learners in unfolding their full potential, and helping them grow and develop into confident, kind and independent human beings more broadly. On the other hand, it is about nurturing their love for languages, their ability to communicate with confidence and to say what they want to say in (an)other language(s) with cultural agility. These words bring forth again the notion of "becoming," illustrating the importance of the map as guiding tool.

A **destination** or outcome is critical here (Allison & Tharby, 2015) on the journey that both mentee and mentor embark on to support the emerging teacher in the transition to becoming an established educational professional with agency and self-efficacy. A vital link can be identified between **self-efficacy**, that is, "the beliefs in one's capabilities to organise and execute the courses of action required" (Bandura, 1997, p. 3), and **"a sense of belonging** in educational transitions" (Gordon, 2020, p. 666). In other words, we must remember the importance of supporting emerging teachers in developing their confidence in themselves and their capabilities, establishing a sense of community, for example by joining languages-specific and wider professional institutions, whilst preparing them for their professional journey ahead. It is important to acknowledge here that the emerging teacher undergoes a journey of transition: In England, critical moments of transition occur for an emerging teacher as they first enter teacher training, then embark on their two-year ECT phase to become embedded in the profession and then again as they move out of this phase to continue their journey towards becoming established practitioners. Here, as Anna Lise Gordon (2020, p. 666) highlights, the term "bridging the gap" is useful to highlight the transition phase that needs to, just like for pupils, be developed through "inclusive, effective and coherent strategies," and acknowledge the emerging teacher as an individual human being. Indeed, it is vital to hear emerging teachers' voices (Ewing & Manuel, 2005).

Research on mentee satisfaction in relation to mentoring, specifically for those who enter the profession as career changers, "indicates the potential need for bespoke training that considers their range of prior life and industry experience" (Bond, 2023, p. 4). Mentors must focus not only on the administrative responsibilities and needs of the teacher but also their professional learning needs and **wellbeing** (Gordon, 2020). Recent research highlights emerging teachers' need for "emotional and psychosocial support" (Bond, 2023, p. 13), as a survey revealed a stark discrepancy between the way mentees (34%) and mentors (69%) felt about being able to share their thoughts, ideas, and worries in a safe environment (Allen et al., 2022). What has been shown to be effective in promoting a nourishing and trusting environment is related specifically to the facilitation of learning through core principles such as cognitive modelling – that is, how to problem-solve and perform tasks – and foundational principles of motivation – looking for example at theories such as self-determination theory – as well as the importance of collaboration, networking, and high-quality professional learning (Bond, 2023). Opportunities for collaboration and networking strengthen a sense of belonging to the wider community and can offer a way to develop and strengthen professional and indeed personal relationships beyond one's own classroom and school which is, as we discussed earlier, vital for emerging teachers during their training and beyond to support them in continuing in their profession. Joining a professional organisation for teaching professionals more generally such as for example the Chartered College for Teaching[1], or a subject association more specifically, e.g. the Association for Language Learning (ALL),[2] can provide emerging teachers with a way to meet others at the same stage of their career, offer space for sharing and provide access both to other professionals who can act as additional points of support, guidance, and inspiration, as well as to high-quality professional learning. These benefits also apply to established professionals.

Task 5.3 offers a framework for a structured reflection on the opportunities for professional learning that you have enjoyed and benefited from.

### Task 5.3 Reflecting on professional learning opportunities

Consider the opportunities for collaboration, networking, and high-quality professional learning that have been useful for you throughout your career and/or look into ways in which you could take up some of these offers.

Reflect on the following and make notes in Table 5.2: How have these opportunities been useful for you and your own evidence-informed classroom practice? In a second step, work with your mentee to agree together which opportunities they should consider, to develop their knowledge(s), skills, and understandings. Finally, consider which opportunities you might want to explore to learn together and develop your collaborative work, much in the spirit of the co-construction that sits at the heart of educative mentoring (see White & Mackintosh, 2022 and Chapter 18 in this volume).

Laura Molway highlights here the crucial importance and "strong appetite for PL [professional learning]" amongst languages teachers that is both evidence-informed and sustained over time (Molway, 2022, p. 647). The latter needs to be highlighted further given that we know from the literature the importance of high-quality professional development to encourage sustained practice over time, which in turn provides a fruitful ground to develop (new) habit formation (Allison & Tharby, 2015). Mentoring can play a vital role in this process. Yet, research has shown that mentors' working hours dramatically increase through the mentoring process, giving them less time for their own professional development and planning. Thus, we need to recognise and indeed reward the efforts of mentors (Cunningham, 2007, p. 86). Literature reveals that effective mentoring can lead to "a range of positive outcomes for mentees, including improved teaching practice, confidence and self-belief, enhanced teacher-student interactions, and an improved classroom environment" (National Institute of Teaching, 2023, para 3). Important here is the note that where emerging teachers are using an **evidence-informed approach** to their teaching, they make "principled changes to practice in response to student needs" (Timperley, 2008, p. 24), helping both their learners and teachers to thrive (Petriwskyj, 2010).

*Table 5.2* Reflections on opportunities for collaboration, networking, and high-quality professional learning

| Task 5.3a: For you, as a Mentor | |
|---|---|
| Opportunities | Professional and Personal Benefits/Outcomes |

| Task 5.3b: For your Mentee | |
|---|---|
| Opportunities | Professional and Personal Benefits/Outcomes |

| Task 3.3: Together as Mentor and Mentee | |
|---|---|
| Opportunities | Professional and Personal Benefits/Outcomes |

**Practical experience** is central to evidence-informed classroom practice, linking the "know that" and "know why" to the "know how to," the application of the lived, embodied experience to the site(s) of learning. Out of the 14 recommendations of the MFLPR2016, key principles can be derived that can support professional learning. In this context, as we have argued, it is critical to also consider how practical experience can be gained in these areas. Interestingly, Shulman (1987) draws attention to an area that is little discussed in relation to classroom teaching and learning, namely that there are ideas which have never been proven by research and would indeed be difficult to prove. Yet, "these maxims represent the accumulated wisdom of practice" (Shulman, 1987: 11). This practical experience is, importantly, next to disciplined empirical or philosophical enquiry and moral or ethical reasoning, the third proposition that Shulman (1987:11) makes. What is more, there is a need to acknowledge the important findings arising from classroom practice that can inform educational theories – and not only vice versa, that is, theory informing practice (see Nelson, 2013; Rifeser and Ros i Solé, 2022).

Make use of Task 5.4 to map how you, as a mentor, and your colleagues in your languages department can support emerging teachers in developing their pedagogical (content) knowledge and enable them to engage in evidence-informed practice to develop their knowledge, understanding, skills, and subject expertise.

---

**Task 5.4 Reflection on the development of specific aspects of language teaching practice**

In your department, explore the following two aspects:

1. Firstly, identify an aspect of pedagogical (content) knowledge that emerging teachers need to learn.
2. Secondly, consider how you can support your mentee to experiment with the application of this knowledge in their classroom practice.

---

Finally, we invite you to explore (Task 5.5) the final proposition put forwards by Shulman (1987), that is **moral or ethical reasoning**:

> [It] reflects the norms, values, ideological or philosophical commitments of justice, fairness, equity, and the like, that we wish teachers and those learning to teach to incorporate and employ. They are neither theoretical nor practical, but normative. They occupy the very heart of what we mean by teacher knowledge ... because they are morally or ethically right.
>
> (Shulman, 1987, p. 11)

---

**Task 5.5 Consideration of your own value positioning**

1. Consider the commitments you make to values (i.e. fairness etc.) in your role as a languages professional. Can you identify what these commitments are for you? Which three are most important to you?
2. As a second step, share your three commitments with your mentee. Then consider, how can you help them identify theirs and support them in developing these?

## Conclusion

As Melina Porto and Michael Byram (2015, pp. 26-27) observe: "foreign language teaching is and should be foreign language education, with all that that means in terms of personal development and societal improvement" and this, so we argue, applies also to the process of professional learning and mentoring to maximise learning and affect change (see Bond, 2023). Continuous development, growth, and critical reflection are all key aims of the mentoring process, involving both the mentor and mentee in this relationship of mutual trust and respect. As we have shown in this chapter, the exploration of teacher knowledge(s) and epistemological beliefs and values is central to this journey. It is here then that "rich mentoring conversations" (Black et al., 2017, p. 13) can emerge whereby both the emerging teacher and the mentor can learn with and from each other, recognising each other's critical role to make the journey a successful one. Indeed, "it is a great privilege to be working with 'tomorrow's teachers' helping to shape, lead and inspire them" (Black et al., 2017, p. 8) and many of us in the teaching profession will attest to the unforgettable impact a mentor – like the character Mentor who supports and guides Telemachus – can have on one's own growth as a languages teacher and the journey to becoming.

## For discussion

Having read this chapter, consider the following:

- At the very beginning of this chapter the importance of trust was highlighted as sitting at the heart of the mentor-mentee relationship. How is a relationship of trust established between you and your mentee?
- Which elements of teacher knowledge identified by Shulman (1987) do you feel were discussed in your own teacher training? Which ones were not explored enough? Has this changed over time in teacher training? Are you aware of any changes?
- If we consider the quote by Porto and Byram (2015) above in terms of the importance of foreign language education (rather than foreign language teaching), how do you think that mentoring can support personal development and societal improvement? What would be your top three goals with regards to this?
- Reflecting upon how you are being supported within your professional learning community: What additional support would you need/wish to receive in your vital role as mentor for the new generation of teaching professionals?

## Further readings

- Black, L., Gordon A. L, Hughes, C., MacArthur, R., & Sandy, S.. (2017). *Effective mentoring of trainee teachers* (pp. 1-33). The Association for Language Learning.
    This is a short guide for mentors produced by the subject association for languages teachers in England (and Wales), the Association for Language Learning (ALL).
- Molway, L. (2022). Which aspects of their practice do modern languages teachers in England's secondary schools say they want to develop? *The Language Learning Journal, 50*(5), 627-649.
    This article gives voice to languages teachers in England by exploring what they think their professional learning needs are and how these might be met.

- Shulman, L. S. (1986). Those who understand: Knowledge growth in teaching. *Educational Researcher, 15*(2), 4-14.

    Despite being written in the 80s, this article is relevant to today's teaching professionals as it explores the types of knowledge that are critical for teachers across all subjects.
- National Institute of Teaching (2023). *Mentoring and coaching of teachers: What can research tell us?* (pp. 1-6). National Institute of Teaching.

    This short guide maps key findings of the investigation commissioned by the National Institute of Teaching (NIoT) into effective mentoring and coaching of teachers at the early stages of their career, namely trainees and Early Career Teachers (ECTs).
- Bauckham, I. (2016). *The modern foreign language pedagogy review* (pp. 1-27). Teaching Schools Council.

    The Teaching Schools Council 2016 commissioned a report on modern languages pedagogy in England. This review was chaired by Sir Ian Bauckham. Both the previous DfE-funded initiative that led to the National Centre for Excellence in MFL Pedagogy (NCELP) based at the University of York, and the current initiative, the National Consortium for Languages Education (NCLE), led by UCL's IOE Faculty of Education and Society in collaboration with the Goethe-Institut London and the British Council, are informed by the Modern Foreign Language Pedagogy Review 2016.

## Notes

1. Chartered College for Teaching.
2. Association for Language Learning (ALL).

## References

Allen, B., Ford, I., & Wespieser, K. (2022). Mentoring and coaching for trainee and early career teachers. Current practice survey, *Report to NIoT*, November 2022. pp. 1-30.

Allison, S., & Tharby, A. (2015). *Making every lesson count: Six principles to support great teaching and learning*. Crown Publishing House.

Bandura, A. (1997). *Self-efficacy: The exercise of control*. Freeman.

Bauckham, I. (2016). *The modern foreign language pedagogy review 2016* (pp. 1-27). Teaching Schools Council.

Black, L., Gordon, A. L., Hughes, C., MacArthur, R. & Sandy, S. (2017) *Effective mentoring of trainee teachers* (pp. 1-33). The Association for Language Learning.

Bond, M. (2023) *Mentoring and coaching of teachers: Thematic synthesis* (pp. 1-30). National Institute of Teaching, University College London, University of Stavanger..

Bruner, J. S. (1960). *The process of education*. Harvard University Press.

Calderhead, J., & Elliot, B. (1995). Mentoring for teacher development: Possibilities and caveats. In T. Kerry & A. Shelton Mayes (Eds.), *Issues in mentoring* (pp. 35-58). Routledge.

Cunningham, B. (2007). All the right features: Towards an "architecture" for mentoring trainee teachers in the UK further education colleges. *Journal of Education for Teaching, 33*(1), 83-97.

Department for Education. (2019a). Early Career Framework. https://www.gov.uk/government/publications/early-career-framework

Department for Education. (2019b). Initial Teacher Training Core Content Framework. Available at: https://www.gov.uk/government/publications/initial-teacher-training-itt-core-content-framework

Department for Education. (2025). *ITTECF Framework (2025)*. Available at: https://assets.publishing.service.gov.uk/media/661d24ac08c3be25cfbd3e61/Initial_Teacher_Training_and_Early_Career_Framework.pdf

Gordon, A. L. (2020). Educate – Mentor – Nurture: Improving the transition from initial teacher education to qualified teacher status and beyond. *Journal of Education for Teaching*, 46(5), 664–675.

hooks, bell. (2018). *All about love: New visions*. HarperCollins Publishers.

Molway, L. (2022). Which aspects of their practice do modern languages teachers in England's secondary schools say they want to develop? *The Language Learning Journal*, 50(5), 627–649.

National Institute of Teaching (2023). *Mentoring and coaching of teachers: What can research tell us?* (pp. 1–6). Available at: https://niot.s3.amazonaws.com/documents/NIOT_mentoring_and_coaching_-_Key_Takeaways.pdf

Nelson, R. (2013). *Practice as research in the arts: Principles, protocols, pedagogies, resistances*. Palgrave Macmillan.

Petriwskyj, A. (2010). Kindergarten transition and linkages to primary school-readiness reconceptualised. In P. Petersen, E. Baker, & B. McGaw (Eds.), *International encyclopaedia of education* (Vol. 2, pp. 120–125). Elsevier.

Porto, M., & Byram, M. (2015). Developing intercultural citizenship education in the language classroom and beyond. *Argentinian Journal of Applied Linguistics*, 3, 9–29.

Rifeser, J., & Ros i Solè, C. (2022). Film-making as creative praxis: Capturing the intimate side of interculturality. *Language and Intercultural Communication*, 22(2), 221–234.

Rogers, C. R. (1969). *Freedom to learn*. Charles Merril.

Shulman, L. S. (1986). Those who understand: Knowledge growth in teaching. *Educational Researcher*, 15(2), 4–14.

Shulman, L. S. (1987). Knowledge and teaching: Foundations of the new reform. *Harvard Educational Review*, 57(1), 1–22. https://doi.org/10.17763/haer.57.1.j463w79r56455411

Timperley, H. (2008). Teacher professional learning and development. *The International Academy of Education*, 1(18), 1–30.

White, E., & Mackintosh, J. (2022). Educative mentoring versus instructional coaching: What approach enables mentors to support student-teacher learning? *University of Hertfordshire Link*, 6(1). Available at: https://www.herts.ac.uk/link/volume-6,-issue-1,-april-2022/educative-mentoring-versus-instructional-coaching-what-approach-enables-mentors-to-support-student-teacher-learning

# 6 Supporting the integration of beginning languages teachers into the community of practice

*Crista Hazell*

## Introduction

Effective and meaningful support of our languages colleagues requires time, focus, and the involvement of the whole language learning community. In this chapter, I shall explore how best we can support the effective integration of beginning teachers, or those new to our educational establishment. Building a network of expert support around new colleagues should facilitate their growth in confidence and deepen their knowledge and understanding. Connecting with a range of different communities of practice (CoP) both inside and outside of school should also help new colleagues to gain a wider perspective of experience, to overcome the challenges they face, and ultimately to stay in the profession. Connecting beginning, or indeed experienced languages teachers into CoP within and beyond our educational establishments advocates continuing self-reflection and professional self-development, empowering our language teachers to develop and build upon their training to date while developing a climate of success. In this chapter, I shall share some personal reflections and link these to current research.

Before reading on, consider Task 6.1.

---

**Task 6.1 Reflect on your own experiences within communities of practice**

Consider your own support network, both within your current school, and beyond. Where do you go to connect with like-minded colleagues, to share experiences and celebrate professional triumphs, seek support, and raise problems of practice?

How did you learn about/build these networks of support?
How often do you engage with these?

---

All languages teachers at interview talk about wanting to engage their learners and take them on a most amazing journey showcasing cultures and language, different sounds and magical words, astounding grammatical constructions which will intrigue, engage, and lead to the ultimate experience; exploration of sights through educational visits, of sounds through music and film, and of smells and tastes through new environments and delicious, but maybe unfamiliar food. The languages classroom can indeed be a magical place and a unique experience for pupils because it is the only lesson in the curriculum where they can be taught through and about another language, and if we are especially lucky two or even three. No beginning teacher sets out with anything less than an aspiration to boost learners at all stages, increasing uptake of higher-level language learning, passionately believing that they have the skill set, and mindset to overcome the challenges that they will face in the classroom. However, we have to be mindful that the "quality of the next generation of teachers will, in large part, depend on the quality of the mentoring support they are given" (Furlong & Maynard, 1995: 195) highlighted by Black, Gordon, Hughes, MacArthur, and Sandy in their collaborative book (2017). We need to ensure that beginning teachers are supported appropriately and effectively to transition from their training establishment, university, or school, into the setting in which we are working. We need to consider cognitive overload when sharing school policies and practices which may be new or different to those previously experienced. As we are developing beginning teachers, we want to allow them to show us all that they can do, create an environment where they will thrive and develop but at the same time help them to understand and integrate systems and approaches which are school and/or trust driven. These need to be adhered to and used in the classroom consistently, as they operate across the school.

Sweller (1998) suggests that cognitive resources are limited, and we know this in the classroom with learners, but we must remember this too with our colleagues. We want to create opportunities for them to be successful in the classroom and as part of this help them understand, know, and feel the support of system-wide institutional practice around starting the lesson, seating the learners, managing behaviour, and finishing the class as successfully as they can. How can we best do this so that we do not overwhelm, bore or cognitively overload them? As Kennedy (2016, p. 6) states "If we break practice into very small bits, our lists become too long and crowded with minutiae." We do not want this either. We need to find a happy medium.

In any interview process, we start to learn a little about each of the candidates, but not everything. We appoint the successful candidate based on their confidence, competence, skill, and ability to connect with the existing members of the languages team, as well as what they can bring. We know they can deliver because, during the interview process, we have scrutinised these areas and have viewed references which attest to this. We need to ensure that we make space to get to know them, in the mîlée that is the end of one and start of the following academic year, we must find time and space to become better cognisant of the teacher's understanding in order that we can better help them. There is of course a variety of considerations – for example if they are a native speaker, they may not need assistance in maintaining subject knowledge, but they may need support with time management or lesson planning and balancing language skills development and grammatical understanding. We won't know until we meet with them.

The journey from initial education to the beginning years is challenging, a balancing act where beginning teachers will be weighing up the subject knowledge and skills they need to be an effective languages teacher but also the pedagogical knowledge and skills required to effectively communicate with their learners. And it doesn't stop there. There are many elements to balance and manage/stabilise therefore the weekly professional mentor meetings are paramount as they create a safe space and build capacity to be reflective and consider different aspects of teaching, learning, the progress of learners, and of course successful integration into the department and school. A timetabled session weekly or fortnightly provides time so that as lead teacher, mentor or head of department, the beginning teacher has that time 1:1 with you so you can home in on aspects that need support. Discussion of these elements brings increased understanding of departmental methods or ways of doing things because there is time created to breakdown these elements and allow the new colleague to ask any questions they may have. These can be routine elements such as support with getting learners in and settled quickly through to looking at policies and how to implement them but equally allow for deepening discussion over time to develop or refine understanding. We know that during Initial Teacher Training according to the Modern Foreign Languages Pedagogy Review (Bauckham, 2016), the subject-specific content should include the following 13 elements as a minimum:

- knowing the distinction between curriculum and pedagogy, and understanding the principles of curriculum planning in modern language
- understanding the role and nature of working memory, long term memory, meaningful practice, and automatisation as applied to languages pedagogy
- developing expertise at integrating language taught and practised into authentic communication in an incremental and planned way
- approaches to the selection, planning, sequencing, and teaching of vocabulary, including a strong basic repertoire of techniques to enable practising, memorising, retrieving, and using new vocabulary
- effective approaches to teaching grammar, including the components highlighted in this report, and including learning to teach, and practising teaching, specific features of the new language (tenses, cases, questions, negatives, agreements, etc.)
- planning and teaching new language phonics effectively
- learning and applying techniques for error anticipation and correction, and understanding when error tolerance is appropriate, and why
- understanding how to design language practice to be progressively less scaffolded and move from comprehension to production and use
- developing a range of approaches for making content meaningful and stimulating
- undertaking a critical evaluation of teaching materials, in particular textbooks
- how to use the new language effectively in the classroom, taking account of the recommendations in this report; understanding the role and limitations of memorised phrases in language progression
- gaining knowledge and understanding of the principles of assessment in languages, including the range of approaches and techniques needed for different purposes
- knowing what has been taught in primary schools in both English and modern languages and knowing how to build on this effectively in KS3 (Bauckham, 2016: 19-20)

Of course, no one will be an expert in all of the areas listed above, but being aware of this we know we have a schema to build upon. There is a difference between knowing that this is a minimum expectation and being able to put it into practice. We also know that there will be additional elements that we may not have thought about in a number of years, but that are a matter of concern for our new colleague (Task 6.2).

---

**Task 6.2 Reflect on your subject-specific knowledge**

Consider the thirteen aspects of subject-specific knowledge listed within the Modern Foreign Languages Pedagogy Review (Bauckham, 2016). Which of these do you feel confident discussing with beginning teachers whom you are supporting. Are there areas where you feel less confident? If so, how could you develop your knowledge in these areas in tandem with your beginning teacher? Who could you turn to for support within your community of practice?

---

I recall my time as a mentor, which I found to be very positive and enriching. The weekly meeting time allocated in the school day, or if not fortnightly was important for me to understand how the new colleague was settling and integrating into the languages team. We may both have had questions or points to raise but this was always done with a cuppa and biscuit in a private space whereby conversations could take place and there would not be a disturbance. Creating time, and space where there are no distractions allows more efficient use of time; equally it shows the new colleague that they are genuinely valued, and that this time is important, and that it is just for them. Foci can be usefully discussed beforehand since they will have questions and things they want to bring with them, but it is up to us to ensure that they successfully integrate into the department and school, so we need to ensure that we cover key elements (e.g. behaviour management or assessment) that are either drawn from the core content framework (Department for Education, 2024) or from more local concerns (e.g. how we reward success in this particular department/school or how we sanction learners that require a reminder of the standards we expect in our classroom).

In terms of reducing cognitive load for our new colleague we want to ensure that we do not tackle all of these elements in one session! In fact, we will want to break this down, as we do with our content in the classroom so that it is sequenced progressively step-by-step. Quite like a flow diagram. The idea is that we are not dismissing something that our new colleague needs support with but equally we are not overwhelming them with all the answers and processes. We make sense of new information by linking this with pre-existing knowledge, which may need reinforcement; we must not assume that our new colleagues can handle it all! Prioritising topics in support and guidance offers clarity therefore does not put too much load on them cognitively. We need to remember that they are learning new policies and practice whilst also establishing themselves as a beginning teacher.

The focus and responsibility do not always have to come only from the department and in fact in my first school I was delighted to have had a buddy from the science department. At first, I wondered how I would fit this into my working week, but he became a firm friend, tremendous support and I am still friends with him and his family now more than 25 years later. A buddy offers an alternate support mechanism to that which you offer your beginning teacher in that they are perhaps an established colleague in their first three to five years of teaching, who have gone through learning the procedural practices in school but also can offer a different perspective. The informal nature of a buddy creates a strong professional relationship which allows the beginning teacher time outside of the department to ask questions they may not ask someone within the languages team. These buddy sessions, although informal are an important addition to the successful integration of a beginning teacher to any school. Sessions may be held within, or outside, school hours are informal perhaps even more casual so that there is no agenda nor person in charge as such. There is often, though not always, no paperwork or review to complete but the session creates opportunities to discuss school processes, matters or procedures and how they work in another department. A buddy can be a huge help with not only day to day matters that arise in school but also encourages the beginning teacher to make friends and links outside of the languages department and perhaps even visit another part of the school.

My most recent beginning teacher needed a push to "get out" of their classroom as they were spending from before 8 am in there, planning, teaching, marking, and talking to learners and tutees. They needed little encouragement to head off to another department to talk to other beginning teachers about their adventures and this provided an opportunity to relax a little and create an environment where meaningful peer discussion could be had. Thankfully this quickly became habit across the fortnight (we had a two-week timetable) resulting in a locked classroom door and the teacher heading off to a different area of the school for a "lunch date" with their peers. Marvellous, I could not have been happier! It was fantastic to see and hear them flourishing through supporting other beginning teachers with their experiences; offering advice and suggestions of how to manage challenges differently and sharing areas with which they needed help in their classroom. The small community helped the beginning teachers realise that whatever the "issue" was, they weren't alone. This powerful realisation helps beginning teachers to be increasingly open with colleagues who they know may have had similar experiences. It also helps the mentor, lead teacher or head of department as their beginning teacher is building a small community of practice within school, which complements the community within the department (Task 6.3).

### Task 6.3 Identify potential allies for your beginning teacher

Consider the possibilities within your own school for buddies in other departments who might support your beginning teacher. Does the languages department share building space with another subject, making connections easier? Or is there a colleague in another part of the school entirely who could support your beginning teacher to make broader links? Would your beginning teacher benefit from a pairing with a drama teacher (who might support them with building presence in the classroom and making effective use of their voice), or perhaps a science teacher (with whom they might discuss shared issues such as the teaching of new and complex vocabulary)?

## Communities of practice beyond the school

CoP are not a new initiative, they are and have been around seemingly forever. According to cognitive anthropologist Jean Lave and educational theorist Etienne Wenger (1991, p. 1) a community of practice is "a group of people who share a concern or passion for something they do and learn how to do it better as they interact regularly." It is wonderful that the teacher interaction described above shows the beginning teacher developing a community of practice outside of the languages team which will offer different perspectives and solutions but within the framework of the policy and practice of the school. Wenger (1998) is said to have developed the concept into a theory of social learning within which there are three identified characteristics (2004): domain, community, and practice.

The domain is the shared interest that acts as the focus around which the community (teachers, practitioners) work collaboratively to develop practice in a particular area or field. There is no specified leader nor required amount of time, there often is no deadline. The focus (domain) is more important, so participants remain part of the community for as long as they feel it has value. Sustained action is required to keep the CoP going towards its focus so the community should engage multiple times.

We should, in time, encourage or provide opportunities for the beginning teacher to join other CoPs beyond the educational establishment, these could be in the form of teaching and learning groups, behaviour management groups or language groups. Finding community with other teachers, beyond their own department and now school is empowering, permitting the beginning teacher to connect with others with a common goal or aspiration. We know all too well that one person cannot do it alone and when our beginning teacher realises this then this is the time we can start to cultivate curiosity about what external CoPs exist. Within languages education we are fortunate to have various CoPs for pedagogy and practice, for specific languages and special interests, across many different platforms. Teachers in the department/team can contribute to and learn from one another in the CoP to great effect, not only giving support, guidance, and advice as a more experienced teacher but also being in receipt of this such as access to new resources and technologies and learning how to use them. CoPs work in transformative ways which engage those within to "do it better." This was reinforced by Koglbauer (2024, p. 181) as he reflected on the pandemic: "experienced teachers reached out to their student teachers, ECTs and mentees for their technological expertise; jointly in teams they adapted classroom-based teaching resources for the virtual classroom."

Whilst training as a teacher I recall one of our lecturers sharing with us the importance of being in a community of likeminded practitioners and advising us to join our subject association. I didn't even know what this was, but once I found myself a member of the Association for Language Learning (ALL) I discovered a vast network of teachers, at all stages of education and careers who came together as a community. I was in awe of the local support for myself and others in the Southwest of England and connected through attendance at local events with other languages teachers to learn, and also share the trials and tribulations and the joys of being a languages teacher. Lamb (2012, p. 4) highlighted the role of the subject association in the "development of professional identity" and also to "foster professionalism by developing a sense of pride and reinforcing values, beliefs and identity." I found this hugely comforting as in the coming together of practitioners I realised that ALL provided support for teachers to help not only the upkeep of their existing subject knowledge but also to develop other new languages I received a newsletter and journal which helped me to keep abreast of the "goings-on" in the languages world. With both formal and informal learning activities I was able to successfully navigate my early years teaching through support from ALL through "clear connections between professional development activity and socialisation" (Rusaw, 1995 in Lamb, 2012, p. 5).

Of course, over time, and since the pandemic technology has created fertile opportunities for new CoPs to come to the fore and flourish. ALL has local branches but also networks and hubs to support members and local teachers. I will discuss the primary school networks first, followed by the secondary school networks below.

ALL Primary hubs locally have sprouted up and now link up online as well as in person, to develop curricula, decolonise the languages curriculum and generate expertise. ALL's Primary hub in Bristol is one of many which are extremely active in supporting primary teachers across an array of languages, ages and across the range of abilities. There are also national events, some of which are held online (PHOrum, Decolonising Primary Languages and the ACAPULCO conference) and some face to face, to draw together this community of practice which offers continuing professional development, training, support, discussion forums and celebration. You will find these on the Association's events pages and also in the Primary Voice areas of the ALL website:

> https://www.all-languages.org.uk/primary-2/
> https://www.all-languages.org.uk/primary-2/primary-voice/
> https://www.all-languages.org.uk/about/community/special-interest-groups/

Secondary colleagues have local branches and hubs, and also online groups such as Secondary Teachers of ALL (STALL) and Decolonising Secondary Languages. There is an action group for German and a Francophonie group (both cross-sector) again to allow people to connect, explore similar challenges and share ideas on different aspects of classroom, or exam practice. Learning from the Classroom is an area of the website for teachers to share classroom research, while the Language Zones feature a variety of contributions from language teachers and researchers. ALL has a mission to support and encourage members to write for others and speak to others, through these outlets:

> https://www.all-languages.org.uk/secondary/
> https://www.all-languages.org.uk/research-practice/learning-from-the-classroom/
> https://www.all-languages.org.uk/about/community/special-interest-groups/

ALL has an active group of teacher educators who work with others to support beginning languages teachers. Volunteers host online and in person conferences, and there is a regular event (the ALL Social Zoom) led by beginning teachers on themes they identify. Expert guests join the social to listen and add support from recent research evidence and from their own experience. The beginning teachers who contribute gain professional experience in creating and delivering their talks and are rewarded with an ALL certificate for their professional file.

To support the learning of all languages in state and community schools, a recently formed home, heritage, and community languages CoP has formed with support of colleagues and various cultural partners, embassies and also Goldsmith's University. ALL hosts the webpage for the HHCL group. This community has a shared vision of raising the profile of languages spoken at home and within communities. It is exciting that this is being recognised as there are many cross-language strategies that we can all share whilst developing genuine community, friendship, and practice:

https://www.all-languages.org.uk/research-practice/language-zones/

There has always been a strong bond with cultural partners and ALL has built a CoP with the Consejería de Educacíon, Goethe Institut, Institut français du Royaume-Uni, the British Council and UK German Connection, as well as The Japan Foundation, the Qatar Foundation International and the newly formed National Consortium for Languages Education here in England (NCLE). This allows members to connect with cultural partners to engage in sharing and achieving their aspirations for their learners. CoPs such as these with a clear focus on one language or stage create opportunities to cultivate a common vision and expertise through sharing and discussion. They empower and encourage individuals in the community by asking them to share their own work or learning journey to date and through further discussion and input from other members facilitates collaboration and sharing of practice by synthesising this new collaborative knowledge and seeing new perspectives can promote real change in teachers' own work.

CoPs have been supporting fellow teachers on social media for a number of years. Follow the hashtag #MFLTwitterati[1] across any social media platform and you will find teachers supporting and advising one another and a rich and varied community going beyond physical or political borders. The LIPS (Languages in Primary Schools), Secondary MFL Matters, Secondary MFL in Wales, and Global Innovative Language Teachers are some of many groups of teacher-practitioners which support one another daily and are in fact a "mass community of practice" as some of these groups have thousands of members. These groups do not often commune other than online. The incredible support that is offered across these online CoPs may help beginning teachers to overcome any challenges they face. Of course, we also want them to have down time to relax, re-energise, and refresh so they are ready for the next working day, and we are consequently wary of promoting too much social media activity. Equally important to mention here is the need for beginning teachers to be aware of the expectations surrounding their use of social media from a professionalism perspective.

## Conclusion

Developing a beginning teacher's skills is not the sole responsibility of the mentor, lead teacher, or head of department nor solely that of the beginning teacher. Schools are learning organisations, as Koglbauer (2024, p. 181) states: "If we understand schools as learning organisations, learning is not just taking place in the classroom by the learners but by everyone involved in the learning process." I firmly believe that connecting with others in the language learning community, and beyond is a robust and healthy way to support the integration of beginning teachers. Active membership of a CoP like ALL provides opportunities for the co-construction of lesson plans and learning activities, creative cultural projects (such as the ALL Literature wiki) and language skills which can be cascaded with the department at meetings and in the languages office whilst the kettle boils. Depending on what we are looking for, I am sure that there will be a nurturing CoP out there which will allow beginning teachers to join and develop their knowledge, skills and understanding to support successful integration into the language teaching community but also to their educational establishments. Koglbauer (2024, p. 184) highlights the need to identify, explore and familiarise ourselves with "common activities of communities of practice" offering explicit language examples. Whether this is sharing articles in ALLNet or Languages Today magazine for discussion to highlighting forthcoming training events which could be helpful. Attending a local ALL event gives an opportunity to meet other teachers at various stages of their careers in languages education and the wealth of experience there knows no limit. My own CoP was deeply enriched by attendance at ALL local events and TeachMeets. I have taken the languages departments I have led to ALL local events in the South West and it was not only beneficial for me to top up my own professional knowledge but equally to see how different sessions came alive to my colleagues and mentees. Interesting personal development projects commenced as a direct result of training, which were shared (and celebrated) at departmental meetings and which improved teaching, learning, behaviour, and engagement across the department. Importantly, it gave each colleague the opportunity to build on what they had learned and experienced and sharing it at departmental level helped us to foster a deeper shared learning experience.

## For discussion

- With which of the CoPs referred to in the chapter were you already familiar? Were any of these new to you?
- Based on your reading of this chapter, what will your first actions be to support your beginning teacher in integrating with relevant COP?

## Further reading

The ALL website is a veritable treasure trove for both beginning and experienced languages teachers, with clearly defined pages offering guidance and support. I recommend the following as a starting point for exploration with your beginning teacher:

- https://www.all-languages.org.uk/events/
- https://www.all-languages.org.uk/student/become-a-language-teacher/
- https://www.all-languages.org.uk/student/ect-years/
- https://www.all-languages.org.uk/student/

The Association for Language Learning in England has produced a guide for mentors. It offers a great starting point for thinking about how to support your beginning teacher.

- Black, L., Gordon, A. L., Hughes, C., MacArthur, R., & Sandy, S. (n.d.). *Effective mentoring of trainee teachers.* Association for Language Learning e-book publication. https://www.all-languages.org.uk/product/effective-mentoring-trainee-teachers-e-book/

## Note

1. #MFLTwitterati was created by Joe Dale, an independent education consultant and former languages teacher to bring the community together.

## References

Bauckham, I. (2016). *Modern Foreign Languages Pedagogy Review*. Teaching Schools Council. https://ncle-language-hubs.ucl.ac.uk/app/uploads/2023/12/Modern-Foreign-Language-Pedagogy-Review-2016.pdf

Black, L., Gordon, A. L., Hughes, C., MacArthur, R., & Sandy, S. (no date). *Effective mentoring of trainee teachers*. Association for Language Learning e-book publication. https://www.all-languages.org.uk/product/effective-mentoring-trainee-teachers-e-book/

Department for Education. (2024). *Initial Teacher Training and Early Career Framework*. https://www.gov.uk/government/publications/initial-teacher-training-and-early-career-framework.

Furlong, J., & Maynard, T. (1995). *Mentoring student teachers: The growth of professional knowledge*. Routledge.

Kennedy, M. (2016). Parsing the practice of teaching. *Journal of Teacher Education, 67*(1), 6–17.

Koglbauer, R. (2024). Professional identity: Becoming an extended professional. In N. Pachler & A. Redondo (Eds.), *A practical guide to teaching foreign languages in the secondary school* (pp. 179–194). Routledge.

Lamb, T. (2012). Language associations and collaborative support: Language teacher associations as empowering spaces for professional networks. *Innovation in Language Learning and Teaching, 6*(3), 287–308. https://doi.org/10.1080/17501229.2012.725255

Sweller, J. (1998). Cognitive load during problem solving: Effects on learning. *Cognitive Science, 12*, 257–285.

Wenger, E. (1998). *Communities of practice. Learning, meaning, and identity*. Cambridge University Press.

Wenger, E. (2004). Knowledge management as a doughnut: Shaping your knowledge strategy through communities of practice. *Ivey Business Journal, 68*(3), 1–8.

# SECTION 3

# Developing beginning languages teachers' pedagogical knowledge, skills, and understanding

# 7 Supporting beginning languages teachers to analyse teaching that they observe

*Sandra Cohen*

## Introduction

Observing experienced teachers is a fundamental part of teacher education. The languages classroom is a highly complex and dynamic environment which can be challenging to understand for beginning teachers. As a mentor, guiding beginning teachers to get the most out of observations is a key part of setting your mentee up for success during the early weeks of their school-based training. Knowing how to effectively observe lessons and how to engage with experienced teachers will help them to enter the lessons they are observing well-prepared and give them the opportunity to engage in meaningful pedagogy-based discussion with the teachers they are observing and with you as their mentor. At the end of this chapter, you should be able to:

- Understand the importance of observation for beginning teachers;
- Have a greater understanding of the main elements that define a successful observation;
- Understand how to set observation goals considering the expertise in your educational setting and how to facilitate access to colleagues' lessons;
- Understand how to help beginning teachers achieve focussed observations through use of schedules;
- Understand how to encourage non-judgemental questioning about an experienced teacher's choices following an observation.

Before reading further, undertake Task 7.1.

---

**Task 7.1 Mentor reflection: reflect on your own experience of observing and being observed**

How would you define a successful observation?
How do you go about setting goals for an observation?
How do you feel about asking a teacher you have observed about their choices during the lesson? How do you feel about being asked about your teaching by your peers?
How do your ideas about what constitutes a successful observation and being asked about your own teaching inform your mentoring practice?

---

DOI: 10.4324/9781003495468-11

## The importance and challenges of observation for beginning teachers

Observation is a key part of the early school experience of beginning teachers; as such, it is built into all Initial Teacher Education (ITE) programmes. Our core beliefs about teaching are shaped by our experience as pupils. The concept of 'teaching as an apprenticeship of observation' (Lortie, 1975, p. 61) suggests that teachers develop their understanding and approach to teaching mainly though observing their teachers while they were pupils themselves. Research also indicates that both trainee teachers and beginning teachers tend to revert to the teaching practices they observed as pupils, unless given the opportunity to compare, reflect, and adapt through training, observation, and per feedback. Bullock's study emphasises the importance of recognising their own 'apprenticeship of observation' to avoid sustaining ineffective or outdated practices (Bullock, 2022). For example, ML teachers may have experienced mainly grammar-based teaching, with limited focus on communicative skills to apply their language to real-life situations. Others may have made limited use of online tools such as language learning websites, or have experienced mainly summative (formal, graded) rather than formative (informal, ungraded) assessments.

Observing other teachers without a clear focus or structure can be overwhelming and ineffective. This is because teaching is highly complex due to its contextual nature. It is helpful to think of teaching as 'dilemma based' (Loughran, 2013, p. 13). A teacher makes numerous decisions throughout a lesson. These can range from pedagogical choices (pausing a lesson to take a step back and provide more explanation) to strategies for classroom management (how to deal with low level disruption) based on their knowledge and experience.

To complicate things further, many decisions are made unconsciously by the experienced teacher. Beginning teachers often find it difficult to identify these decisions. This is because they are often in the 'conscious incompetence' or 'unconscious incompetence' stages of the Conscience Competence Learning Matrix. This research highlights the need to include strategies to explicitly teach beginning teachers how to recognize and interpret the decision-making processes of experienced teachers. These include 'modelling'; observation of experienced teachers making decisions in a classroom setting, 'Think-Aloud sessions' where experienced teachers verbalise what they are thinking, and 'Decision-Making Frameworks' to help beginning teachers analyse and categorise the decisions made by experienced teachers, with the aim of making process more transparent and understandable (Jaggede et al., 2000).

A further challenge when it comes to observing experienced teachers is 'tacit teacher knowledge.' Tacit knowledge is like an iceberg; everything the teacher is doing that cannot be easily seen on the surface. (Polanyi, 1958). An example of tacit knowledge on display in language lessons can be found in the use of target language by teacher who is a native speaker. As using the target language comes naturally to a native speaker teacher, they will likely use it more, exposing pupils to a wider variety of vocabulary they can use for themselves. Another example is how much target language is used for certain explanations. An experienced teacher may decide to partially or fully explain a grammar point or set up a task in L1 to maximise pupil understanding and engagement (Task 7.2).

---

**Task 7.2 The focus of observation**

Think about a lesson you observed recently: what was the purpose of the observation? Was it a beginning teacher teaching, a peer observation or perhaps an interview lesson? Did this influence your focus during the lesson?

Was there a pro forma for you to complete? Did you speak to learners and look in books, or did you just observe? How did this influence your focus and the notes you took?

---

## Identifying areas of observation and setting observation goals

Prior to a beginning teacher's first observations, it's good practice to prepare them by agreeing a focus and guiding them on the lesson elements to pay attention to.

Arrange to meet prior to any observations starting and guide them to reflect on what their ideas and philosophies regarding teaching are. It is helpful for them to acknowledge that their ideas and opinions are likely influenced by their own experience as learners, as described above. In an MFL setting, this can often mean a beginning teacher was educated abroad. This is an important consideration, as they may have different perspectives due to cultural differences, differences in teaching styles, approaches to discipline, questioning and teacher/pupil relationships, curricula, homework, and assessment practices. This means they will naturally notice different things from a trainee teacher educated within the same national setting. For example, beginning teachers educated abroad in Europe often notice the strict rules regarding uniform as most schools in France, Germany, and Spain don't have uniform. Approaches to detentions also vary widely across different countries, both in frequency and scope.

## What are the elements that define a successful observation?

The areas for observation depend on beginning teachers' prior experience and interests as well as your school's policies. The key is to prepare them to identify observable behaviours that evidence effective teaching and learning. A starting point might be to consider the 10 areas outlined below:

1. Lesson Outlines
2. Starting, finishing and linking the segments
3. Oral Interaction: Teacher talk/Pupil talk
4. Oral Interaction: Procedural instructions (for setting up activities)
5. Oral Interaction: Questions and Answers
6. Oral Interaction: Classroom Language
7. Approaches to Reading
8. Approaches to listening (to audio and video material)
9. Pupil Writing
10. Homework

Table 7.1 Two examples of observation notes detailing lesson outlines

**Example 1**

| Class | Activity | Skills developed | Comments |
| --- | --- | --- | --- |
| Year 10 | Oral presentation of a topic 15 minutes | Memorisation; speaking | Pupils lacked confidence; pronunciation OK |
| | Listening to an audio file 6 minutes etc.... | Listening - ability to pick out certain key phrases | Teacher stopped the recording after every question |

**Example 2**

| Time | Activity | Comments |
| --- | --- | --- |
| 9.00 | Class enters, books handed out, write objectives | All routine instructions in the target language but objectives in English |
| 9.05 | Questions on weekend activities | Teacher nominates pupils, does not wait for hands up. Seems to be a revision of things previously learned. |
| 9.15 | Writing activity - matching questions to answers etc.... | Pupils working in pairs, allowed to talk quietly |

I recommend arranging a joint observation of an experienced colleague, including a meeting before and afterwards. This enables you as mentor to highlight for the beginning teacher things they may observe. For example, if you are at a school where the schedules for starting and finishing a lesson, as well as target language use are clearly defined, it is likely they will notice consistency between lesson starts and finishes in different year groups and with different teachers.

## Achieving focussed observations through the use of schedules

Below I provide further details of the 10 structured lesson observation schedules listed above, together with questions beginning teachers could ask experienced teachers about their practice. These observation schedules, which are linked in full under further reading, can be valuable tools to help new colleagues deconstruct and understand what is going on in the classroom.

### *Lesson outlines*

Every lesson has some kind of overall plan, outline, or sequence. A frequent example might involve the following (depending on the length of the lesson):

- an introduction to new language using the interactive whiteboard
- a question-and-answer session
- pair work by pupils
- pupils note down the new language
- the setting of a homework in which pupils will use the new language in written exercises.

A beginning teacher can choose lessons from those they have observed and write out their outlines and sequences of activities, noting the approximate allocation of time to each of the main parts of the lesson. See Table 7.1 for examples of this.

*Supporting beginning languages teachers to analyse teaching* 81

*Table 7.2* Example of observation notes focussed on linking the segments

| Activities and links | Examples of words used by teacher | Other things teacher does | Working conditions |
|---|---|---|---|
| Activity | Bon, Aujourd'hui ... (sets up starter task) | Turns on projector, logs on to computer, loads PowerPoint | Pupils silent |
| Link | Maintenant prÈparez le dialogue | Points to board where the parts are exemplified | A few whispered conversations |
| Activity | Talking in pairs | Scans the room | Rumble of talk |
| Link | | Walks round the room monitoring talk but also handing out a worksheet (next activity?) | |
| Activity | etc... | | |

### Starting, finishing, and linking the segments

Crucial parts of the lesson are the start of the lesson, the end of the lesson and any point where the nature and focus of the activity changes. Effective management of these parts of a lesson is essential to the smooth-running of the lesson. See Table 7.2 for an example of observation notes focussed on linking the segments.

### Oral interaction – teacher talk/pupil talk

What, roughly, is the proportion of teacher talk to pupil talk? What sorts of things do teachers and pupils actually say? In many lessons pupils are involved in talking to each other in the target language. To what extent are pair- and groupwork effective teaching strategies?

In the 1:30 situation (whole class, teacher up front), estimate the amount of time pupil(s) actually spend talking in the second language (L2). What are the functions of the classroom discourse? Specifically:

- what sort of talk/language does the L2 teacher talk consist of – e.g., information/explanation/procedural instructions/questioning? What is the proportion roughly of each?
- what sort of talk/language does the L2 pupil talk consist of – e.g., information, questions, requests, spontaneous remarks? Do learners ever initiate an exchange? What types of mistakes do they make?
- what is the topic of the discourse?
- is there any deviation from the intended topic? Why (not)?

### Oral interaction: procedural instructions (for setting up activities)

The efficient organisation of activities plays an important part in lessons running smoothly. Clear procedural instructions are vital to ensure that pupils know what they have to do. But are these given in the target language, and if so, how?

### Oral interaction: questions and answers

Question and answer in the target language is a technique that many languages teachers employ at some time during most lessons. It is important to develop the very difficult skills which ensure that all pupils are given opportunities to answer without causing embarrassment to more reticent pupils.

### Oral interaction: classroom language

We define classroom language as 'the types of utterances normally only found in the classroom'. If pupils are taught to understand and produce such utterances in the target language and are encouraged to use them on a regular basis, this can be one step towards making the classroom a place of genuine, spontaneous oral interaction in the L2.

### Approaches to reading

Most secondary school pupils can draw on their existing first language (L1) literacy skills to support their learning of the L2, potentially making it much more efficient. For example, reading can be an important vehicle for introducing new language, reinforcing familiar language, and demonstrating language use in context. It can also provide a window into the target language culture and can facilitate access to many other exciting resources (e.g., web pages). However, none of this will be very effective if pupils are not able to 'retune' their literacy skills to the second language. For example, they might not be able to 'decode' from print to sound very effectively.

### Approaches to listening (to audio and video material)

Listening is often considered a difficult skill to develop, because of the fleeting nature of the spoken word. Most teachers expose learners to quite a lot of listening texts, but it is often claimed that these are used mainly to assess pupils' listening proficiency, rather than to help them develop their listening proficiency.

### Pupil writing

Written work is often used as a way of recording new language and of practising language that has just been introduced in controlled ways, with an emphasis on accuracy. But how often do pupils have the opportunity to undertake more creative, 'free writing' tasks in which the emphasis is on expressing themselves? To what extent do the writing tasks they are set help them to develop their proficiency in l2 writing?

### Homework

Two or three hours a week in class is very little time in which to learn a language! Homework provides an opportunity for learners to extend their language learning outside the classroom.

The internet provides a world of opportunities to practise the language and to encounter authentic L2 resources at home. However, the teacher needs to think carefully about how to set up homework tasks, to ensure that learners can access them and get the most out of them in the absence of support from the teacher.

The categories covered above are designed to assist beginning teachers to undertake a comprehensive programme of observation of experienced teachers. Of course, it would be possible to 'deconstruct' a lesson using different categories to the ten used here.

## Post-observation questioning about a teacher's choices

Before reading on, please complete Task 7.3.

---

### Task 7.3 Post-observation questioning

Think about a recent lesson you observed and write down the positive elements you noticed along with the areas for development.

How would you phrase the post-observation questions for the positive elements you observed? How about the questions regarding the areas for development?

Is there a difference? Reflect on how the way you phrase your questions could affect the observing teacher and determine the quality of the answer you receive. Did the answer you received help you to understand the reasoning behind their decisions? Did you feel there was an open dialogue? Why?

---

Encouraging beginning teachers to initiate meaningful discussions following observations is key for their learning and development. It is helpful for mentors to also communicate to colleagues that they are likely to get some questions, so they are prepared and can give this some of their time. While using an observation protocol is likely to prompt beginning teachers to ask meaningful questions, it can feel uncomfortable for them to engage with experienced teachers about a lesson they observed. Harrison et al. (2005) discuss the importance of non-judgemental questioning techniques to support reflective practice among trainee teachers. This is fundamental in the mentor-mentee relationship as it builds trust, mutual respect and paves the way for effective habits of reflective practice to achieve professional growth.

As a mentor, you can prepare your mentee for questioning experienced teachers by talking to them about questioning techniques following an observation by linking this to the way you engage with each other in your mentor-mentee relationship. Non-judgemental questioning promotes a safe, positive, supportive, and reflective environment where beginning teachers can learn from their observations. It is valuable for mentors to model how to ask non-judgemental questions during debrief sessions, by modelling to show respect and curiosity rather than criticism. Non-judgemental questions focus on understanding what was observed rather than evaluating it. Talking your mentee through scenarios they may observe and how to formulate questions to the teacher afterwards can be a helpful way to prepare them.

Scenario 1: Pupils in a Y9 Spanish lesson are calling out, chatting to each other while the teacher is addressing the class, and playing with heir pencil cases rather than doing independent work. Instead of asking, 'Why didn't you deal with behaviour better?' a non-judgemental question would be, 'What strategies do you find most effective for managing behaviour with this group?'

Scenario 2: Pupils in a Y7 French lesson are asked to play a dice boardgame where they answer a question in French when they land on a square. Pupils are answering questions in English, throwing the dice at each other, and shouting across the room. Encourage beginning teachers to ask reflective questions such as, 'What was the purpose of this activity?' or 'How did you decide to handle that situation?' This encourages an open dialogue and critical thinking and will help them understand the reasoning behind an experienced teacher's choices.

It is worth encouraging a beginning teacher to finish a discussion about a lesson by asking the experienced teacher whether they noticed something about the lesson. A simple: 'Did I miss anything of note?' can pave the way for meaningful discussion and enable a teacher to explain some of their tacit or less visible elements of the lesson. An example of these could be any challenge and support questions asked or materials given out during independent work, or a teacher's choice to use or not use the target language in an explanation.

Discussing a lesson with a teacher straight afterwards is ideal. However, school days can be incredibly busy, and this is not always possible in practice. Encourage your mentee to agree a suitable time after the lesson to engage in a meaningful discussion with the teacher they observed. Writing down questions on the observation protocol can be helpful in this regard.

### Focus on the expertise available in your school setting

As a mentor, it is helpful to have an overview of which teachers or departments within your setting are experts in various aspects of teaching. Once you have guided your mentee to reflect on their preconceptions and the areas they feel may of interest or challenging to them, you can then point them in the direction of experienced teachers with a particular strength in that area. Behaviour is often cited by beginning teachers as an area they find challenging, so observing lesson where an experienced teacher with a particular skillset in behaviour teaches a challenging class, a specific year group, or even a particular pupil can instil confidence. The same logic applies for any other element of teaching. Setting up tasks, use of TL, setting homework, etc. Following an individual pupil or a form group for a full school day can also give a beginning teacher a valuable perspective on the way in which different teachers approach certain pupils or groups of pupils within their setting.

Creating an observation timetable containing a mixture of languages and other subjects is an effective way to expose beginning teachers to a variety of settings and subjects. With the help of the abovementioned observation schedules, this enables beginning teachers to observe and reflect on the widest possible range of teaching settings and scenarios to inform their practice.

When creating an observation timetable, it's helpful to share this with the teachers being observed beforehand to inform them and give them an opportunity to feed back if necessary. Most teachers appreciate advance notice of visitors to their lessons and may want the opportunity to evaluate a lesson they plan against any observation foci your mentee has.

Finally, a beginning teacher would most certainly value the opportunity to shadow you as their mentor or another member of the languages team for a full day to give them an idea of a 'day in the life' of a teacher in your setting. Taking in teaching, PPA time, pastoral duties with a form group, and any duties or meetings is often an eye-opening experience.

## Conclusion

Supporting beginning languages teachers to analyse teaching through structured observations is vital for their professional growth. Guiding them to reflect on their own preconceptions of teaching, often based on their own experiences of being taught, enables beginning teachers to avoid sustaining ineffective or outdated practices. One of the challenges in observing experienced teachers in 'tacit teacher knowledge', the idea that so much of that is valuable in the way a class is taught is innate in the teacher's skills and as such not easily observable by the untrained eye.

Using the observation schedules described in this chapter, and attached in full in Appendix 1, along a sample set of questions to ask teachers about their practice can be a helpful starting point to enable beginning teachers access to experienced teachers' knowledge. These observation schedules can be valuable tools to help beginning teachers understand what is going on in the classroom. In order to get the most out of post-observation questions, using non-judgemental questioning can be considered an effective tool to foster open professional discussion. Mentors can model this, by asking questions that show respect and curiosity, rather than criticism and judgement.

There are various ways mentors can leverage expertise within their setting to benefit mentees. Creating an observation timetable based on a mentee's self-identified interests and challenges is a powerful way to do this. This timetable can follow a teacher for a day, a class (form group) or an individual pupil or indeed contain a mixture of teachers, year groups and subjects. It is best practice to accompany your mentee to at least one observation to guide them on how to approach it.

By understanding the importance of observation, setting clear goals, leveraging departmental expertise, facilitating access to lessons, using focused schedules, and encouraging non-judgemental questioning, mentors can create a supportive and reflective learning environment. This not only enhances the beginning teacher's skills but also contributes to a culture of continuous improvement within the school.

## For discussion

1. Consider the systems and protocols and schedules regarding the running of lessons available in your school – how can these be presented to your mentee for them to use these in addition to the schedules presented above to observe lessons?
2. Before your first, ideally joint observation of a colleague, ask your mentee to observe one of your lessons and to ask you 'probing questions' afterwards, using non-judgemental questioning, enabling you to feed back to them.
3. Consider how the ML observations schedules could be used or adapted for use in your setting. Copy the ML observations schedules from this book or download them from the book's accompanying website. Discuss with your mentee how to use these during their observations.

## Further reading

Modern Languages Observation Schedules (see Appendix 1)

These observation schedules are valuable tools to help beginning teachers understand what is going on in the classroom. Observations using these should ideally begin early in a teacher's training year, rather than spending time engaged in 'general observation' without a specific focus – which can be an overwhelming and unproductive experience.

## References

Bullock, S. M. (2022). Apprenticeship of observation: Avoiding the perpetuation of ineffective or outdated practices. *Frontiers in Education, 7*, 06 April [online]. https://doi.org/10.3389/feduc.2022.754759

Harrison, J., Lawson, T., & Wortley, A. (2005). Mentoring the beginning teacher: Developing professional autonomy through critical reflection on practice. *Reflective Practice, 6*(3), 419–441.

Jaggede, D., Taplin, R., & Chan, K. (2000). *The unconscious competence matrix: A framework for understanding skill acquisition*. Wiley.

Loughran, J., 2013. *Developing a pedagogy of teacher education: Understanding teaching and learning about teaching* (2nd ed.). Routledge.

Polanyi, M. (1958). *Personal knowledge: Towards a post-critical philosophy*. Routledge.

# 8 Supporting the lesson planning process of beginning languages teachers

*Sophie Vauzour*

## Introduction

Planning languages lessons is a complex process that encompasses knowledge and skills often beyond the beginning teacher's stage of development in terms of understanding of pupils' needs, curriculum, and languages pedagogy. In addition, planning also involves elements of classroom practice, such as classroom management, assessment for impact, adaptive teaching (Johnson, 2018). Most of this process has often been internalised by experienced teachers, and effective mentoring in this area requires the ability to deconstruct planning practices, making the implicit and the internalised explicit, and accepting the limitations that come with earlier stages of teacher development, providing scaffolding as necessary (Wright, 2018).

Exploring the planning process also requires considering the multi-faceted and complex nature of the subject and the debates around how to best teach it (Driscoll et al., 2014), as well as the ever-changing examination requirements and curriculum constraints, and schools' individual contexts. What is considered effective planning will differ from school to school, depending on the communities they serve, and also common expectations in terms of routines and pedagogical choices. Other differences will be linked to teacher identity, individual preferences, and level of experience (Johnson, 2018).

In this chapter, we explore practical approaches to support beginning teachers in developing effective planning practices, as this will support pupils' long-term learning and engagement with languages in their classes (Mackay, 2019).

At the end of this chapter, you should be able to:

- Reflect on the planning process in your context and your beginning teacher's stage of development in relation to this process
- Identify approaches to develop beginning language teachers' understanding of the 'big picture'
- Consider how to use lesson plan proforma effectively to scaffold beginning language teachers' planning practice
- Develop beginning languages teachers' understanding of a purposeful approach to the planning process
- Consider feedback, readiness to learn and workload in the learning to plan process.

Before reading further, undertake Task 8.1.

---

**Task 8.1 Reflect on the planning process in your context and your beginning teacher's readiness for this process**

- What constitutes a successful lesson plan in modern languages in your school context? What is the pedagogical model used in your department? Can you describe these explicitly and recommend key readings?
- What implicit knowledge and skills are necessary to plan a lesson successfully in languages (e.g. anticipating common mistakes/misconceptions or evaluating the time needed for an activity)? To what extent has your beginning teacher acquired these and what needs to be scaffolded?
- How have your planning practices evolved throughout your career? Why? What could have helped you (if anything) to develop effective planning practices earlier in your career?
- How much is it realistic to expect from your beginning teacher at their current stage of development and with their emerging understanding of the school context?
- What support should you provide at this stage? How could this be progressively removed?
- What are the resources available in your department to support planning? How easy/difficult will they be to use for a beginning teacher?

---

The process of learning to plan is not linear. It can be frustrating for mentors to consider how difficult beginning teachers find the planning process initially, despite being given lots of support. It might be helpful to consider Mackay's cycle of 'plan, do, review' (2019). Experiences of planning will not be enough in themselves for beginning teachers to become better at planning. What matters is what they learn from these experiences, with your support, by reviewing, evaluating, and reflecting in relation to the underlying theories which underpin effective planning practice.

## The big picture

Before starting the planning process, it is worth considering the wider context and the purpose of the lesson or series of lessons in the overall scheme of work or curriculum (Pachler et al., 2014). How will this segment of learning support the pupils' overall progress in acquiring linguistic competence, gaining an understanding of other cultures, and experiencing success in examinations? This understanding of the endgame is crucial and might not be usable at an operational level by the beginning teacher until they have experienced the full cycle of learning and teaching in your context, so systematic modelling and scaffolding will be needed (Department for Education, 2024).

Whilst it is not recommended to 'teach to the test', as it might limit the scope of the subject and the engagement of pupils with it, it is helpful for a beginning teacher to understand examination requirements, as they often precisely describe the knowledge and skills that pupils are expected to develop over the phase and inform curriculum design (Bauckman, 2019).

Systematically referring to the big picture might seem counter intuitive in the early stages, as your beginning will probably plan at micro level (segments of lessons and individual lessons) before they do it at macro level (medium- and long-term plans). But for beginning teachers to be able to see the 'big picture' as an essential part of the planning process, it needs to be explicitly discussed, modelled, and scaffolded from the earlier stages of their practice, for instance, through the activities presented in Task 8.2.

### Task 8.2 Encouraging beginning teachers to consider the big picture

Colour code the list of activities below, by highlighting in green what you already do with your beginning teacher, in orange what you are planning to do in the future, and in red things you are unsure about. Pick at least one red activity to trial with your beginning teacher. You might want to discuss this with another mentor, the initial teacher education (ITE) tutor or early career coordinator.

- Share and discuss schemes of work, curriculum plans etc. before the beginning teacher even starts teaching, and revisit regularly throughout the mentoring period
- Use every opportunity to discuss how a particular segment of learning fits into the bigger picture (medium-term plan, scheme of work, curriculum, etc.)
- Involve beginning teachers in departmental discussions around curriculum building
- Invite beginning teachers into post-16 lessons if available in your setting
- Prompt beginning teachers to look at available resources critically, assessing what elements of content will need to be acquired, within the constraint of curriculum time and considering the classes' particular needs
- Encourage beginning teachers to read and discuss exam specifications (even if they are not responsible for exam classes) and sit the exam (in their specialist language or even better, in their second or third language)
- Involve beginning teachers in marking and moderation exercises, progressively moving from scaffolded and collaborative practice to independent marking.

## The planning process in modern languages: rationale and purpose

The big picture will drive the first step of the planning process, the determination of learning objectives (also called outcomes or intentions) of individual lessons/series of lessons. Research suggests that 'language practice [should] be progressively less scaffolded and move from comprehension to production and use' (Bauckham, 2019, p. 19). Whilst learners benefit from developing receptive knowledge before moving onto productive practice, 'structured receptive practice is often under-represented in classrooms and textbooks' (Marsden & Hawkes, 2019a, p. 1). Receptive and productive meaningful practice of linguistic features must be extensive, frequent, and spaced to allow learning to take place (Marsden & Hawkes, 2019a).

In the long term, the sum of learning outcomes should also be multidimensional, developing the many skill areas necessary in language learning: lexical, grammatical, phonological, communicative, cultural, transferable, etc. (Pachler et al., 2014). Learning outcomes should also be realistic, as research indicates that some linguistic features (like the word order in sentences) will not be acquired before the learners are ready, despite extensive quality instruction (Lightbown & Spada, 2018). This will inform planning decisions such as whether to present a linguistic feature as a formulaic chunk or explore the feature in detail in an explicit way. Such decisions require an extensive understanding of how pupils learn in languages, and in your context, and your beginning teacher is likely to need your support and input as they build up this level of understanding.

In the early stages, due to the complexity of the process described above, you might want to provide learning outcomes of lessons, moving away from the temptation to limit pre-planning discussion to providing resources and/or activities (pages of the textbook, sentence builder, or core-text). Whilst this might be sufficient for a more experienced teacher, beginning teachers need to understand the 'why' in order to effectively plan the 'how', and this will require you as a mentor to analyse your own planning practice to explicitly model it to your mentee (Wright, 2018).

## A carefully crafted sequence of suitably challenging and purposeful learning activities

Once the learning objectives have been established (by the beginning teacher or you), the next step is to think of the lesson as a series of learning episodes (each with assessable desired outcomes) that will be carefully sequenced and organised to allow pupils to meet the desired overarching outcomes. Again, beginning teachers might find this process challenging as they might lack the understanding of required prior knowledge/common misconceptions/difficulties learners will face, in general and in your context. In addition, assessment for impact should be at the core of this process. As highlighted by Black and Jones, 'if teachers want to find out what pupils understand and/or can do, then these pupils need to be challenged by activities that make them think and perform' (2006, p. 5). In other words, the process of assessing pupils' learning should inform the choice of planned learning activities themselves, instead of being an afterthought.

In addition, beginning teachers should be encouraged to explore how the four skills of listening, speaking, reading, and writing are interconnected and can be taught together (Bauckham, 2019). For instance, a written text could support work on reading skills and comprehension, writing skills (model answer or redrafting process), pronunciation and presentation or recall of sound spelling correspondences (SSC), grammar, vocabulary, culture, etc. Exploiting one resource for several purposes instead of creating multiple resources will also support workload management (Department for Education, 2018; see also Chapter 13).

In the early stages of their development, beginning teachers might adopt a very structured and teacher-led approach such as presentation practice production (PPP), as this offers a reassuring and clear model, a default setting from which they can develop basic class management and teacher exposition skills (Harmer, 1998). They might also adopt your own planning and teaching style (Mackay, 2019) as a necessary step until they have internalised basic planning and teaching skills, and it might take a while before the beginning teacher is ready to introduce creativity, variety, and independent learning. Whilst it is important for beginning teachers to embrace your department's pedagogical choices, there needs to be space for them to develop their own teacher identity. They might need a bit of encouragement from you to do so initially. One way to achieve this is to ask beginning teachers to draw a list of new things they would like to try (that they have learnt about during their ITE programme, observed in other schools, discussed with peers, read about, etc.), and get them to consider if they could be suitable activities to meet the learning outcomes of the lessons they plan.

In the planning process, the choice of the best pedagogic approach and appropriate teaching and learning activities are the areas most influenced by school context and teacher identity, as there is no ideal way to teach a language (Broady, 2014). That said, whatever your and your department's positions on the numerous debates around how best to teach languages (Driscoll et al., 2014), as a mentor, you should always re-centre the discussion about learning activities around purpose, and desired/measured impact on pupils' learning. It is essential for beginning teachers to develop a secure understanding of purposeful planning, and some examples of activities to support this process are presented below (Task 8.3).

### Task 8.3 Supporting the planning process

Invite your beginning teacher to pick up to three activities from the list below, and sequence them to address their priorities for development in terms of planning. Do the same on your side. Compare and discuss similarities and differences in your plans. What does this tell you about your mentee's understanding of the planning process? Finally negotiate a plan of activities over the next half term. This will encourage a dialogic approach that is tailored to your mentee.

Practical collaborative activities to develop beginning language teachers' understanding of a purposeful approach of the planning process:

- Analysis of scheme of work focussed on an aspect of language learning
  This activity encourages beginning teachers to focus on how a particular aspect of language learning, such as SSC or culture, is/could be developed throughout the period covered by the scheme of work. This could be done independently at first by the beginning teacher, then discussed with you, or in a departmental meeting.
- Discussion of the mentor's own lesson resources, plan or medium-term plan, exploring rationale and purpose
  This is an opportunity for mentors to deconstruct their own planning practices, and to create a positive dialogue around planning, that doesn't focus on what went wrong or what needs changing in their beginning teacher's

planning. It allows beginning teachers to ask the essential 'why' questions in a safe and positive environment.
- Resource analysis, observation and debrief

    Provide your beginning teacher with the resources and plan for the lesson they are going to observe in advance. Ask them to predict the overarching learning outcome from the resources/plan, and to decide on the rationale for activities included in the lesson. After the observation, give an opportunity to your beginning teacher to reflect on the similarities and differences between their analysis and the observed lesson, then debrief, in a similar way as above. This is an excellent way to model how to use shared resources.

- Scaffolded co-planning

    Provide your beginning teacher with the overarching learning outcome of a lesson, and a list of steps they should take to achieve this (not precise activities, but outcomes such as: practice verb recognition, ascertain prior knowledge of auxiliary verbs in the present tense, introduce past participle formation, revise adjectival agreement, etc.). Ask your beginning teacher to design activities to fulfil these steps in order to meet the overarching outcome. Once the outline of the lesson is clear, you can model the process of planning for behaviour and classroom management, assessment for learning and adaptive teaching, as appropriate.

- Joint planning

    This is an opportunity for mentors to narrate and model the planning process, making explicit the steps they are taking and the rationale for their choices. This activity needs to be carefully planned by the mentor as taking shortcuts only appropriate for experienced teachers who have internalised a large part of this process might reinforce the misconception that planning is an unnecessary hurdle. A systematic approach will be more appropriate (for instance using a lesson plan proforma) and a dialogic approach could be adapted to the beginning teacher's stage of development.

## 'But they do not plan!'

Beginning teachers might not immediately see the point of lesson planning. Instead, they might focus on mechanically planning activities to occupy pupils for the duration of the lesson/series of lessons (Wright, 2018). Some beginning teachers navigate planning like a ship without destination, keeping the boat afloat and organised, ensuring the crew is entertained to avoid mutiny, but letting winds and currents determine the destination (if any)! This could potentially lead to activities whose purposes do not go further than providing light entertainment for pupils (Marsden & Hawkes, 2019b) and to a 'culture of low expectations which poses little intellectual and linguistic challenge to pupils', which in turns, will affect motivation and engagement (Wingate, 2018, p. 442).

This view that individual lesson plans are a waste of time is sometimes supported by the misconception that experienced teachers do not plan lessons, as their planning process is more instinctive, implicit, and private, and therefore invisible to beginning teachers (Mackay, 2019). In addition, as experienced teachers 'carry syllabuses around in their head, developed through years of experience', they often make the activity the starting point of the planning process, a shortcut that might not be helpful for less experienced teachers (Johnson, 2018, p. 283). It is therefore important to create frequent opportunities to explicitly deconstruct the planning process to make it visible, explicit, and understandable by beginning teachers (and hence different to your own planning process).

## Lesson plan proforma: friend or foe?

Lesson plan proformas are designed to centre the planning process around rationale. They are mostly used in the early stages of the beginning teacher's practice but can be useful at other points. As for the planning process itself, beginning teachers might not understand the point of the proforma straight away and they might see it as an unnecessary burden. For example, I have known some beginning teachers to even complete the proforma after the lesson resources have been designed! If not modelled, used collaboratively, debriefed and adapted (to become a friend), proformas will have no training value (and will stay a foe). Table 8.1 provides an example of part of a lesson plan proforma for consideration.

Whilst the process of modelling the use of the proforma (see Task 8.4) is initially a time-consuming process, it soon empowers the beginning teacher and supports their progress. To be effective, proformas need to be tailored to the beginning teacher's needs and stage of development (Pachler et al., 2014). For instance, once the beginning teacher has automatised aspects of classroom and resource management (such as making the most of circulating in the classroom during independent work to give out resources needed in the next activity), there will be very little training value in completing the seventh column in the example above and this could be deleted completely. In contrast, some elements of the proforma could be used years into the beginning teacher's early career to develop specific aspects of their

*Table 8.1* Lesson plan proforma example

| Class information: | | | | | | |
|---|---|---|---|---|---|---|
| Overall learning objectives/outcomes/intentions of the series of lessons/lesson: | | | | | | |
| Required prior learning to recall/re-activate: | | | | | | |
| Opportunities for cross-curricular and spiritual, moral, social, and cultural development: | | | | | | |
| Time | Activity and rationale – skill practiced (e.g. listening, phonics recognition, translation etc.) | Expected pupils' output (including minimum expectations) – and anticipated misconceptions/ difficulties | Assessment for Learning opportunities | Talk for Learning: target language/ transitions/ explanation and modelling/ questioning | Adaptive Teaching | Class and resource management |

practice, such as stimulating spontaneous speaking by carefully planning their own use of the target language (Christie, 2016). In this case, the second, third, and fifth column only will be necessary.

---

**Task 8.4  Using a lesson plan proforma: modelling, scaffolding and adaptation**

Try out some of the activities below with your beginning teacher to help them understand the value of a lesson plan proforma. Evaluate/discuss with your beginning teacher the impact on their practice and reflect on any activities that would have been beneficial at an earlier stage. Make a note of those for future beginning teachers.

- Before your mentee's first solo taught lesson, or at any stage if planning is not going well, model the use of the lesson plan proforma, narrating the process whilst you complete it. Then your mentee produces the resources for the lesson.
- Ask your beginning teacher to complete a lesson plan proforma for lessons they observe (select headings as appropriate). This exercise will be more fruitful if you have done the previous activity beforehand.
- Offer scaffolding, providing the elements that require an understanding beyond the beginning teacher stage of development. Remove the scaffolding progressively, starting with the least challenging element (step 6) and working upwards:

    1. The overall learning outcome or intention and the expected overall pupils' output;
    2. Any required prior learning to recall/revisit;
    3. Common mistakes/misconceptions/difficulties;
    4. Needs of particular pupils/groups of pupils in relation to the outcome;
    5. Series of mini-outcomes necessary to meet the overarching one;
    6. Ideas of activities to meet and assess the intended outcomes.

- Ask the beginning teacher to write the lesson plan proforma for shared resources they will use (e.g. a PowerPoint). Discuss the outcome.
- When teaching is established, request the lesson proforma before the lesson resources have been designed, and offer feedback on the clarity of rationale and purpose. Whilst a lot of beginning teachers struggle to plan purposeful activities in relation to the learning outcome, they become quickly effective at designing resources.
- Most importantly, adapt the lesson plan proforma to the needs of the beginning teacher, removing or adding columns as necessary. Make this a regular discussion point in mentor meetings as it is important to balance workload with developmental needs. Move onto medium term planning as soon as the beginning teacher is ready (see Table 8.2).

*Table 8.2* Medium-term plan template example

| Class information: | | | | |
|---|---|---|---|---|
| Overall learning objectives/outcomes/intentions of the series of lessons: | | | | |
| Final pupils' output/assessment: | | | | |
| Required prior learning to recall/re-activate: | | | | |
| Opportunities for cross-curricular and spiritual, moral, social, and cultural development: | | | | |
| Lesson – date | Learning outcome(s) | Learning activities | Assessment of impact | Retrieval – interleaved practice |
| Lesson 1 – date | | | | |
| Lesson 2 – date | | | | |

## Moving to planning a sequence of lessons: medium-term planning

Whilst planning over a series of lessons might be a step too far at the earliest stages of teacher development, learning to plan medium-term is a necessary skill to develop effective planning and teaching practices. Only then will beginning teachers start to apply the knowledge gained about the 'big picture' and purposeful planning, and be able to consider and plan the extensive, frequent, and spaced receptive and productive meaningful practice necessary for the acquisition of linguistic features (Marsden & Hawkes, 2019a). In addition, medium-term planning will support reflection on variety of activities and balance of input and output. As always, the starting point is the learning objectives as set out in the scheme of work, but it might also be helpful for the beginning teacher to consider the end of sequence pupils' output (or production of language), and work backwards to equip pupils to achieve this by the end of the sequence (Deane, 2002).

To achieve this, your beginning teacher could look critically at a textbook module they are going to teach, come up with the final productive output (e.g. talking about relationships with friends using reflective verbs in the first and third persons singular and plural in three tenses), then look critically at the resources deciding what content will support meaningful practice towards this, and what content should be adapted, or just ignored. Beginning teachers are often reluctant to do this as they feel that any content in published resources needs to be taught. They could then map out how each lesson will build towards the final outcome in a scaffolded and structured way (Bauckham, 2019). If your department uses end of module/term assessments, it is also very important that beginning teachers look at the assessment before they start teaching the unit of work, as it is crucial for pupils' motivation to experience success in a context of high expectations and strong challenge (Maxwell, 2019).

As per the process of individual lesson planning, you should carefully scaffold and model the use of any medium-term planning template (Table 8.2). To begin with, you could provide the beginning teachers with the first two columns (use your own medium-term plan and empty the other columns as appropriate), until they are ready to plan independently. Joint planning, regular feedback, and professional dialogue will also support their progress (Mackay, 2019). Please note that whilst this is a process that beginning teachers may have explored earlier in their ITE school placements, it might be worth modelling and scaffolding again whilst they are getting used to the specific context of your school.

## Final thoughts on feedback, readiness to learn, and workload

Evaluation and feedback will be explored further in subsequent chapters, but it is worth pointing out that the link between planning and learning should be made explicit to ensure beginning teachers can learn from their experiences (Black et al., 2017) (also see Figure 8.1). It is also important to tailor your feedback to the stage of development of your beginning teacher. Early feedback is likely to be based around the planning of classroom management and teacher exposition (e.g. timing, organisation, explanation and modelling) as you will have provided a lot of scaffolds for the other elements – see Task 8.3. The feedback can then progress onto the new areas of autonomy (e.g. choice of purposeful activities). Make sure you pick the areas of feedback that will have the most impact on the beginning teacher's practice (as long as they are ready for this). Whilst it will not be difficult for a beginning teacher to identify that they have not allocated sufficient time to a listening activity and address this in subsequent lessons, they might not realise that, even if the class appeared engaged, very little learning was taking place due to low challenge, purposeless activities.

Beginning teachers are often their own harshest critics and might experience feedback fatigue (Wright, 2018) so feedback needs to be meaningful, manageable, and motivating. For more on feedback, see Chapter 10. It might be useful here to refer to Reeves' (2008) idea that feedback on planning should be medical rather than post-mortem. Feedback should be looking forward rather than backwards, shifting the focus from correcting to learning to plan. Giving extensive feedback on a lesson that is already fully planned and resourced, but not yet taught, will likely cause distress, especially at a stage when beginning teachers spend hours planning an hour lesson. Asking beginning teachers to re-plan the lesson is also likely to create resentment and workload issues. Instead, provide the beginning teacher with the scaffold they need (see Task 8.3), so they can operate in their 'desirable challenge' zone, rather than being thrown out of their depth. Later on, when the beginning teacher is ready to plan independently, you could ask

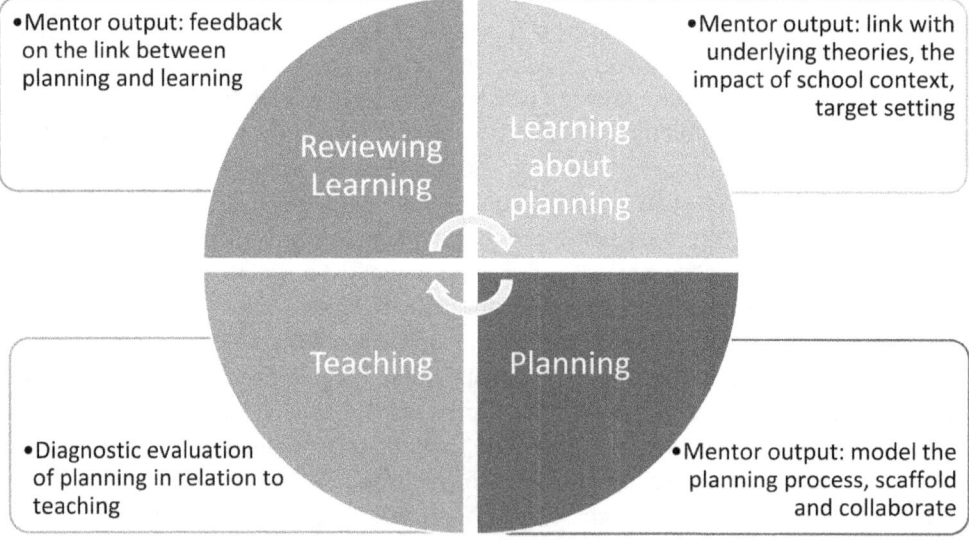

*Figure 8.1* Learning to plan cycle. (Adapted from Mackay, 2019.)

*Supporting the lesson planning process* 97

for an outline of the lesson a few days ahead (e.g. asking for columns one, two, three and four on the lesson plan proforma in Table 8.2). You could then give feedback before the lesson is fully planned and resourced as this has been shown as having the most impact on emerging planning practices of beginning teachers (Mackay, 2019).

It can be disconcerting and frustrating for mentors that some beginning teachers spend so long planning (ineffective) lessons when they are given all resources. Whilst there is a consensus that beginning teachers will take longer to plan than experienced teachers (Mackay, 2019), this chapter has highlighted another possible reason. The beginning teacher might simply not be ready for finding rationale and purpose in resources and linking them to the big picture. This does not mean that you should not share resources with beginning teachers, as one of your roles as a mentor is to ensure they can have a reasonable work-life balance (Black et al., 2017). However, as for the rest of the planning process, using pre-made resources effectively should be modelled and scaffolded. A quick conversation (or email), clearly stating the desired outcomes of the lesson, how it translates in terms of meaningful practice (input and/or output), the required prior knowledge to reactivate and common mistakes/difficulties to pre-empt will go a long way, especially in the early stages.

And finally, whilst lessons need to be well-planned and resourced purposefully, with a focus on pupils' long-term progress, it is important that beginning teachers feel empowered to adapt these plans to the emerging needs of pupils, and to make the most of learning opportunities that might occur during the planning process but also during lessons. Johnson highlights the importance for beginning teachers to learn to be opportunistic as well as organised, to make the most of 'golden opportunities to teach something, too good to miss' (2018, p. 284), even if this involves diverting from their carefully designed plan.

## Conclusion

Learning to plan is a complex and demanding process that brings together most of the knowledge and skills necessary to become an effective languages teacher. Mentors can have a deeply positive impact on the Learning to Plan process by adopting collaborative and scaffolded approaches.

In this chapter, we have considered the importance of:

- Being aware that experienced teachers' intuitive planning practices might not be appropriate for beginning teachers.
- Understanding the complex processes involved in planning a lesson/series of lesson and being able to deconstruct your own planning practice, to explicitly analyse and model the 'why'.
- Encouraging beginning teachers to consider the big picture from the start (even when they only plan at micro level). This is probably an implicit and instinctive part of your practice so modelling should be intentional (as it will not be natural).
- Focusing on rationale and purpose.
- Considering that beginning teachers might not see the point of planning or using scaffolding tools such as lesson plan proformas and that this should be explicitly modelled and scaffolded.

- Modelling individual parts of the process separately through collaborative planning, considering beginning teachers' readiness to learn these at their stage of development, and providing scaffolding as necessary until the beginning teacher is ready to undertake these in an integrated way.
- Moving to medium-term planning as soon as the beginning teacher is ready as this will unlock important aspects of language teaching and learning (such as spaced practice).
- Making the link between planning and learning explicit in lesson feedback.
- Providing feedback on lesson outlines rather than fully resourced lessons.
- Giving beginning teachers the confidence to step away from their carefully designed plan in response to in-the-moment pupil needs/interests.

## For discussion

- Explore the No-Go pedagogy from the NCELP (National Centre for Excellence for Language Pedagogy) with your beginning teacher/department: https://resources.ldpedagogy.org/concern/resources/z316q160c?locale=en
  How does this list relate to your department teaching and planning practices?
- To what extent do your mentoring practices in regard to the Learning to Plan process meet the need of your beginning teacher (or have met the need of former beginning teachers)?

## Further reading

- NCLE (National Consortium for Languages Education) Universal CPD, available at https://ncle-language-hubs.ucl.ac.uk/universal-cpd/
  Whilst still under development at the time of writing, this section of the website announces three free universal CPD modules on planning: Planning for Success 1 – The Three Pillars: Phonics, Vocabulary and Grammar; Planning for Success 2 – Curriculum Design and development; Planning for Success 3 – The Intercultural Dimension. The Planning for Success sessions 1 and 3 might be particularly relevant to beginning teachers.
- LPD Language Driven Pedagogy (ex NCELP National Centre for Excellence for Language Pedagogy) – Meaningful Practice: Definitions, Rationales, and Principles, available at https://resources.ldpedagogy.org/concern/resources/ng451h506?locale=en
  This is a guidance document for teachers, outlining what constitutes practice in language teaching and learning, what it is for, how it develops, and the principles for creating the best conditions for its success. It summarises useful information to support your beginning teacher's medium-term planning and would constitutes a good basis for initial discussions around this.
- ALL (Association for Language Learning) – Decolonise the MFL Curriculum Special Interest Groups, available at https://www.all-languages.org.uk/about/community/special-interest-groups/de-colonising-the-curriculum/
  We cannot talk about the big picture in MFL teaching and learning without exploring decolonising the curriculum and embedding anti-racist education. The ALL Decolonise the MFL Curriculum Special Interest Groups webpage is regularly updated with the ongoing collaborative work and development on the topic of anti-racist education. It

presents amongst other things an extensive collection of reading/research and training resources, as well as a resource bank.
- https://themillennial.home.blog/2021/02/04/making-the-curriculum-lgbt-inclusive-with-mfl-examples/

    This blog offers a great starting point to making the modern language classroom more inclusive of LGBTQ+ identities, with some concrete ideas to plan inclusive resources for languages lessons, which aim towards normalisation and embodiment. The principles of this blog could also be used to create resources more racially inclusive.

## References

Bauckham, I. (2019). *Modern Foreign Languages Pedagogy Review: A review of modern foreign languages teaching practice in key stage 3 and key stage 4*. Accessed November 18, 2023, https://ncelp.org/wp-content/uploads/2020/02/MFL_Pedagogy_Review_Report_TSC_PUBLISHED_VERSION_Nov_2016_1_.pdf.

Black, L., Gordon, A. L., Hughes, C., & Sandy, S. (2017). *Effective mentoring of trainee teachers (e-book)*. Association for Language Learning.

Black, P., & Jones, J. (2006). Formative assessment and the learning and teaching of MFL: Sharing the language learning road map with the learners. *Language Learning Journal*, 34(1), 4–9.

Broady, E. (2014). Foreign language teaching: Understanding approaches, making choices. In N. Pachler & A. Redondo (Eds.), *A practical guide to teaching foreign languages in the secondary school* (pp. 1–10). Routledge.

Christie, C. (2016). Speaking spontaneously in the modern foreign languages classroom: Tools for supporting successful target language conversation. *The Language Learning Journal*, 44(1), 74–89.

Deane, M. (2002). Planning MFL learning. In A. Swarbick (Ed.), *Aspects of teaching secondary modern foreign languages: Perspectives on practice* (pp. 147–165). Taylor & Francis Group.

Department for Education (2018). *Addressing teacher workload in initial teacher education (ITE): Advice for ITE providers*. Crown.

Department for Education (2024). *Initial teacher training and early career framework (ITTECF)* [Online]. Accessed February 19, 2024, https://www.gov.uk/government/publications/initial-teacher-training-and-early-career-framework.

Driscoll, P., Macaro, E., & Swarbrick, A. (2014). *Debates in modern languages education*. Routledge.

Harmer, J. (1998). *Default settings: What models do for trainees*. Melbourne Exhibition Centre.

Johnson, K. (2018). *An introduction to foreign language learning and teaching*. Routledge.

Lightbown, P. M., & Spada, N. (2018). *How languages are learned* (4th ed.). Oxford University Press.

Mackay, C. (2019). *Learning to plan modern languages lessons: Understanding the basic ingredients*. Routledge.

Marsden, E., & Hawkes, R. (2019a). *Meaningful practice: Definitions, rationales and principles*. [Online] Accessed February 19, 2024, https://resources.ncelp.org/concern/resources/ng451h506-Meaningful_practice_definitions_rationale_principles.pdf.

Marsden, E., & Hawkes, R. (2019b). *No-Go Pedagogy* [Online]. Accessed February 19, 2024, https://resources.ldpedagogy.org/concern/parent/z316q160c/file_sets/n870zq82k.

Maxwell, J. A. (2019). *Making every MFL lesson count: Six principles to support modern foreign language teaching*. Crown House Publishing.

Pachler, N., Evans, M., Redondo, A., & Fisher, L. (2014). *Learning to teach foreign languages in the secondary school: A companion to school experience* (4th ed.). Routledge.

Reeves, D. (2008). Leading to change: Effective grading practices. *Educational Leadership, 65*(5), 85-87.
Wingate, U. (2018). Lots of games and little challenge – A snapshot of modern foreign language teaching in English secondary schools. *The Language Learning Journal, 46*(4), 442-455.
Wright, T. (2018). *How to be a brilliant mentor: Developing outstanding teachers*. Routledge.

# 9 Helping beginning language teachers to analyse their own planning and teaching

*Trevor Mutton*

## Introduction

This chapter explores the significant role that a languages mentor has in helping the beginning teachers with whom they are working to think in a critical way about their planning and their teaching. There are several approaches to this issue. First, the chapter will consider the way in which beginning teachers might reflect on their planning and their practice, and some of the potential limitations of the "reflective" approach. The chapter will also discuss the different forms of knowledge that beginning teachers can draw on in order to inform their reflection as they start to develop well-informed rationales for the decisions that they make (both when planning and when in the classroom itself). Critical interrogation of these sources of knowledge will also enable beginning teachers to identify clear criteria by which to evaluate their practice, and they will thus start to move from their initial dependence on the professionals with whom they are working (particularly their mentor). Your role, as a mentor, is to guide beginning teachers as they plan, teach, and evaluate their teaching but you will also want to develop greater levels of independence as these beginning teachers start to take on more responsibility for all aspects of their practice as part of the process of becoming a full professional. In doing so, it is useful for you to be aware of the different types of knowledge that a teacher needs. Winch, Oancea and Orchard (2015) argue that "teaching as a professional endeavour" (p. 210) brings together different forms of knowledge which are necessary to avoid limited and limiting conceptualisations of teaching. They focus on the role of "situated understanding" and "technical knowledge" but argue that, to be fully professional, teachers also need to engage in "critical reflection" (p. 204). Careful and thoughtful mentoring of beginning teachers is therefore essential in developing the capacity for critical reflection and, in doing so, to establish the foundations for teachers' career-long professional learning and development (Task 9.1).

---

**Task 9.1 Reflecting on a range of mentoring strategies to support beginning teachers' planning**

Before reading any further, it might be useful to consider what you think are the most and least effective aspects of the strategies that you, as a languages mentor, might use when working with a beginning teacher to support them in analysing their planning and their teaching. Below are 10 things you might do, although the list is by no means exhaustive. What do you think are the strengths/limitations of each of these approaches? You might also like to consider discussing the potential strengths and limitations of these suggested approaches with other colleagues who might be working with the beginning teacher (Table 9.1).

*Table 9.1* Reflecting on a range of mentoring strategies to support beginning teachers' planning

| Strategy | Advantages/strengths | Disadvantages/limitations |
|---|---|---|
| Ask to see a lesson plan at least 24 hours before the lesson and sending written feedback | | |
| Discuss a lesson plan with your beginning teacher at the "first draft" stage | | |
| Ask your beginning teacher to "script", in advance, a grammatical explanation they plan to cover in the lesson | | |
| Ask your beginning teacher to teach a lesson plan that has been produced by somebody else, and then observing and feeding back on the lesson | | |
| Observe a lesson and then feed back to your beginning teacher as to what their strengths and/or areas for development might be | | |
| Encourage your beginning teacher to try out new ideas in the classroom | | |
| Use feedback to highlight any issues around subject knowledge/target language accuracy | | |
| Focus on your beginning teacher being able to follow the school/department approach to planning and teaching | | |
| Focus on your beginning teacher being able to follow the school's behaviour management policy | | |
| Asking your beginning teacher to keep a reflective journal, which you look at each week | | |

## Developing beginning teachers' reflection

The contribution of mentors to the learning of beginning languages teachers is distinctive, and draws on the accumulated experience and expertise you offer as a mentor. While generic approaches to mentoring, such as those encapsulated within the *National Standards for school-based initial teacher training (ITT) mentors* (DfE, 2016) in England, may provide a broad framework for general mentoring approaches, they say little about the way in which languages mentors might work effectively with beginning teachers as part of a programme of professional formation. Such generic models also give no indication of what mentoring a beginning teacher within a specific subject area might look like. Mentoring can be conceptualised as occurring at different levels (see McIntyre & Hagger, 1994) with "zero level" (p. 86) characterised by generic approaches and "developed mentoring" (p. 94) characterised as drawing effectively on the mentor's full range of expertise. The latter requires you to have an enhanced understanding of the nature of beginning teachers' learning, as well as a range of mentoring strategies that provide appropriate learning opportunities within the practicum context and which enable beginning teachers to develop their professional knowledge "through interpretation, application and reflection on experience" (Loughran, 2019, p. 527). So how can languages mentors help the teachers with whom they are working to analyse their practice and support them in reflecting effectively on their experiences?

First, it is useful to discuss what we mean by teacher reflection, which has been a key component of teacher education programmes for several decades, drawing on the ideas of John Dewey (1933, 1938) but rooted particularly in the seminal work of Donald Schön (1983, 1987). The concept of "the reflective practitioner" is now common across a number of professions, and reflection is a key component of teacher education programmes, but it is not necessarily always a straightforward issue and we have to be clear about the nature and purpose of such reflection. Schön was interested in the relationship between theory and practice and the way in which reflection contributed to teachers' decision making in the moment (reflection-in-action) and how teachers might reflect on teaching that has already taken place (reflection-on-action). Reflection-in-action is considered to be an essential part of the process of developing the capacity of a teacher to draw on their knowledge in order to inform how they respond in the moment. Given the "multidimensionality, simultaneity, and unpredictability" of the classroom (Doyle 1977, p. 54) this in-the-moment decision making is important and is what Rowland et al. (2005) refer to as "contingency knowledge", which they define as "knowledge-in-*inter*action" (original emphasis). This represents "the ability of the teacher to 'think on her feet' and respond appropriately to the contributions made by her students during a teaching episode" (p. 266). Nevertheless, the almost universal call for reflection within programmes of teacher education is not without issues. Beauchamp (2015), in her review of the research literature on teacher reflection, provides an overview of these critiques which, among others, include a lack of theoretical understanding of the nature of reflection, the fact that models of teacher reflection often fail to take account of context or individual identity, and that often "the push for accountability in teaching has resulted in forced reflection, or in a routinization of reflective practice that undermines the notion of reflection as deep thinking" (p. 127). In terms of the *context* in which reflection takes place, and the importance of taking account of individual teacher *identity* when encouraging beginning teachers in particular to engage in reflection, the mentor has a key role to play to address both of these issues. Reflection cannot be seen to be an isolated and individual pursuit that the beginning teacher is expected to carry out on their own – it is a social process that requires you, as the mentor, to co-reflect with the beginning teacher, and to support the latter, through open dialogue and discussion, as they seek to model what the reflective process looks like and how it might be of benefit. The context, therefore, has to be one that is supportive of professional learning but this cannot work if there is a hierarchical relationship between mentor and beginning teacher. In terms of teacher identity, it needs to be acknowledged that this is closely bound up with a beginning teacher's sense of self, their aspirations, their own ideas about teaching and learning (including what may be quite strong preconceptions) and their emotions.

As reflective practice is an often used and, sometimes, misunderstood concept, it is worth pausing to consider in further depth, at this stage, the actual process of reflection. McIntyre (1993) sees learning to reflect as being an important goal for beginning teachers as it is central to the process of developing what he calls "practical reflectivity" (p. 45), that is to say, the ability to articulate criteria by which to evaluate and develop one's practice. McIntyre was concerned about the way in which theory and practice needed to be closely integrated within programmes of initial teacher education (ITE) and that critical evaluation had to be a central feature of beginning teachers' practice, leading him to conceptualise a model for teacher professional leaning that he later called "practical theorising" (McIntyre, 1995, p. 365). He sees this as being a dialectic process, through which beginning teachers are supported in developing their ability to draw on and interrogate different sorts of knowledge (both theoretical and practical). Reflection of this kind will then inform the decisions they take in relation to their own developing practice (Burn & Mutton, 2015). Practical theorising places the beginning teacher at the heart of the process of learning to teach and addresses the need, discussed above, to acknowledge the complex role that both the learning context and the individual teacher's identity and beliefs play in the development of professional learning.

Supporting beginning teachers to be able to analyse and reflect on their own teaching is therefore not an easy process. We need to consider what critical reflection actually involves, and how it can be developed through careful mentoring. Kriewaldt and Turnidge (2013) suggest that teachers need to exercise critical reflection through a process of what they call "clinical reasoning", and which they understand to be "the analytical and intuitive cognitive processes that professionals use to arrive at a best judged ethical response in a specific practice-based context" (p. 106). This depends on the teacher's need to draw on different sources of knowledge and to collect and analyse the data available to them in order to make the informed ethical decisions in relation to their teaching. The issue with beginning teachers, however, is that they are expected to be acting competently within a professional context from a very early stage of their training, so the accumulated expertise and accompanying evidence on which they can draw in order to make informed practice-based judgements is therefore understandably limited. The mentor's role is therefore vitally important in engaging beginning teachers in educative conversations which will enable them both to draw on, and to make sense of, all the information available to them. Kriewaldt and Turnidge (2013) see the clinical reasoning model as comprising four elements:

- respectful and reciprocal dialogue
- iterative use of data and evidence
- probing personal assumptions and theories
- articulating reasoning (visible thinking) (p. 108).

If you are to support beginning teachers in this way, then this has to be a two-way process (respectful and reciprocal dialogue) in which both you and the beginning teacher are adopting an inquiry stance (which involves collecting and analysing appropriate data), and which involves carefully managed discussions (requiring questioning, reflective responses, and active listening on the part of each participant) and both the space and openness to explore and articulate key ideas and rationales. These professional dialogues will be informed by a range of evidence, drawing directly on both your practical experience and knowledge, *and* the practical experience and knowledge of the beginning teacher, as well as wider understandings of the nature of languages teaching and what can be learnt from research and the practice of others.

The clinical reasoning model could be applied equally usefully, for example, to discussions of lesson planning (including planning for any collaborative teaching), post-lesson reflection and analysis, or more general discussions around pedagogical approaches in the modern languages classroom. In each case the key purpose would be to support the developing thinking of beginning teachers in relation to their practice and, over time, to support them in being able to identify appropriate criteria by with which evaluate that practice (i.e. both their planning and their classroom teaching) (Task 9.2).

### Task 9.2 Questions to promote beginning teachers' critical reasoning

Below is a short scenario featuring Jake, a beginning teacher who is towards the end of the first term of his ITE programme.

> Jake has just taught a lesson (that you observed) where the topic in question was school life in Spain. The lesson plan showed that he had planned a starter activity to re-cap the vocabulary covered in the previous lesson (school subjects and the school timetable) and then, in his words, to 'do a listening,' the text of which involved various Spanish children talking about their school day. The lesson plan indicated that he was going to follow this up with a short reading task, and finish the lesson with a structured writing activity. In the event, Jake only got as far as revising the vocabulary (which took a lot longer than he had anticipated) and completing the listening activity, with which many of the pupils struggled and there was some off-task behaviour and low-level disruption. Repeated attempts to replay the short dialogues did not seem to help some pupils with the task of identifying the Spanish children's likes and dislikes.
>
> You begin by asking how Jake thought the lesson went and he is very negative – he says he is generally disappointed with the way things went. He says that he had decided at the last minute to introduce, during the starter activity, some cultural input about what school life is like in Spain, since he is really keen to introduce the pupils to aspects of Spanish culture when he can. This aim did not feature in his lesson plan. He says that the pupils were 'awful' today and just didn't seem to want to learn.

Looking at the following list of questions, how useful is each one likely to be in terms of facilitating a dialogue which will enable Jake to articulate his reasoning effectively?

Rate each one as being not useful at all/reasonably useful/very useful/extremely useful:

- What were you trying to achieve in that lesson?
- What led you to plan the lesson in that particular way?
- How much of what happened was down to the way you planned the lesson?
- What led to the starter activity over-running by so much?
- What do you think led to the pupils' poor behaviour?

- Why did you not issue a warning to student x?
- Where did your ideas for the listening activity come from?
- What are the challenges of using recorded material to develop the pupils' listening?
- What have you learnt, from observing other teachers, about carrying out a listening task?
- Why do you think you weren't you able to complete all the activities you had planned to do in the lesson?
- From the lessons you have taught with other classes and lessons that you have observed others teaching, what would say is the link, if any, between lesson content, different pedagogical approaches, and pupil behaviour?
- In general, do you think it is better to get through the activities you have planned or to go at the pace of the learners, which may mean that you don't get to cover everything in a lesson?
- Do the pupils generally appreciate your attempts to introduce some aspect of the target language culture into lessons?
- I noted that the majority of the pupils were able to/not able to .... (for example, pronounce the names of the sports correctly in the starter activity). Why do you think that was?
- What would you do differently next time?
- What alternative use, if any, could you have made of the taped recording and the transcript of the listening text?
- Why do you think that pupils find listening and understanding Spanish such a difficult skill?
- What could we do about making listening tasks in Spanish easier for our pupils?
- So, what are your key take-aways from that lesson?

If you only got to ask three of the above questions in a post-lesson feedback session, which would these be and why?

What further questions could you ask that might enable you to probe further any personal assumptions and theories that Jake might have?

## Drawing on different sources of knowledge

When considering the sources of knowledge on which the beginning teachers might be drawing, it is unlikely that any single source will be sufficient to enable them to reflect critically and work out potential approaches that they might explore further in their practice. Although not an exhaustive list, the sources on which beginning teachers can draw will include the following:

- **Theoretical knowledge** which may be found in research journals, books, or research publications produced by language-specific subject associations, such as the Association for Language Learning in the United Kingdom. Much of this literature will focus on the extensive body of international applied linguistics research around second language acquisition (SLA). In addition to publications which may focus on very specific issues, some will provide more general overviews of SLA theories (for example Mitchell et al., 2019). Beginning teachers may have been introduced to some of this literature by their ITE provider and should be able to read and analyse the literature critically in order to gain access to research-informed approaches to teaching languages. Beginning teachers will also be accessing more theoretical ideas around both general pedagogy and languages-specific pedagogy, all of which they will need to read critically and draw on in their decision-making in relation to their own practice.

- **Personal knowledge, identity, and beliefs.** As noted above, individual identity plays an important part in teacher learning, along with what may potentially be strongly held beliefs and preconceptions, so much so that beginning teachers need to engage with these fully and even apply to them similar critical judgement that they use to interrogate the literature. This requires not only a high degree of self-awareness, but also a willingness to subject what may often be long-held beliefs to scrutiny. Furthermore, they are more likely to engage with this process if they recognise that you are also willing to ask similar questions of your own preferred approaches to teaching. The benefits of critically examining their own beliefs and preconceptions will enable beginning teachers to facilitate the process of integrating their personal selves and their professional lives, but Buehl and Beck (2014) demonstrate that the relationship between teachers' beliefs and their practice is complex, and that there is often incongruence between the two for a number of different reasons. They conclude that "teacher educators should be attuned to the role that reflection and awareness play in supporting the congruence between teachers' beliefs and practices" (p. 81). For mentors, this might mean a number of things such as: exploring fully what those beliefs are and how they influence the decisions the beginning teacher is taking; encouraging the beginning teacher to explore these beliefs further and to test out the viability of their application in the classroom context; and then you observing what happens when these ideas are tried out, followed by supported reflection in relation to the actual outcomes. Giving beginning teachers the opportunity to explore their beliefs in this way, even in the face of particular obstacles and challenges (for example, trying things that may not align with a particular school, departmental or even an individual teacher's approach) is important since otherwise any incongruence between beliefs and practice is likely to remain and cause potential problems.
- **The knowledge gained through beginning teachers reflecting on their own experience of planning and teaching.** Teaching is rooted in classroom practice and beginning teachers have to gain experiential knowledge through engaging in the process of planning and teaching. The decisions they take during the pre-active (planning) and active (actual teaching) phases of their practice clearly have an effect on the outcomes, and these decisions and their impact need to be evaluated. Your role is crucial here in encouraging the beginning teacher, after the teaching itself has taken place, to articulate their goals for the lesson and the rationale behind the choices that they made; to explore any alternative approaches, drawing on both theoretical and practical considerations (and whether these may or may not have been considered); and to evaluate the outcomes against agreed criteria.
- **Knowledge about the learners.** Beginning teachers need both to know about their learners, and to learn from them. They use this knowledge to inform all aspects of their planning and teaching, but this needs to be driven by a close attention both to the level

of progress that the learners are achieving and analysing the information that they have about this effectively in order to determine their ongoing learning needs. Mentors will encourage beginning teachers to draw on specific evidence (both formal and informal) to inform their critical reflection on the lesson outcomes as they begin to take increasing responsibility for evaluating their own practice.

- **The professional practical knowledge of established teachers** is another key source of the beginning teacher's learning, which is often called "craft knowledge", a term which has been interpreted by some as being unhelpful as it potentially diminishes the status of teaching and reduces the role of teacher to that of a craft worker. The idea of craft knowledge has, however, generally been considered in a more positive light and has been used to define the knowledge that is rooted in teachers' classroom practice, but also the thinking and rationales that underpin that practice, with the latter often being tacit and not necessarily easy to articulate. The concept of craft knowledge acknowledges that teaching is complex and that "dilemmas and challenges are part of teachers' everyday practice" (Black-Hawkins & Florian, 2012, p. 570). This sort of knowledge is also an important source of learning for beginning teachers but the process through which they might acquire such knowledge needs to be planned and managed carefully. Beginning teachers need opportunities to observe experienced teachers, and this is particularly beneficial not just at the beginning of a programme, but also later, when they have a greater appreciation of the classroom and teacher decision-making. Hagger (1997) and Hagger and McIntyre (2006) have shown that providing guidance as to how beginning teachers might ask appropriate questions in relation to the teaching they have observed can promote effective dialogue, which leads to enhanced understandings of experienced teachers' classroom practices and the rationales that underpin it.

To give an example of how these different sources might be providing different perspectives for a beginning teacher of languages, let us consider one issue that is likely to arise, that is to say, the extent to which the target language is used within the languages classroom. Consider the example of Emily as follows and then complete Task 9.3:

> Emily has very positive memories of her own secondary school and particularly of her French teacher whom she still looks up to as a role model. Emily's teacher used French most of the time and expected her students to do the same. Emily feels that this helped her to develop both her listening and speaking skills, as well as her love of the language in general. This approach continued during her undergraduate programme and, as a Foreign Languages Assistant, teaching English at a lycÈe in France during her year abroad, her classes all took place in the target language. In the first few weeks of her ITE programme she had read some of the literature and had concluded, from a number of different studies, that high quality oral interaction in the target language is important if the learners themselves are to be able to communicate effectively. Having observed several lessons in her placement school, Emily notices that one experienced teacher (a native speaker of French) is using the target language fairly consistently, two teachers are using it occasionally (but using English to give instructions and grammatical explanations), and one is hardly using it at all. When Emily talks to the teacher who hardly uses the target language at all, she is told that in an ideal world using the target language

would be fine, but not with this particular class on a Thursday afternoon. Other teachers tell her that the more target language you try and use, the greater the risk of the pupils going off-task and being poorly behaved. She talks to a few pupils about what they think, and they tell her that they like it when the teacher talks in French, but that they struggle to use French themselves in the classroom and feel embarrassed when asked to do so. Emily concludes that she would like to use the target language more, but is worried about potential classroom management issues. She is also anxious not to come across as being critical of the practice of other teachers (including, perhaps yourself, because she does not want to upset you) yet she feels that she does need to find a way forward.

---

**Task 9.3 Exploring beginning teachers' thinking, and developing strategies to provide targeted support**

What might a mentoring conversation look like which aimed to explore the range of sources of knowledge on which Emily might be drawing? What questions might you ask?

What sort of questions would you, as a mentor, ask Emily in order to elicit her beliefs and preconceptions about languages teaching and learning?

How might you develop a better understanding of any tensions that Emily might be experiencing in terms of what approach she ought to be taking?

What might Emily want to ask you?

Following the mentoring conversation, you decide to offer Emily more support around helping her to reconcile some of the tensions she is experiencing around to how much of the target language she could be using. Assess each of the following strategies in terms of whether you think they might be very helpful/fairly helpful/not particularly helpful/not helpful at all:

- Co-planning a lesson with Emily, that she will teach, discussing the rationales for the planning choices made and taking into account opportunities for use of the target language.
- Co-planning a lesson with Emily, that you will both co-teach, discussing the rationales for the planning choices made and taking into account opportunities for use of the target language.
- Asking Emily to plan a lesson where she will identify where, and where not, to use the target language. You will observe the lesson and give feedback afterwards.
- Suggesting some strategies that Emily might use to increase her use of the target language.
- Ask Emily to share what she has read about the use of the target language in the literature and then discuss these ideas with her.
- Asking Emily to observe again the teacher who does use the target language fairly consistently and to note the factors that seem to facilitate this practice, and then to reflect what support she might need to enable her to implement some of these approaches herself.
- Going through the school's behaviour policy with Emily.

## The role of an inquiry-based approach to support and develop teacher reflection

As noted above, one strategy for ensuring that beginning teachers reflect effectively on their planning and their classroom teaching, is for you and your beginning teacher to take an inquiry approach. At its simplest, this means identifying pedagogical issues or puzzles and then exploring approaches that might lead to improvement in the quality of teaching and learning. In fact, it could be argued that reflective practice is wholly dependent on teachers adopting an inquiry stance. Mann and Walsh (2013) who researched the role of reflective practice in English as a Second Language (ESL) settings, argue "for a more dialogic, data-led and collaborative approach to reflective practice" (p. 291) and that a "(G)reater understanding of professional practice is more possible when a process of inquiry is carried out in the teacher's natural environment, using a teacher's own data" (p. 301). In the case of beginning teachers, it is you, as the mentor, who can offer support by adopting a different approach to providing feedback following an observed lesson. Instead of using the observation of a lesson to measure and record progress against a set of generic descriptors or standards (which is often the case) you and your beginning teacher can agree what data it might be useful to collect to inform a discussion about a specific aspect (or aspects) of their classroom practice that you have *both* identified as being something that might be developed further. Examples of what data might be collected are:

- The overall amount, and/or nature, of both teacher-talk and pupil-talk during the lesson
- The amount of target language used (by both teacher and pupils)
- Wait times, during question and answer sequences
- The level of participation of individual pupils
- The frequency and nature of error correction
- The strategies that individual pupils seemed to be using to decode a reading text
- The extent of "teacher echo" (the verbatim repetition of a pupil's response) during question and answer sequences
- Recording what occurred at moments in the lesson where in-the-moment contingent decision making took place
- Pupil outcomes which would be difficult to monitor/assess without somebody else there to record these outcomes (for example, a detailed assessment of the quality of the pupils' pronunciation during a pair-work speaking task)

The post-lesson discussion would then focus on any data collected by both you and your beginning teacher, without any judgement as to whether the findings indicated a particular level of teaching competence or otherwise, but rather the discussion would focus on highlighting potential changes to practice that the professional dialogue around the data may have suggested.

## Developing beginning teachers' own criteria by which they might evaluate their planning and teaching

If we want to encourage beginning teachers to be able to evaluate their planning and teaching effectively, particularly those who have already had a reasonable amount of experience of

- Emily receives support from her mentor in terms of suggestions for ways to incorporate more target langauge into her lessons
- Emily experiements using a number of different strategies that she has learnt from her discussions with colleagues and from her reading
- Emily has received quite extensive feedback, which has suggested ways of increasing her own use of the target language
- Emily now sets herself a target of developing greater student use of the target language and has a clear idea of what she wants to achieve
- Emily asks her mentor to record instances of student target language use - and note both how much there is, and its quality

*Figure 9.1* Enabling beginning teachers to identify for themselves areas of development and related evaluation criteria.

the classroom, there needs to be a sense of progression in the way that mentors guide and support those with whom they are working (Figure 9.1). This may require a shift from an approach which is more about "offering short-term support for immediate problems" (Hagger & McIntyre, 2006, p. 169) – an approach which may sometimes characterise feedback in the earlier stages of a programme – to one which leads to the beginning teacher "acquiring the habit of evaluating their own teaching against a wide range of criteria and drawing on a wide range of kinds of knowledge" (p. 170).

If we return to the example of Emily above, this might be realised in the following way.

As your beginning teacher moves towards this greater level of independence, your role becomes even more collaborative, with discussions around teaching and learning becoming less mentor-led and post-lesson dialogue driven predominantly by the agenda of the beginning teacher.

## Conclusion

The aim of this chapter has been to show the way in which beginning languages teachers can be supported in developing their capacity to analyse and reflect on their planning and their teaching. Professional reflection is not as straightforward as is sometimes assumed – it is not just a matter of deciding whether a lesson was successful or not and what the reasons for that judgement might be. If reflection is to enhance professional learning (both for the beginning teacher, and for the mentor) it needs to be carried out critically, drawing on different sources of knowledge which are used to interrogate each other. Theoretical and practical considerations have to be weighed in the balance, along with their own beliefs and personal understandings, to ensure that decisions made in relation to both planning and teaching are informed by appropriate evidence in order to arrive at the "best judged ethical response in a specific practice-based context" (Kriewaldt & Turnidge, 2013, p. 106). Beginning teachers will not necessarily be able to achieve this level of reflection without being encouraged to adopt a critical stance towards what they are discovering (from a range of different sources) but, if supported in doing so, it is likely that they will go on to develop as full professionals, using strategies to evaluate their own practice that will sustain them throughout their teaching career. As a mentor, you have a crucial role in enabling this to happen.

## For discussion

- What can you do to ensure that the mentoring conversations with the beginning teacher(s) with whom you are currently working reflect the four elements of the clinical reasoning model described above?
- What, if any, are the challenges of developing critical reflection with beginning languages teachers in the specific context in which you are currently working?
- What, if anything, is unique to the mentoring of languages beginning teachers when it comes to encouraging the development of more critical reflection in relation to their planning and teaching?

## Further reading

If you are interested in exploring these ideas further the following two publications provide some useful follow-up reading.

1. Kriewaldt, J., & Turnidge, D. (2013). Conceptualising an approach to clinical reasoning in the education profession. *Australian Journal of Teacher Education*, 38(9), 103-115. https://doi.org/10.14221/ajte.2013v38n6.9

    Underpinning this chapter is the concept of clinical reasoning which the authors argue "can produce teachers who are better able to articulate their reasoning for pedagogical choices drawing on both school-based and research-based evidence so as to improve their own teaching and improve the teaching of others". The paper sets out the underlying principles of the approach and gives guidance as to the way in which mentors can support beginning teachers' developing reflection on their practice.

2. Mann, S., & Walsh, S. (2013). RP or 'RIP': A critical perspective on reflective practice. *Applied Linguistics Review*, 4(2), 291-315.

    This paper offers a critique of reflective practice in the context of language learning (albeit from an ESL perspective) and argues for (i) more dialogic approaches to reflective practice; (ii) approaches which are data-led; and (iii) the use of appropriate tools to ensure that reflective practice can support teacher professional learning more effectively. The paper draws on extracts from dialogues, which are rooted in actual practice, to illustrate these approaches.

## References

Beauchamp, C. (2015). Reflection in teacher education: Issues emerging from a review of current literature. *Reflective Practice*, 16(1), 123-141. https://doi.org/10.1080/14623943.2014.982525

Black-Hawkins, K., & Florian, L. (2012). Classroom teachers' craft knowledge of their inclusive practice. *Teachers and Teaching, 18*(5), 567–584.

Buehl, M. M., & Beck, J. S. (2014). The relationship between teachers' beliefs and teachers' practices. In H. Fives & M. G. Gill (Eds.), *International handbook of research on teachers' beliefs* (pp. 66–84). Routledge.

Burn, K., & Mutton, T. (2015). A review of 'research-informed clinical practice' in initial teacher education. *Oxford Review of Education, 41*(2), 217–233.

Department for Education (2016). *National Standards for school-based initial teacher training (ITT) mentors*. Accessed October 20, 2023, from https://assets.publishing.service.gov.uk/media/5a803fe4ed915d74e33f9541/Mentor_standards_report_Final.pdf.

Dewey, J. (1933). *How we think*. Heath & Co.

Dewey, J. (1938). *Experience and education*. Collier Books.

Doyle, W. (1977). Learning the classroom environment: An ecological analysis. *Journal of Teacher Education, 28*(6), 51–55.

Hagger, H. (1997). Enabling student teachers to gain access to the professional craft knowledge of experienced teachers. In D. McIntyre (Ed.), *Teacher education research in a new context: The Oxford internship scheme* (pp. 99–133). Paul Chapman.

Hagger, H., & McIntyre, D. (2006). *Learning teaching from teachers: Realising the potential of school-based teacher education*. Open University Press.

Kriewaldt, J., & Turnidge, D. (2013). Conceptualising an approach to clinical reasoning in the education profession. *Australian Journal of Teacher Education, 38*(9), 103–115. https://doi.org/10.14221/ajte.2013v38n6.9

Loughran, J. (2019). Pedagogical reasoning: The foundation of the professional knowledge of teaching. *Teachers and Teaching, 25*(5), 523–535. https://doi.org/10.1080/13540602.2019.1633294

Mann, S., & Walsh, S. (2013). RP or 'RIP': A critical perspective on reflective practice. *Applied Linguistics Review, 4*(2), 291–315.

McIntyre, D. (1993). Theory, theorizing and reflection in initial teacher education. In J. Calderhead & P. Gates (Eds.), *Conceptualising reflection in teacher development* (pp. 45–58). The Falmer Press.

McIntyre, D. (1995). Initial teacher education as practical theorising: A response to Paul Hirst. *British Journal of Educational Studies, 43*(4), 365–383.

McIntyre, D., & Hagger, H. (1994). Teachers' expertise and models of mentoring. In H. Hagger, D. McIntyre, & M. Wilkin (Eds.), *Mentoring: Perspectives on school-based teacher education* (pp. 86–102). Routledge.

Mitchell, R., Myles, F., & Marsden, E. (2019). *Second language learning theories*. Routledge.

Rowland, T., Huckstep, P., & Thwaites, A. (2005). Elementary teachers' mathematics subject knowledge: The knowledge quartet and the case of Naomi. *Journal of Mathematics Teacher Education, 8*, 255–281.

Schön, D. A. (1983). *The reflective practitioner*. Basic Books.

Schön, D. A. (1987). *The reflective practitioner: Toward a new design for teaching and learning in the professions*. Jossey-Bass.

# 10 Observing your mentee's teaching and giving written feedback

*Francesca Knight*

## Introduction

One of the most important and potentially transformational aspects of your role as a mentor of beginning teachers is to regularly observe their teaching practice and to provide feedback both orally and in writing. The impact that your observation and subsequent feedback will have on your beginning teacher is contingent on how you approach this key feature of your mentoring and indeed on the relationship you have established with your mentee. The importance of establishing a trusting and supportive relationship between mentor and mentee has been discussed in previous chapters and, whilst it is not the main subject of this particular chapter, it bears mentioning here due to the significance it holds in terms of observation and feedback.

This chapter will discuss the role of the mentor in developing beginning teachers' classroom practice through careful consideration of observation as a formative process, exploring practical tips on how to observe your beginning teacher as well as considering how to provide written feedback as both a record of their development and a tool for formative assessment.

At the end of this chapter, you should be able to:

- Reflect on the importance of observation for the development of your beginning teacher
- Consider how best to observe your beginning teacher from a non-judgemental and formative standpoint
- Compare and contrast three different models of observation and the potential impact each could have on your beginning teacher's development
- Have a greater understanding of the importance of written feedback and how this differs from oral feedback or post-lesson dialogue

Before reading further, please undertake Task 10.1.

---

**Task 10.1 Reflecting on your experiences of being observed**

Think of a time when you have been observed recently and consider the following questions.

- Was the purpose of the observation made clear to you?
- How did the observer's behaviour during the observation make you feel?

---

- How was the feedback given to you? Verbally? In writing? Both? Which did you most value and why?
- How might the way you have been observed in the past impact on how you observe or will observe your beginning teacher?

## Why observe?

From the moment we embark on a career in teaching, our teaching practice is subject to observation from colleagues. Indeed, whether we like it or not, our lessons will be watched, commented on and potentially judged. Hobson (2016) discusses the potential problematic nature of observation from a beginning teacher's perspective, describing it as inducing anxiety and potentially provoking feelings of being criticised. However, Hobson (2016) also draws on studies from researchers (notably Hobson, 2002, and Bullough, 2005) that indicate that, despite some aforementioned limitations, most beginning teachers do, in fact, value observation feedback from their mentors, in particular when that feedback indicates practical strategies to improve. Furthermore, observation is recognised by many mentors and beginning teachers as being of value in terms of professional development (Beek et al., 2019).

The perceived value of observing your beginning teacher notwithstanding, most initial teacher training (ITT) courses will require regular observation as part of an ongoing formative process to support the beginning teacher in making progress as a competent classroom teacher. As such, a mentor's role will be to ensure this experience is as positive and impactful as possible in continuing to develop the beginning teacher.

## How to observe your beginning teacher

This section begins by reflecting on Hobson's (2016, p. 88) advice that we consider beginning teachers as 'vulnerable learners' due to their position within the 'pecking order' of the school. With Hobson et al. (2009) describing beginning teachers self-identifying as 'voiceless' and 'powerless', Hascher et al. (2004) encourage mentors to truly examine their role as being one that provides both emotional and psychological support to beginning teachers with a view to raising their self-esteem. Whilst Hobson (2016) questions the need for continual observation, stating that some beginning teachers can perceive this as unnecessarily critical and not always a positive experience, mentors are not always in a position to choose the frequency of observation, nor whether they have the possibility to opt out entirely. Indeed, as previously discussed, observation is valued by many beginning teachers so the question is really how we ensure that the process is as effective as possible. Research highlights the critical role that the relationship between the observer and observee plays in terms of how positive the experience of observation is for the observee (see for example: Hobson, 2016; Tilstone, 1998; Wragg, 1999). Giving the observee some degree of agency is also suggested as a way to empower and involve your beginning teacher in the observation process (O'Leary, 2012). This would also enable the mentor/observer to move away from an asymmetrical approach to the observation, instead acting as more of a peer, promoting a developmental model to the process (Gosling, 2002) (Table 10.1).

Table 10.1 A simplified version of Gosling's (2002) models of observation

| Evaluation model (EM) | Developmental model (DM) | Peer review model (PRM) |
| --- | --- | --- |
| • Senior staff observe other staff<br>• Highly performance related<br>• Potential pass/fail outcome<br>• Asymmetry of observer/observed relationship<br>• Risks alienation and lack of co-operation<br>• Appears summative in nature | • Between educational developer and less senior teacher<br>• Demonstration of teaching competencies, with a view to improvement<br>• Assessed by report or action plan<br>• No shared ownership; power imbalance in relationship between observer and observed<br>• Somewhat more formative than EM | • Teachers observing each other<br>• Post observation discussion; self and mutual reflection encouraged<br>• More equality, mutuality, and less judgement<br>• Constructive feedback given<br>• Mutual learning; teaching is valued<br>• Potential risk for being unfocused, too conservative<br>• More formative than summative in nature |

According to Gosling's (2002) models, both the Evaluation and Developmental models assume a deficit in the observed, with the observer almost tasked to 'fix' this. However, the Peer review model implies more of a collaborative approach, with the observed genuinely seeking constructive ways to improve their practice. Adopting such a peer review approach with your beginning teacher would support recommendations from Hobson (2016) as well as being welcomed by most beginning teachers, particularly as it feels inherently more supportive and less judgemental. Based on evaluation feedback from university-based beginning teachers, mentors with whom trusting relationships had been established were described as 'gentle', 'sensitive', 'supportive', 'kind', and 'helpful'. It is, of course, worth mentioning that this will not be a universal range of qualities desired or expected in a mentor, and more on this is discussed in the subsequent paragraph. These responses from beginning teachers indicate that research into the impact of mentor/mentee relationships on beginning teacher development resonates in practice too. The more positive the relationship, the less judged a beginning teacher is likely to feel, therefore the more accepting of feedback from observation they are likely to be.

It is important to note, however, that this type of relationship may not always be appropriate or desirable between mentor and beginning teacher. For example, we cannot neglect to acknowledge that the mentor's ultimate role is significant in the beginning teacher's professional success, creating a natural asymmetry. Furthermore, not all beginning teachers are ready to be observed in such a collaborative way; being attuned to the individual needs of your beginning teacher is crucial, recognising that at times they may need a more directive approach with practical advice and strategies (Hobson, 2016). Indeed, Shute (2008) indicates that beginning teachers value guidance from mentors that is specific and demonstrative of how they can improve their teaching. As such it can be beneficial at the start of a beginning teacher's journey to act as a more instructive observer who provides clear ideas on how to move forward. This is both appreciated by many beginning teachers as well as appropriate for their stage of development.

In Task 10.1 you were asked to reflect on your own experiences of being observed and in doing so perhaps you recognised the significance of the role of the person observing you and the resultant feelings of power imbalance, or indeed collaboration, depending on the relationship you had with your observer. Gosling (2002) warns that differences in power can really bias the outcome of an observation and suggests instead that both parties can learn from the experience with the right approach. Indeed, trusting the observer is most likely to ensure that any comments or reflections made are valued and contribute to the learning process, regardless of the potential power imbalance from the beginning teacher/mentor dynamic (Gosling, 2002).

## Practical advice for observing your beginning teacher

### Agree a focus with your observee

As previously discussed, the nature of the mentor/beginning teacher relationship can generate feelings of a power imbalance. Involving your beginning teacher in the decision regarding what you will focus on during the observation will serve several purposes. First of all, your beginning teacher will have some agency within the observation, hopefully addressing potential feelings of powerlessness (Hobson, 2016). Additionally, this will reassure the beginning teacher that you are not there to observe every minor error they may commit, but rather to support them in developing one specific area of their practice. This will also allow both parties to be aware of emerging priorities for the development of the beginning teacher. Developing one aspect at a time would be more manageable for anyone, especially a beginning teacher. That is not to say that you will not comment on anything other than the focus, particularly if you have positive reflections to make. Indeed, encouragement and praise are usually appreciated by anyone being observed and have been found to be of particular importance to beginning teachers (Soares & Lock, 2007). Finally, this will support you as a mentor in deciding which aspects of the lesson are worthy of note and comment.

### Ensure your agreed focus allows the beginning teacher to develop as a subject specialist

Research by Lock et al. (2009) suggests that mentors often focus on general aspects of teaching such as classroom management when observing beginning teachers. Whilst it is natural that both mentor and beginning teacher are concerned with the behaviour of the class, especially when starting out, we must recognise that our role is also to support the development of a beginning teacher of languages and, as such, our observation focus should reflect this. I would also argue that providing beginning teachers with feedback on how to improve their pedagogical approach is more immediately actionable and within a beginning teacher's control than 'fixing' behaviour management issues which may require a more longitudinal approach. For example, were a mentor to advise a beginning teacher that a grammar explanation had been too complicated for the pupils to follow, suggesting the pupils needed more opportunities to practise the grammar point, the beginning teacher could adapt this in a subsequent lesson through redesigning an explanation and planning activities that facilitated pupil practice. You might also at this point encourage your beginning teacher to reflect on the potential positive impact that such an approach to a grammar explanation might have on the pupils' behaviour, particularly if this is also an area for development. Compare this with a classroom management situation in isolation, and the beginning teacher will need to invest time to build a relationship with their pupils, important and valuable too but not as quickly overcome.

### Keep your facial expressions and body language neutral and non-judgemental

As we have discussed, beginning teachers can find the performative nature of observation daunting and anxiety inducing (Bjørndal, 2020; Hobson, 2016). As such, part of our role as an observer is to reduce negative feelings towards the process, instead creating a supportive and positive environment in which the observation feels like a constructive part of the beginning teacher's development. A reassuring smile should you catch your beginning teacher's eye or even a thumbs up, if appropriate, is likely to reduce any feelings of negative evaluation.

Before reading any further, please undertake Task 10.2.

> **Task 10.2 What kind of observer will you be?**
>
> In light of the previous discussion, take a moment to consider how you will establish yourself as a supportive observer. Are there any steps you can take to reduce the power imbalance within the relationship? Could you seek feedback from a colleague whom you have previously observed?

## Written feedback from lesson observation

In the next section, we will focus on both the value and importance of providing written feedback as well as considering how we can ensure the written feedback we give is of value to our beginning languages teachers.

### Why give written feedback?

'… good feedback can significantly improve learning processes and outcomes, if delivered correctly' (Shute, 2008, p. 154). Policy and research abounds in the educational field about the value and importance of giving feedback to learners within our classrooms to improve their performance (Black & Wiliam, 1998; Hattie, 2008; Higgins et al., 2014). Equally, effective feedback from a mentor has been shown to be of significant gain to beginning teachers (Shute, 2008).

Whilst beginning teachers will receive the majority of their feedback verbally (Bunton et al., 2002; Hudson, 2005; Spear et al., 1997), beginning teachers greatly value receiving written feedback (Monk & Dillon, 1995). First of all, written feedback can be referred back to whilst verbal feedback can be forgotten or mis-remembered (Bunton et al., 2002). Puttick and Wynn (2021, p. 153) also highlight that 'heightened emotions' during post lesson dialogue can contribute to a beginning teacher's inability to accurately recollect all verbal feedback. Additionally, beginning teachers may be keen to 'save face' when receiving verbal feedback perceived as critical whereas written feedback can be digested in their own time and space, thus potentially reducing this feeling (Bjørndal, 2020). Given that in our context of languages many beginning teachers may not have English as their first language, the written record of their observation may be of even more value as a tool to refer back to and digest in one's own time (Bunton et al., 2002).

Beginning teachers can also infer that what has been recorded in writing will be the most salient of points observed, comments which can be returned to and reflected on as necessary (Puttick & Wynn, 2021). Written feedback may also be quicker to disseminate than a dialogue, welcomed in a busy teacher's and indeed beginning teacher's daily life (Soares & Lock, 2007). However, despite some clear benefits to written feedback as a record to be revisited, we should also recognise that verbal feedback can be of great value to clarify what has been written and, as such, written feedback should not replace post-lesson dialogue (Bunton et al., 2002).

Notwithstanding the outlined benefits of written feedback, there can, of course, be limitations. For example, handwritten comments may not always be legible and the clarity of communication could be compromised, potentially with no opportunity for oral clarification (Bunton et al., 2002). Furthermore, some beginning teachers have expressed frustration at receiving mere descriptions without explanation or comment, thus compromising the value of the written feedback (Soares & Lock, 2007). Some logical strategies to overcome these potential limitations could be to type rather than hand write feedback and to invite your beginning teacher to seek clarification on any statements they perceive to be ambiguous. There is also the potential, as with verbal feedback, for an emotional response to written feedback perceived as negative (Dowden et al., 2013). Attempting to give feedback which is non-evaluative and more supportive in nature will hopefully address such a response (Shute, 2008). Stating positive outcomes of a beginning teacher's approaches in the lesson will highlight to them specifically what was successful. For example; 'Using no-hands up really encouraged some of the quieter students to participate'; 'Your use of mini white boards to allow students to practise the grammar point enabled you to engage all learners and to assess their understanding'.

## How to give written feedback to your beginning teacher

Taking into consideration our previous discussion around favouring a non-judgemental observation approach, it may also be important that this is reflected in your written feedback.

As we discussed in previous sections, there may be times that, contrary to the idea that facilitating reflection and encouraging a learner to come to their own conclusions is desirable, adopting a directive approach is more effective (Hobson, 2016). Indeed, Shute (2008, p. 163) tells us that 'some research has shown that directive feedback may actually be more helpful than facilitative'. This is particularly likely to be the case at the start of a beginning teacher's practice, although it may be appropriate to gradually move to a more facilitative approach as the beginning teacher's competence increases (Hobson, 2016; Shute, 2008). With this in mind, a mentor should not fear giving explicit examples and direct advice on how their beginning teacher could improve their teaching when giving written feedback. In fact, this may be one of the most effective aspects of giving written feedback, and more details are provided below.

Although there is not necessarily one ideal way to give feedback as this will depend on the needs of the recipient (Beek et al., 2019), some commonalities present themselves on consultation with research and indeed in the views of beginning teachers therein.

Key desirable features of written feedback:

- The feedback should be supportive and non-evaluative (Dowden et al., 2013; Shute, 2008).
- Feedback should be positive in nature, praising successes of the observee (Bunton et al., 2002; Dowden et al., 2013). Feedback that is more negative than positive in nature is unlikely to enhance the learning of the recipient (Voerman et al., 2012).
- Written feedback should be personalised and specific. Vague comments, even ones largely positive in nature, do not contribute to the learning of the recipient (Bunton et al., 2002; Shute, 2008). Specific feedback can be defined as a comment that the beginning teacher is able to directly link to an episode in their teaching whereas non-specific feedback might be a comment such as 'great!', not clearly related to something that occurred in the teaching (Beek et al., 2019). Indeed, non-specific feedback may be viewed by the beginning teacher as frustrating or without merit (Williams, 1997, cited in Shute, 2008).
- The observer should offer guidance and suggestions to overcome particular observed difficulties (Bunton et al., 2002; Shute, 2008; Soares & Lock, 2007). This has been highlighted as desirable by beginning teachers themselves who perhaps do not always feel in a position to reflect independently on how to improve, therefore valuing the guidance of an expert colleague.
- Feedback should be delivered in manageable chunks (Shute, 2008). In considering the cognitive load of our beginning teachers, it is important to recognise that they will not be able to assimilate high volumes of feedback and presenting it in such a way could compromise the efficacy, thus rendering the message useless (Shute, 2008).
- The beginning teacher should receive the written feedback in a timely manner (Shute, 2008). In order for the beginning teacher to be able to act on their feedback, it is important that they receive their written feedback as soon as possible after the observation. This will also ensure the beginning teacher has more opportunities to connect the written feedback to their teaching as it will be more prominent in their memory. At the very least, it would be of most benefit for the beginning teacher to receive the feedback prior to teaching the same class again so that they may digest the feedback and attempt to implement advice. It is also likely that your beginning teacher will be observed by other colleagues. To avoid overwhelming them with potentially diverse and possibly conflicting feedback, share with colleagues which areas of development the beginning teacher is prioritising so that colleagues can focus their feedback accordingly.
- Written feedback should be subject specific (Puttick & Wynn, 2021; Soares & Lock, 2007). Ideally, if an impartial colleague were to read the written feedback of your beginning teacher, it should be clear through your comments that the lesson observed had been a languages lesson. This will help your beginning teacher to develop as a teacher of their subject as well as a classroom practitioner.

Before reading any further, please complete Task 10.3.

---

**Task 10.3 Analysing an example of mentor written feedback**

Look at the example of written feedback below. To what extent does it reflect the advice and guidance in the previous section? Is it clear that this feedback is from a languages lesson? What is the balance between positive and negative comments? Are there clear suggestions and guidance for how the beginning teacher can progress in their teaching? How specific is the feedback?

---

The example in Table 10.2 is the summary sheet from a template used in a university-based ITE programme, and additional written comments will have been provided to the beginning teacher. The template itself encourages the observer to balance the feedback in that it demands them to provide three areas of strength and an equal three (or two as the third is optional) areas for

*Table 10.2* Example of written feedback

| PROGRESS / STRENGTHS – Please identify emerging areas of progress observed with specific detail. Also, please ensure that each observation highlights a subject specific strength and an area for development. | |
|---|---|
| **Strength 1: Subject knowledge/subject pedagogy:** You take opportunities to bring culture into the lesson, educating the pupils on reguetón music and discussing the origins of Flamenco. You also bring in your own experiences as a language learner to motivate pupils to attempt the pronunciation of the Spanish 'r'. | |
| Strength 2: Praise is used effectively to motivate pupils, you show them with your body language, your tone of voice and your awarding of points that you value their efforts and contributions. This helps to create a positive environment for learning and a culture of mutual respect. | |
| Strength 3: The lesson is planned to engage the pupils with a range of activities that allow revisiting of prior learning as well as building on this through encountering new conjugations of the verb 'gustar' as well introducing new vocabulary. | |

| Areas for development – Please be specific and clear with examples if appropriate | Ideas of how to address these areas of development |
|---|---|
| **Area 1: Subject knowledge/subject pedagogy:** Some of your more able linguists need stretching more. Consider how you can empower the high prior attainers to develop their understanding of the language. | Look at activities and think of your high prior attaining linguists – what more can they do? E.g. with the mini white boards they could have added their opinion or added 'pienso que es...' |
| Area 2: Increase wait time when questioning; you have a quick pace but make sure pupils have time to think. | Ask the question, pause and count in your head 'one, two, three, four, I must wait a little more'. |
| Area 3: (OPTIONAL) Please write in this box if there is a third area you wish to set this week. Make your expectations clear so that all pupils understand what you require from them in terms of behaviour. | Don't be afraid to stop them, remind them of basic rules and expectations. Try to avoid too much 'please' Try to get out of the habit of saying 'ok' so much Work on transitions between the activities to avoid dead time. This can give pupils the opportunity to go off task and exhibit undesirable behaviours. |

development. This supports the research discussed above that mentors should prioritise positive over negative feedback. Additionally, the way the template is laid out demands that the observer provide practical guidance and advice to address the suggested areas for development, also one of the recommendations above. As such, a template such as this could be used when observing, helping to structure your written feedback, also suggested by Puttick and Wynn (2021). This will help to guide and remind you of some of the recommendations above to ensure that your written feedback is as effective as possible in helping your beginning languages teacher to develop.

## Conclusion

Observation and providing written feedback are key aspects of your role as a mentor of a beginning teacher of languages. You have the opportunity through both of these important elements of mentoring to make a significant difference to the progress of your beginning teacher. These are also likely to be aspects of your role that are highly enjoyable as you witness first-hand the progress your beginning teacher is making based on your feedback. In this chapter we have discussed the following:

- The importance of establishing a trusting and supportive mentor/mentee relationship
- Aiming to be non-judgemental and non-evaluative as an observer and in giving feedback
- Giving your beginning teacher agency in the decision around the focus for the observation
- Some key ideas and strategies to ensure your beginning teacher gets the most out of your written feedback including being specific and offering guidance and practical strategies
- The need for balance between praise and positivity and giving constructive ways to improve
- Giving subject specific feedback to ensure you are developing your beginning teacher as a teacher of languages

## For discussion

1. What steps can you take from the moment you meet your beginning teacher to start to establish a trusting relationship when you observe and provide feedback?
2. What qualities would you value most in an observer? How would you like to be made to feel empowered in the process? What steps can you take to ensure that your beginning teacher experiences the observations you undertake positively?
3. How can you make sure your feedback is concise so as not to be overwhelming, but also specific enough so that your beginning teacher knows what action to take? Look at examples of colleagues' written feedback (either within your school or from university tutors) to help you assess what good written feedback looks like.

## Further reading

Hobson, A. (2016). Judgementoring and how to avert it: Introducing ONSIDE Mentoring for beginning teachers. *International Journal of Mentoring and Coaching in Education*, 5(2), 87–110. https://doi.org/10.1108/IJMCE-03-2016-0024

This article should help you to develop the importance of a trusting and collaborative relationship between you and your beginning teacher, examining the importance of non-judgemental observation.

Gosling, D. (2002). Models of peer observation of teaching. ResearchGate. Accessed December 30, 2023, from https://www.researchgate.net/publication/267687499_Models_of_Peer_Observation_of_Teaching

Here you can visit the observation models discussed in the chapter in more detail to help guide you towards which model is most appropriate for you to adopt in observing your beginning teacher.

## References

Beek, G. J., Zuiker, I., & Zwart, R. C. (2019). Exploring mentors' roles and feedback strategies to analyze the quality of mentoring dialogues. *Teaching and Teacher Education, 78,* 15-27.

Bjørndal, C. R. P. (2020). 'Student teachers' responses to critical mentor feedback: A study of face-saving strategies in teaching placements. *Teaching and Teacher Education, 91.* Available at: https://doi.org/10.1016/j.tate.2020.103047

Black, P., & Wiliam, D. (1998). *Inside the black box: Raising standards through classroom assessment.* Kings College.

Bullough, R. V. Jr (2005). Being and becoming a mentor: School-based teacher educators and teacher educator identity. *Teaching and Teacher Education, 21*(2), 143-155.

Bunton, D., Stimpson, P., & Lopez-Real, F. (2002). University Tutors' practicum observation notes: Format and content. *Mentoring & Tutoring, 10*(3), 233-252. https://doi.org/10.1080/1361126022000037060

Dowden, T., Pittaway, S., Yost, H., & McCarthy, R. (2013). Students' perceptions of written feedback in teacher education: Ideally feedback is a continuing two-way communication that encourages progress. *Assessment & Evaluation in Higher Education, 38*(3), 349-362. https://doi.org/10.1080/02602938.2011.632676

Gosling, D. (2002) 'Models of peer observation of teaching'. ResearchGate. Accessed December 30, 2023, from https://www.researchgate.net/publication/267687499_Models_of_Peer_Observation_of_Teaching.

Hascher, T., Cocard, Y., & Moser, P. (2004). Forget about theory – Practice is all? Student teachers' learning in practicum. *Teachers and Teaching: Theory and Practice, 10*(6), 623-637.

Hattie, J. (2008). *Visible learning: A synthesis of over 800 meta-analyses relating to achievement.* Routledge.

Higgins, S., Katsipataki, M., Kokotsaki, D., Coleman, R., Major, L. E., & Coe, R. (2014). *The Sutton Trust-Education Endowment Foundation teaching and learning toolkit.* Education Endowment Foundation.

Hobson, A. (2016). Judgementoring and how to avert it: Introducing ONSIDE mentoring for beginning teachers. *International Journal of Mentoring and Coaching in Education, 5*(2), 87-110. https://doi.org/10.1108/IJMCE-03-2016-0024

Hobson, A. J. (2002). Student teachers' perceptions of school-based mentoring in initial teacher training (ITT). *Mentoring and Tutoring, 10*(1), 5-20.

Hobson, A. J., Ashby, P., Malderez, A., & Tomlinson, P. D. (2009). Mentoring beginning teachers: What we know and what we don't. *Teaching and Teacher Education, 25,* 207-216. http://dx.doi.org/10.1016/j.tate.2008.09.001

Hudson, P. (2005). Identifying mentoring practices for developing effective primary science teaching. *International Journal of Science Education, 27*(14), 1723-1739.

Lock, R., Soares, A., & Foster, J. (2009). Mentors' written lesson appraisals: The impact of different mentoring regimes on The content of written lesson appraisals and

The match with pre-service teachers' perceptions of content. *Journal of Education for Teaching: International Research and Pedagogy*, 35(2), 133-143. https://doi.org/10.1080/02607470902770963

Monk, M., & Dillon, J. (Eds.). (1995). Observing science teachers at work. In M. Monk, & J. Dillon (Eds.), *Learning to teach science: Activities for student teachers and mentors* (pp. 14-29). Falmer Press, Taylor and Francis.

O'Leary, M. (2012). Exploring the role of lesson observation in the English education system: A review of methods, models and meanings. *Professional Development in Education*, 38(5), 791-810. https://doi.org/10.1080/19415257.2012.693119

Puttick, S., & Wynn, J. (2021). Constructing 'good teaching' through written lesson observation feedback. *Oxford Review of Education*, 47(2), 152-169. https://doi.org/10.1080/03054985.2020.1846289

Shute, V. (2008). Focus on formative feedback. *Review of Educational Research*, 78(1), 153-189. https://doi.org/10.3102/0034654307313795

Soares, A., & Lock, R. (2007). Pre-service science teachers' perceptions of written lesson appraisals: The impact of styles of mentoring. *European Journal of Teacher Education*, 30(1), 75-90. https://doi.org/10.1080/02619760601120056

Spear, M., Lock, N., & McCulloch, M. (1997). The written feedback mentors give to student teachers. *Teacher Development*, 1(2), 269-80.

Tilstone, C. (1998). *Observing teaching and learning - Principles and practice*. David Fulton.

Voerman, L., Meijer, P. C., Korthagen, F. J., & Simons, R. J. (2012). Types and frequencies of feedback interventions in classroom interaction in secondary education. *Teaching and Teacher Education*, 28(8), 1107e1115. https://doi.org/10.1016/j.tate.2012.06.006.

Wragg, E. C. (1999). *An introduction to classroom observation* (2nd ed.). Routledge.

# 11 Holding pre- and post-lesson discussions with beginning languages teachers

*Laura Dixon, Lynda Hamilton, and Lisa Madden*

## Introduction

A large part of your role as a mentor will involve giving advice to beginning teachers on how a lesson plan might benefit from adjustment, or supporting beginning teachers to evaluate the success of a lesson that you have observed. This is a vital part of the training process, and we often underestimate the power of our feedback. Just as important as this kind of evaluation is the way that discussion, joint thinking and decision making about how a lesson might be structured can help a beginning teacher develop understanding of their practice (Sherrington & Caviglioli, 2020; Sweller et al., 2011).

In 2015, the Carter Review of initial teacher training (ITT) recommended access to support for beginning teachers with a longer induction period, going so far as to describe ITT programmes as: 'limiting if they are not built upon in ways that take teachers' professional understanding and skills further forward in a structured way' (Carter, 2015, p. 22). Following this review, the Early Career Framework (Department for Education [DfE], 2019a) extended the induction of teachers following the award of QTS from one to two years. The Core Content Framework (CCF) (DfE, 2019b) was introduced to provide consistency across routes into teaching and link beginning teachers' ITT programmes with their induction. A weekly mentor meeting was one of the key changes to the process and this makes mentoring central to the professional development of beginning teachers. The mentor's role is vital to act as an expert colleague who works consistently to help beginning teachers at all stages of their training and induction to develop key skills as they teach (Forster et al., 2021). The National Mentoring Standards (DfE, 2016b) were devised to guide mentors in understanding effective practice as ITT provision requires increased mentoring time in school (Task 11.1)..

---

**Task 11.1 Reflect on your understanding of a mentor's role over time**

- What do you think a mentor's priorities should be when they start working with a beginning teacher during their training year?
- What do you think a mentor's priorities should be when a teacher approaches the end of the induction period?
- Are you familiar with where you can access support from your subject association, The Association for Language Learning (ALL), on effective mentoring?

---

This chapter provides some practical guidance on how to approach holding pre- and post-lesson discussions which encourage the beginning teacher to take responsibility for their own development. We will suggest questions to engage beginning teachers in the reflective process which will continue to feature throughout their career (Brandom et al., 2023) and use some scenario activities to help you consider how this form of dialogic mentoring can influence beginning teachers in improving their teaching. We would also like to emphasise that personalised mentoring should evolve over time towards a coaching approach which prioritises space for self-evaluation, enabling beginning teachers to gain confidence and experience in both their practice (Gordon, 2020) and dealing with change (Day & Gu, 2014).

At the end of this chapter, you should be able to:

- have a greater understanding of the role and purpose of pre- and post-lesson observations
- gain an appreciation of effective questions which encourage beginning teachers to engage in the reflective process and how these might change over time
- increase your awareness of the importance of mentoring in encouraging good practice
- compare and contrast three common scenarios and how these could be used to support your role as a mentor

## The purpose of pre- and post-lesson discussions

Discussions with colleagues prior to and following beginning teachers' lessons offer many opportunities for developing knowledge and understanding about teaching. Being mindful of how much beginning teachers are investing in developing their planning in the early stages of their training and how difficult it might be not to take feedback personally, we recognise the value of mentors modelling key techniques (Hobson & Malderez, 2013). As teachers gain experience, we increasingly do not need to provide the answers and often it can be good practice to co-develop the answers to a pedagogical problem, as an example of the way that teachers make decisions about their practice. For example, the mentor could pose questions such as 'what would happen if ...?/how could we have improved x/y?' instead of issuing instructions such as 'avoid doing x/y ... /change the way you...'.

There are some things that beginning teachers need to know, and in the early stages of a teacher's development your mentoring may be focused on the specific skills that beginning teachers are learning in their ITT curriculum, and the context of using these in the classes with which they are working. However, the focus of your pre- and post-lesson discussions will change during the ITT programme/ECT induction period. Over time it is important for mentors to move away from a judgemental form of mentoring to a non-directive approach. Manning and Hobson (2017, p. 576) agree with Clutterbuck's position (2004) that: 'a non-directive approach to mentoring will tend to be more developmental and empowering'.

Beginning teachers should be guided to reflect on their practice and identify their areas for growth. Mentors can use a combination of questioning and active listening, which prompt this reflection (Kullman, 1998, cited in Delaney, 2012). Mentors can build trust and set ground rules for the mentoring relationship with the beginning teacher, providing emotional support to boost confidence (Malderez & Wedell, 2007) and avoid setting too many targets which can be overwhelming (Burn et al., 2015).

Effective mentoring involves different approaches to pre- and post-lesson discussions over time with a definite shift from directive mentoring of very beginning teachers towards a more dialogical coaching approach as they gain more experience in the language classroom (Task 11.2).

---

**Task 11.2 Reflect on your understanding of the role of pre- and post-lesson observations.**

Think of a time when you were mentored effectively in the past.

- What kinds of behaviours did your mentor exhibit?
- What kind of language was used to promote your learning?

---

## Effective questions to engage beginning teachers in the reflective process

The following questions and strategies for holding pre- and post-lessons discussions have been adapted from the works of Buck (2020), Sherrington and Caviglioli (2020), Scott (2017), Ager and Wyatt (2018), and Black et al. (2017).

### Pre-lesson discussions

'If you start all your conversations by asking great questions, you are giving colleagues the chance to work out their own solutions' (Buck, 2020, p. 131). During the pre-lesson discussion, it is essential that the mentor maximises the use of the time available to guide the beginning teacher to decipher the best plan of action for themselves, with increasingly less intervention from the mentor as time progresses. Buck (2020, p. 75) refers to this meeting as a 'pre-mortem' where beginning teachers benefit from deciding on appropriate actions and priorities. Below is a list of possible questions which could feature in pre-lesson discussions, prompting the beginning teacher to reflect on the content and structure of their language lessons. These questions also require the beginning teacher to anticipate barriers and devise strategies for overcoming them (Table 11.1 and Task 11.3).

*Table 11.1* Scenarios of teachers at different stages of development and some examples of how pre-lesson discussions might encourage engagement in reflective practice

| Beginning of beginning teacher's training programme | During transition to a new placement school | Beginning teacher is becoming more independent in the classroom |
|---|---|---|
| How will you sequence/scaffold these activities to ensure your lesson objectives are met? How and when will you use target language to support and challenge learners? | What prior knowledge do pupils need to access? Which sound spelling links will pupils need to be reminded of? | How will you know your grammar explanation has been successful? Last time we identified an area for growth of reducing the amount of vocabulary in your resources to avoid overloading working memory. How will you decide what vocabulary to include? |
| How do you anticipate pupils will develop skills in the lesson? | How will you know the pupils are learning the vocabulary in the lesson? | What will this learning look like? |
| Where does this fit into the scheme of work? What will challenge pupils in this lesson? | Which misconceptions do you anticipate the pupils having with this language point? | How could you avoid these misconceptions? |
| How will you engage pupils with the topic of (work and future plans)? | What could prevent you from meeting your lesson objectives? | How will you help the pupils to commit this vocabulary to their long-term memory? |
| Which activities will pupils finish at the same time? Which activities involve pupils working independently/in groups/in pairs/as a class? | When do we need everyone's attention? What if some pupils finish the reading task more quickly than the others? | Which activities will stir/settle learners and why is this important? |
| How can you develop intercultural awareness in this lesson? | How can you link the target culture(s) with today's objectives? | How can pupils develop their understanding outside the lesson? |

### Task 11.3 Reflect on pre-lesson discussions

Reflect on a pre-lesson discussion you have had with a beginning teacher and consider the following points.

- How many questions did you ask?
- Who was talking more, the mentor or the beginning teacher?

Look at a lesson plan and resources a beginning teacher has sent you.

- What questions could you use or adapt from the prompt list above for the beginning teacher to improve their plan and delivery of the lesson?

## Post-lesson discussions

Knowing the beginning teacher's specific goals and targets at any one time is going to help structure post-lesson discussions, perhaps also changing the kind of feedback that beginning teachers need over time. In the early stages of mentoring, you might provide lots of reassurance as well as questions about what your beginning teacher hoped to achieve and the extent to which that was done. Later on, the focus may shift towards questions about the pupils' understanding, their pre- and misconceptions, the extent to which they learned what was planned, moving (over time) to your beginning teacher taking responsibility for evaluating the lesson independently.

During the post-lesson discussion, it is vital that the mentor provides positive feedback on the beginning teacher's actions or behaviours and guides the beginning teacher to reflect on what went well during the lesson. This discussion is both an opportunity for reflection and for professional growth. Beginning teachers can often be overly self-critical and take negative feedback very personally. Beckett (2010) warns of the potential impact of inconsistent or ill-planned feedback. Throw-away comments can be damaging to beginning teachers' confidence and can stay with them for a lifetime. Do not underestimate the power of your feedback!

When delivering constructive advice, it is helpful to depersonalise feedback to reduce the risk of harming a beginning teacher's confidence. Ager and Wyatt (2018) highlight the benefits of mentors creating a safe, non-judgemental environment for self-evaluation in their work with beginning teachers. Beginning teachers need to feel they can be honest about their experience and have freedom to set their own next steps and targets in-line with the framework within which they are working (e.g. in England at the time of writing, the framework for the first three years of teaching can be found at DfE, 2024).

Effective mentors are able to use techniques for 'interpreting classroom events' (Delaney, 2012, p. 190) such as Sherrington and Caviglioli's Three-Point Communication (2020) where a mentor and mentee sit side by side as a step towards de-personalising feedback. Looking at the descriptors against which beginning teachers are evaluated (DfE, 2011, 2024) and prompting them to track their progress against each descriptor can make it easier to: 'keep the accent on the teaching and not the teacher' (Sherrington & Caviglioli, 2020, p. 157).

As the beginning teacher's journey develops from unconscious incompetence to unconscious competence (Taylor, 2007), our purpose as their guide develops too, from directive mentoring to dialogic coaching. Our pre- and post- observation meetings must evolve with this in mind. Three distinct phases of development could be experienced within the mentee-mentor relationship. The first, a beginning teacher who believes they are being more effective than they are (unconsciously incompetent,) secondly, a beginning teacher who knows they cannot get an aspect of practice quite right and is seeking support (consciously incompetent), and lastly a trainee who is consciously competent for their career stage, who needs to be introduced to the next stage of practice and to reflect on how to automatise their practice so that they become 'unconsciously competent'. Figure 11.1 illustrates potential questions you may ask at different stages in key areas of language lessons.

## Behaviour

### Core Pre and Post Questions

- How do you plan to use the rewards policy?
- How could you gain their attention after activity number…?
- How do you need to plan for x's engagement?
- Which behaviours and engagement do you ideally want to see when students are doing the activity?
- What could the barrier to their attention be with activity …
- What would happen if you used rewards with that activity?
- What would happen if you changed where …x… sat?
- What would happen if you used quiet prompts with …x… then?
- Which 3 things went well and what would you change next time?

### Activities

| Settlers | Stirrers |
|---|---|
| translation | running dictation |
| dictation | picture back to back description |
| faulty transcript | fan and pick |

## Speaking Skills

### Core Pre and Post Questions

- How have you planned for accuracy in phonics?
- How are you planning to monitor quantity of speech?
- How will you model good speaking?
- How have you planned to scaffold students' confidence?
- How (much) are you going to correct student speaking?
- How do you need to plan for x's engagement?
- What would happen if you had focused on phonics?
- What would happen if you had taken away the scaffolds?
- How would you improve student fluency next time?
- Where were students most and least confident?
- What would good speaking scaffolding look like next lesson?

### Activities

| Phonics | Scaffolding | Fluency |
|---|---|---|
| chinese whispers | I do we do you do | trap door |
| Multiple choice quiz | gap fill | finger point of view |
| Dodgy spelling | dodgy transcript | bullseye |

## Progress

### Core Pre and Post Questions

- How have you planned for recap and retrieval of core knowledge?
- How will you engage and scaffold for reluctant learners?
- How have SEND needs been catered for in 'x' activity?
- What are the misconceptions that might come up in the lesson?
- How successful were the students in avoiding 'x' misconception?
- What's the plan to move from receptive to productive skills?
- How did disadvantaged and SEND learners progress at the same rate as their peers in 'x' activity?
- Where did students engage the most? Why?
- How effective was your questioning for checking disadvantaged learners?
- How are you going to support students to bridge open book activities to performance close book?
- What are the next steps in making all students reach their target in their next assessment?

### Activities

| Phonics | Scaffolding |
|---|---|
| Metacognition reading and listening skills wrappers | deconstruct - reconstruct WAGOLLs |
| Multiple Choice quizzing | DIRT redrafting |
| Success Criteria | Questioning: hands down |

Mentoring ← → Coaching

*Figure 11.1* Subject-specific examples of questions that can be used in pre- and post-lesson discussions. (Based on advice from Warren (2019), Hunton (2015), and Smith and Conti (2023).)

## Scenarios

Beginning languages teachers often need to develop skills around developing a specific language skill such as speaking. Here are some subject-specific examples of how the questions you use in pre- and post- lesson discussions can support the reflective process. We have also included some examples of the types of activities you might encourage them to include to work on this area, based on advice from Warren (2019), Hunton (2015), and Smith and Conti (2023). You may find it useful to reflect on where your current beginning teacher is and their areas of focus to improve their practice, devising three key questions to support them in evaluating their lessons in the coming week.

Regarding the structuring of your post-lesson conversations, below is a suggested structure based on Buck (2020), with potential questions or sentence starters for different stages of the beginning teacher's development.

### Provide praise in relation to the beginning teacher's actions and behaviours within the language lesson.

*Examples:*
- I noticed you picked up on a number of pronunciation errors and you confidently diverted from your lesson plan to address these.
- I noticed you were using 'cold calling' questioning to check understanding of the grammar point.
- There was a real buzz in the room during the speaking task! Pupils were all participating and having a go.

Scott (2017) advocates these three key elements that mentors can use to describe their observations of beginning teachers' practice and stimulate reflection:

**Situation:** *After the grammar explanation, most pupils were still using incorrect word order.*
**Behaviour:** *You stopped the lesson and wrote more examples on the board, involving pupils using questioning.*
**Impact:** *This meant that the pupils had a better understanding and could apply the correct word order in their translations.*

### Ask the beginning teacher to reflect on the positives (Task 11.4).

*Examples:*
- What else did you feel went well during the lesson?
- What else went well for you that I have missed?
- What do you think the pupils thought went well in the lesson?

---

**Task 11.4 Reflect on stage 2 of Buck's (2020) suggested feedback structure**

Can you identify at which stage of the training/induction programme the above questions would be most appropriate?
Can you add more examples in discussion with colleagues in your department?

---

### Highlight areas for development and growth

*Examples:*
- How well did pupils grasp the content of the listening task?
- What did you notice about the length of pupils' written answers?
- Some pupils were talking during the listening task, making it hard for others to concentrate. How could you avoid this in future?
- I'm curious about what made you decide to remove the speaking task?
- How would you rate the instructions you gave during the lesson out of ten and why? How could you improve that rating for next time?
- When will you take the language scaffolding away?
- I noticed that some pupils were not challenged and finished the writing task quickly. How could you adapt activities to challenge them?
- What are the challenges regarding subject knowledge on this topic? What steps could you take to improve that?
- What was it about that pupil's answer that made you respond in that way?
- I noticed a number of missing accents in your board work. How could you ensure the correct spelling in future?
- Let's look at the different descriptors for subject knowledge in the course handbook. How would you rate yourself against each descriptor and what evidence do you have to support your rating?

Sometimes the beginning teacher may be struggling to grasp the areas for development. In this case, they need to be told directly if there is an issue. This feedback needs to be as impersonal as possible (Scott, 2017) and focus on a particular behaviour or action.

### Setting next steps

*Examples:*
- What would you do differently next time?
- When will you revisit this vocabulary?
- If you were teaching this lesson on the past tense again, what would you change?
- What scaffolding would you provide in future?
- I can you see you've already put a lot of effort into adapting teaching and resources for lower-ability pupils, how could you refine that further?
- You've decided on a target of researching ways to build fluency. What do you need to help you do this?
- What's the first thing you need to do to work towards meeting your target of anticipating common misconceptions?
- Can I offer you some suggestions with how to model longer written pieces?
- How confident do you feel with modelling translation tasks if you were to rate it out of ten? (If it's a high score, encourage the beginning teacher to push themselves out of their comfort zone to try something more challenging to them.)
- I've used some strategies from this teaching guide in the past. Have a look and see which ones may be useful.

- I have a colleague who is an expert at setting up speaking tasks. When are you free to observe them?
- Can I demonstrate another way of modelling the writing answer?

> **Task 11.5 Reflect on good practice and what to avoid in post-lesson discussions**
>
> Think about a professional growth meeting that didn't go well. How did you feel? How might this meeting have been more productive and positive?
>
> After reflecting on this from your own experience, take a look at Table 11.2. Did you identify similar things to avoid or were your own suggestions different?

Before reviewing Table 11.2, consider Task 11.5 as you consider how to offer feedback effectively. Table 11.2 summarises the authors' suggestions for mentors' input in the form of comments and questions in post-lesson discussions to encourage beginning teachers to reflect on their progress. We also note some phrasings that we suggest are best avoided.

*Table 11.2* The authors' suggestions for how mentors could phrase their questions and comments, and what might be best avoided

| Do | Don't |
|---|---|
| Initiate the post-lesson discussion by stating some positives. 'The sequence of activities enabled the pupils to build on their prior knowledge of the free time topic'. | Ask how the beginning teacher thinks the lesson went before providing a positive comment. |
| Encourage the beginning teacher to reflect on what went well during the lesson: 'What did you feel went well during the lesson?' | Avoid using the 'feedback sandwich' model (positive-negative-positive), as this method does not encourage the beginning teacher to identify their own areas for growth. (Ager & Wyatt, 2018, p. 108) |
| Use open questions and ask one question at a time to open up a discussion: (Buck, 2020) 'What activity from your lesson enabled students to best learn the vocabulary?' | Avoid using closed questions unless really trying to focus the beginning teacher's attention on a specific issue (Buck, 2020). |
| Use 'What...?' (Buck, 2020): 'What made you cut the listening task short and move onto the game?' | Use 'why...' as this appears judgemental (Buck, 2020): 'Why did you think it was a good idea to cut the listening task short?' |
| Use 'three-point communication' through use of a framework such as the Teachers' Standards, the ECT framework, a school policy or curriculum vision. This depersonalises potentially negative feedback. (Sherrington & Caviglioli, 2020, p. 157) 'Our curriculum vision states that students should spend at least fifty percent of lesson time doing speaking tasks. How much time is spent on speaking in your lessons?' | Don't give purely subjective opinion-based feedback: 'I personally like these speaking activities, so I want you to use them next time instead of the ones you used today'. |

*(Continued)*

*Table 11.2* (Continued)

| Do | Don't |
|---|---|
| Use data-led feedback through presenting data to the beginning teacher collected during the observation. This also depersonalises feedback. 'I noted a number of students answering in the wrong tense who were not corrected'. | Use critical, judgemental language: 'How on earth didn't you notice that they were answering in the wrong tense?' |
| Guide the beginning teacher to reflect on their own strengths and areas for growth. They are more likely to be committed to their next steps if they have identified them. (Black et al., 2017) 'How clear did you feel the grammar explanation was?' | Tell the beginning teacher what to do. 'Your grammar explanation was really unclear and next time you need to write out what you are going to say'. |
| Use the Situation, Behaviour, Impact model for delivering praise and highlighting areas for growth (Scott, 2017). | Give a subjective judgement such as 'it was good'. |
| Be direct if there is an issue that the beginning teacher is not picking up on but depersonalise this as much as possible from the beginning teacher. | Avoid raising something you see as a current issue or a potential issue, as it may become harder to rectify in the future. |
| Signpost other information, advice and guidance, as appropriate. 'We have copy of a book on how to structure MFL lessons in our staff library, I will give you the name and you can borrow it to help with lesson sequencing'. | Think you should know all the answers as there is a wealth of resources that can be signposted to beginning teachers. |

## Conclusion

In this chapter we have outlined the importance of dialogic feedback and effective questioning in mentor conversations; leading beginning teachers towards reflective practice where they are able to reflect and build their own repertoire with expert guidance rather than imitating practice seen elsewhere. We have emphasised the criticality of a mentor's role in developing this professional practice in teaching professionals through the tool of pre- and post-lesson discussions. This guidance enables the agency and autonomy which is so important in developing as a professional. The pre- and post-lesson discussions mentors have with beginning teachers will change over time with directive mentoring shifting towards dialogic coaching as teachers gain more confidence and experience. Effective mentoring facilitates the development of autonomy in beginning teachers and, whilst the processes involved are time consuming, their impact and importance are as obvious and beneficial to the beginning teacher as they are rewarding for the mentor.

## For discussion

- Having read this chapter, consider the type of post-lesson conversations you typically have with your beginning teacher(s). Where on the journey from directive mentor to dialogic coach do these conversations fall?
- What three actions might you prioritise in your future pre- and post-lesson discussions with a beginning teacher?

## Further reading

- Buck, A. (2020). *The BASIC coaching method.* Cadogan Press.
  This book offers a more detailed exploration of a framework for post-lesson discussions that is briefly explored in the chapter above.
- Farrell, T. (2024). *Reflective practice for language teachers.* British Council. https://www.teachingenglish.org.uk/sites/teacheng/files/2024-03/Farrell_Reflective_Practice_Final.pdf
  This short, open-access publication is aimed at teachers of English but contains a framework and other tools for reflecting on practice that are highly relevant to teachers of any language.

## References

Ager, E. O., & Wyatt, M. (2018). Supporting a pre-service English language teacher's self-determined development. *Teaching and Teacher Education, 78,* 106–116.

Beckett, H., (2010). 'How to deal with constructive criticism', TES Magazine, May 7. Accessed November 23, 2023, from https://www.tes.com/magazine/archive/how-deal-constructive-criticism.

Black, L., Gordon, A. L., Hughes, C., MacArthur, R., & Sandy, S. (2017). *Effective mentoring of trainee teachers* [Online]. Association for Language Learning. Accessed November 23, 2023, from https://www.all-languages.org.uk/product/effective-mentoring-trainee-teachers-e-book/.

Brandom, A.-M., Richardson, C., Shepherd, J., & Wright, A. (2023). The role of the mentor in initial teacher education. In S. Gibbons, R. Brock, M. Glackin, E. Rushton, & E. Towers (Eds.), *Becoming a teacher: Issues in secondary education* (pp. 342–355). Open University Press.

Buck, A. (2020). *The BASIC coaching method.* Cadogan Press.

Burn, K., Hagger, H., & Mutton, T. (2015). *Beginning Teachers' learning: Making experience count.* Critical Publishing.

Carter, I. (2015). *Carter review of initial teacher training.* Department for Education.

Clutterbuck, D. (2004). *Everyone needs a mentor.* Mc Graw-Hill Education.

Day, C., & Gu, Q. (2014). *Resilient teachers, resilient schools.* Routledge.

Delaney, Y. A. (2012). Research on mentoring language teachers: Its role in language education. *Foreign Language Annals, 45*(1), 184–202.

Department for Education. (2011). *The teachers' standards.* Crown.

Department for Education. (2016a). *Standards for teachers' professional development: Implementation guidance for school leaders, teachers, and organisations that offer professional development for teacher.* Crown.

Department for Education. (2016b). *National standards for school-based initial teacher training (ITT) mentors.* Crown.

Department for Education. (2019a). *Early career framework.* Crown. https://assets.publishing.service.gov.uk/media/60795936d3bf7f400b462d74/Early-Career_Framework_April_2021.pdf

Department for Education. (2019b). *ITT core content framework.* Crown. https://assets.publishing.service.gov.uk/government/uploads/system/uploads/attachment_data/file/974307/ITT_core_content_framework_.pdf

Department for Education. (2024). *Initial Teacher Training and Early Career Framework.* https://www.gov.uk/government/publications/initial-teacher-training-and-early-career-framework.

Forster, C., Wire, T., Eperjesi, R., Hollier, R., Howell, E., & Penny, J. (2021). Exploring the impact of expert guidance from school-based mentors on student teachers' professional learning. *Practice, 4*(10), 1–11. https://doi.org/10.1080/25783858.2021.1997338

Gordon, A.-L. (2020). *Educate – Mentor – Nurture: Improving the transition from initial teacher education to qualified teacher status and beyond. Journal of Education for Teaching*, 46(5), 664–675. https://doi.org/10.1080/02607476.2020.1807296

Hobson, A. J., & Malderez, A. (2013). Judgementoring and other threats to realizing potential of school-based mentoring in teacher education. *International Journal of Mentoring and Coaching in Education*, 2(2), 80–108.

Hunton, J. (2015). *Fun learning activities for modern foreign languages: A complete toolkit for ensuring engagement, progress and achievement*. Crown House Publishing.

Malderez, A., & Wedell, M. (2007). *Teaching teachers: Processes and practices*. Continuum.

Manning, C., & Hobson, A. J. (2017). Judgemental and developmental Mentoring in further education initial teacher education in England: Mentor and beginning teacher perspectives. *Research in Post-Compulsory Education*, 22(4), 575–595.

Scott, K. (2017). *Radical Candor*. Macmillan.

Sherrington, T., & Caviglioli, O. (2020). *Teaching WALKTHRUs: Five step guide to instructional coaching*. John Cart Educational Ltd.

Smith, S., & Conti, G. (2023) *The language teacher toolkit* (2nd ed.). CreateSpace Independent Publishing.

Sweller, J., Ayres, P., & Kalyuga, S. (2011). *Cognitive load theory*. Springer.

Taylor, W. (2007). *Developing conscious competence*. National College of Natural Medicine.

Warren, D. (2019). *100 ideas for secondary teachers: Outstanding MFL lessons*. Bloomsbury.

# 12 Accelerating mentorship: coaching insights for empowering mentor meetings

*Candida Javaid*

## Introduction

In my 19 years of teaching, I've observed the education sector's ongoing struggle with challenges like teacher retention and burnout. Despite various efforts to address these issues, they have remained remarkably unchanged. Many teachers leave because they seek to make an impact and find other avenues to do so, while others burn out and disappear from the profession.

If you are mentoring beginning teachers, you have a crucial opportunity to equip them with the skills and support they need to successfully navigate the challenges they will encounter throughout their careers. As mentors, you play a pivotal role in shaping the future of these educators, directly influencing their ability to remain resilient and effective in the classroom. Don't underestimate the positive power you hold. We need to remember that if too many teachers leave the profession, it is the children who will ultimately suffer, as they will not receive the necessary support and quality education they deserve. A reimagined approach to supporting teachers is earnestly called for.

In this chapter, I advocate for a coaching approach aimed at cultivating a conducive thinking environment (Kline, 1999) with the aim to encourage autonomy and growth. Coaching is fundamentally rooted in conversations and relationships. We remember the people who cared about us during our careers and those who enabled us to grow. Munro (2022) emphasises that conversations are what enable or inhibit our growth, and that the powerful role coaching can play lies in developing more intentional conversational habits. Through this, coaching becomes a catalyst for professional learning. To increase ownership and accountability, we need to encourage reflective practice. By taming our 'advice monsters' (Stanier, 2020), we can foster creativity and innovation in our mentees' development.

This chapter is designed for those involved in mentorship within language education, whether you are mentoring teachers, being mentored, or engaged in peer support. The primary emphasis is on exploring the ways in which coaching principles can be applied to mentoring relationships. By adopting a coaching mindset, we can create a more supportive, resilient, and effective teaching community. Let's embark on this journey to transform our mentoring practices and, ultimately, improve the educational experiences of our pupils. At the end of this chapter, you should be able to:

- Understand what is meant by a 'coaching mindset' and how this might differ from more directive mentoring
- Have an awareness of the range of different models of practice associated with mentoring and coaching teachers at different stages of teacher development

## Exploring coaching mindsets in languages mentoring

So, what is the context and why are we talking about mentoring in languages? In England, beginning teachers receive mentorship, targeted training, and a dedicated induction phase, nurturing continuous growth and establishing a robust foundation for effective teaching. Introduced in September 2019, the early career framework (ECF) offered a concise, yet comprehensive two-year support programme tailored for beginning teachers. Designed to elevate teaching proficiency, confidence, and classroom impact, the framework covers crucial aspects such as behaviour management, pedagogical approaches, assessment techniques, and subject expertise. An enhanced framework, the initial teacher training and early career framework (ITTECF) (Department for Education, 2024), replaces the ECF from September 2025 and aims to enhance content to better equip teachers in supporting pupils with special educational needs and disabilities (SEND), implement measures to reduce workload for mentors, and offer more subject-specific training opportunities. These changes reflect ongoing efforts to improve teaching standards and support for early-career teachers and acknowledge evidence that mentoring a beginning teacher can significantly impact their professional growth and the quality of education they provide to their learners (Murtagh et al., 2024). Despite these ongoing changes, the fundamental reason we discuss mentoring remains straightforward: it is the primary method for inducting beginning teachers.

Induction frameworks keep changing, and there is very little that individual teachers can do about it. But what if there was something we could do that might not only help our beginning teachers but also improve our own skills? This is where coaching comes in. Interestingly, coaching and mentoring are often mentioned in the same breath (Garvey et al., 2021; Lancer et al., 2016; Oberholzer & Boyle, 2023) and yet, the two terms are defined and applied differently across various contexts, at times resulting in conflicting practices and misconceptions (Booton et al., 2023, p. 8). It often seems that everyone has their own opinion on what coaching and mentoring is and isn't, often holding viewpoints that differ significantly from one another. For instance, consider Knight's Instructional Coaching (2017) and the Graydin approach (https://www.graydin.com/). While both focus on improving teaching practice, Knight's model emphasises a structured, evidence-based approach with clear roles for coaches, often aimed at teachers working to improve specific teaching strategies (what is referred to as 'instructional strategies' in some contexts). On the other hand, the Graydin approach places a strong emphasis on the development of reflective, growth-oriented relationships between coaches and teachers, offering more flexibility in the coaching process. Despite their differences, both approaches aim to support teacher development and foster a coaching mindset, though their methods may vary. To avoid any frustration, I won't be discussing or evaluating different coaching models. My intention is to acknowledge their existence but to clarify that this discussion isn't about any specific approach or model, such as GROW (https://www.mindtools.com/anOfzpz/the-grow-model-of-coaching-and-mentoring). Instead, I'm interested in exploring why it might be useful to view coaching as a mindset and what we can learn from the field of coaching.

So, what is coaching, and why does it deserve a place in this book? 'Coaching is about finding a way to change what isn't working or improving on something that is working' (Franklin, 2019, p. 11) This idea of 'finding a way' is one way to distinguish coaching from mentoring.

In coaching, it is usually the coachee who finds the way to improve, not the coach. Viewed this way, coaching and mentoring could be envisaged on a continuum, with coaching being 'less directive/facilitative' and mentoring 'more directive' (Munro, 2020, p. 40). In the less directive/more facilitative stance, the coach adopts a 'beginner's mind', putting aside their expertise to fully understand the coachee's perspective. The coach aims to stimulate profound reflection and insights from the coachee (Munro, 2020, p. 40). It is easy to assume that our expectations for the mentoring relationship align with those of the mentee, the training provider, or what we believe is the correct approach to mentoring. This assumption can lead to misunderstandings and missed opportunities for growth.

I believe mentors could benefit from reflecting on their roles and what they might learn from the field of coaching. I will share insights from my training to become a coach and my experience teaching coaching skills to adult learners. These experiences reshaped my perspective on mentoring in teacher education. One key insight was that changing the narrative—or the purpose of the mentor/mentee relationship—can be beneficial. I propose that as mentors, we consider shifting from a default position of wanting to 'help' our mentees to one where we clarify the roles each of us plays in this relationship. In the mentor-mentee relationship, there's a risk of slipping into the dynamics of Karpman's drama triangle (1968), where the mentor unintentionally assumes a rescuer role, disempowering the mentee. West (2020) highlights this potential pitfall, emphasising the importance of adopting coaching principles to facilitate effective professional growth. However, amidst the pressure to cover the relevant induction framework, these coaching skills may be overlooked. Striking a balance between meeting framework requirements and fostering a coaching oriented mentorship is crucial to ensure the beginning teacher's holistic development.

Applying coaching principles, as outlined by organisations such as the International Coaching Federation (ICF) and the Association of Coaching (AC 2012), involves a shift from being an expert to serving as a facilitator of the mentee's growth. This transition empowers beginning teachers to develop into independent, confident practitioners. Drawing from my own journey as a coach, I grappled with the temptation to provide answers instead of guiding my coachees to find their own solutions. This challenge is common among new coaches who may feel compelled to rely on their expertise. Even seasoned coaches encounter this tension. Quiney (2022) underscores this by emphasising that coaching is not about moulding others to resemble oneself but rather guiding your coachee to embrace their authentic self (Task 12.1).

### Task 12.1 Reflecting on the nature of past mentoring relationships

- Reflecting on past experiences as a mentor or mentee, have you noticed a tendency for relationships to be more directive or self-directed?
- Can you think of factors that contributed to the development of these dynamics within the mentorship relationship?

## Coaching in languages mentoring relationships

Effective mentors for beginning teachers create environments where mentees independently unravel solutions to challenges and gain insights, thereby cultivating confidence in their practice. This process hinges on adeptly listening, posing probing questions, and showing unwavering support and guidance. By prioritising this approach, mentees assume ownership of their objectives, explore different solutions to their problems, and drive their progress. Consequently, they evolve into more self-reliant practitioners capable of effectively navigating forthcoming obstacles, paving the way for enduring professional development. A mentee's motivation is a key driver of progress and helps steer discussions. As a mentor, your effectiveness is enhanced when the person you mentor has clear goals or aspirations. Without this focus, conversations may lack direction, leading to unfulfilling outcomes for both parties (Starr, 2021, p. 41)

Some of the typical areas languages beginning teachers have to navigate are listed below:

1. Classroom Management
2. Workload and Time Management
3. Assessment and Feedback
4. Language Proficiency
5. Technology Integration
6. Responsive and adaptive teaching
7. Parental Engagement
8. Curriculum Design and Implementation
9. Cultural Competence
10. Adaptation to New Environments

Of course, the above list is not exhaustive. How do we start supporting someone without knowing where their starting point is?

As educators, our default position is to help others and to pass on our knowledge to our mentees, especially, if we think that we have the solution to their problems. We have all heard the idea of 'helping someone to help themselves', especially with the aim to accompany them on their journey to self-actualisation (Frager & Maslow, 1987) but what does that really mean? I argue that if our instinct is to help (or even rescue) our mentee, the power balance can unintentionally shift in the direction of the mentor holding the power (Berne, 1968). What if the beginning teacher you are working with does not require the help we assumed they might need, or doesn't wish to participate in this perceived power dynamic? In such scenarios, where do we pivot? What alternative actions can we take? This is where coaching can be helpful, because it prompts us to carefully establish what each partner will bring to the relationship. A fundamental aspect of coaching involves what is known as 'contracting'. Berne (1966) described three levels of a contract: administrative, professional, and psychological. It can be beneficial to emphasise to your beginning teacher the importance of addressing and discussing all three aspects during meetings. Seeing these three aspects as a common thread running through our relationship can provide clarity and coherence for both sides.

In addition, Latimer (2024) advocates for a non-directive approach to coaching that focuses on three key aspects: absolute clarity on the current reality, absolute clarity on the desired future, and absolute clarity on the steps needed to bridge the gap between the two. Thinking through these three aspects allows both the mentor and the mentee to develop a shared understanding of what is required of the mentee, aligning their efforts and expectations as they work together towards the desired outcome (Task 12.2).

> **Task 12.2 Reflect on your own positioning and possible approaches to establishing administrative, professional and psychological expectations with your mentee**
>
> - Have you ever felt the urge to rescue or provide solutions to your mentees' challenges? How did this impact their autonomy?
> - How can you balance providing guidance with fostering autonomy in your mentees' professional development?
> - How do you ensure that all aspects of your contract with your mentee—administrative, professional, and psychological—are addressed in your mentor meetings? Could visualising these aspects, along with gaining clarity on the current reality, the desired future, and the necessary steps to bridge the gap, enhance the mutual understanding and effectiveness of your relationship?

## Mentorship in practice

If you are a beginning teacher under the guidance of a mentor, utilise their experience, knowledge, and support, but remember that the responsibility of becoming an exceptional teacher ultimately rests on your shoulders. At the outset, you might not foresee mastering the skills expected of you, whether through the statutory framework or the unique demands of your school setting. Stay open to your mentor's guidance, acknowledging that much of your journey involves building independence. While your mentor and other colleagues will provide observations and feedback, you will also often be required to teach or fulfil professional responsibilities independently, such as lesson planning, classroom management, and pupil assessment. Keep notes of questions and topics to discuss with your mentor to maximise your time together. Consider strategies like preparing an agenda for your meetings, seeking specific feedback on your teaching practices, and setting personal development goals. Regular reflection on the feedback you receive and on your own experiences is crucial.

The mentoring relationship varies depending on the stage of your teaching career. In my own teacher training, I was fortunate to have a mentor who was deeply invested in my growth. He recognised that my learning needs extended beyond language teaching skills to understanding the cultural nuances of the UK education system, as I had only arrived in the United Kingdom four months earlier. He guided me in learning a very different approach to teaching than I had experienced in my own schooling. He also connected me with a German native-speaking colleague who helped me understand the subtler distinctions between the English and German education systems, something he might have found more difficult to share himself. This holistic support significantly enriched my learning experience, and I remember him as an experienced teacher truly invested in my development.

Mentors don't need to be experts on everything. One of their roles is to guide the mentee to appropriate sources of support, much like teachers who don't have to be perfect walking dictionaries for their pupils. If they were, pupils wouldn't learn the dictionary skills necessary for independence. By fostering a relationship that balances guidance with opportunities for independent problem-solving, mentors help beginning teachers develop the skills they need to thrive in the long term.

## Adult learning theories

Drawing from adult learning theories, it is important to recognise the parallels between coaching and mentoring. Successful mentoring requires active participation from both parties and transcends the conventional teacher-student roles. Mentees are not children, and mentors are not traditional teachers, necessitating a different approach to fostering growth and development. By understanding and implementing these principles, mentors can enhance the effectiveness of their mentoring relationships and avoid common pitfalls.

Exploring key principles derived from adult learning models can provide valuable insights to mentors. While some begin their teacher training straight out of university, a significant number choose teaching as a second career, often bringing diverse skills and experiences from other professions. This latter group may be older and might have different learning needs; although those coming directly from university might more readily adapt to the mentor's style, utilising adult learning models benefits both cohorts, enhancing the mentoring process for everyone involved.

As mentioned above, adult learning theory differs from pedagogy we learn about as educators of young people. I would like to mention here three theorists who contribute to our understanding of how adults learn and the factors that influence their learning experiences. In your sessions, you might want to explore different dimensions of the learning process your mentee will go through, with reference to these three thinkers. Knowles' (1978) model of andragogy provides insights into the unique characteristics and motivations of adult learners, Mezirow's (1996) transformative learning theory sheds light on how adults can undergo significant personal and cognitive changes through education, and Zimmerman's social cognitive theory (Schunk & Zimmerman, 1997) offers perspectives on self-regulated learning and motivation. In the next few paragraphs, I will give a very brief introduction to these three thinkers.

Andragogy, attributed to Knowles (1978), is a model that highlights the significance of self-directed learning, acknowledging that adults excel in learning when actively engaged in planning and evaluating their educational journey. Unlike pedagogy, which is more teacher-centred and commonly associated with the education of children, andragogy places emphasis on the autonomy and experience of adult learners. An example of andragogy in action might be seen in a professional development workshop for teachers. Instead of a traditional lecture-style approach, the workshop could encourage teachers to set their own learning goals, participate in collaborative activities, and reflect on their teaching practices. For mentors working with beginning teachers, leveraging this model involves empowering them to take charge of their learning objectives. Knowles' andragogy has been influential in shaping how educators approach designing courses for adult learners. It underscores the importance of recognising the autonomy and life experiences of adults, promoting a learner-centred approach that considers adults' unique needs and motivations (Task 12.3).

---

**Task 12.3 Considering the implications of the theory of andragogy**

- In what ways can you encourage beginning teachers to set and monitor their own learning goals related to language instruction and assess their progress?

---

A different lens in adult education is transformational learning, pioneered by Mezirow (1996), which highlights the importance of creating learning environments that encourage critical reflection, open dialogue, and the exploration of new perspectives, fostering personal and cognitive transformations in adult learners. Critically examining one's assumptions and beliefs can drive personal change. In the realm of mentoring beginning teachers, this model serves as a robust framework as mentors play a pivotal role in guiding mentees to question their existing assumptions about teaching. They actively encourage exploration of diverse perspectives and teaching approaches beginning teachers have encountered during their training, fostering a mindset that is receptive to re-evaluation and transformation. Through this process, beginning teachers can embrace new insights and methodologies, sparking significant growth in their teaching practices. Consider a scenario where a mentee is used to a traditional lecture-style teaching approach. The mentor, applying the principles of transformational learning, encourages the mentee to critically examine the underlying assumptions about effective teaching methods. For example, the mentor might suggest observing and collaborating with a colleague who uses a variety of learner-centred strategies in their classroom. This exposure challenges the mentee's preconceptions and opens up a dialogue about the potential benefits of adopting more engaging instructional methods (Task 12.4).

---

**Task 12.4 Considering the implications of transformational learning model**

- How can beginning teachers critically examine their assumptions about effective language teaching methods? What strategies can both beginning teachers and mentors use to facilitate open dialogue about diverse perspectives and approaches to language education?
- How can both beginning teachers and mentors foster a mindset receptive to transformation and growth by exploring teaching methodologies that challenge existing beliefs and practices?

Lastly, we turn to the theory of Self-Regulated Learning, credited to Zimmerman (see Schunk & Zimmerman, 1997), which focuses on individuals taking an active role in their learning journey through setting goals, monitoring their progress, and adapting strategies to achieve success. Within this model there are four levels of development: observation, imitation, self-control, and self-regulation. In the mentorship of beginning teachers, this framework may help mentors to chart the development of these skill levels with their mentees, assisting them in effectively navigating their professional development. By guiding them to establish clear goals, promoting self-awareness in progress monitoring, and facilitating the adjustment of strategies, mentors empower beginning teachers to evolve into skilled, self-directed learners who engage on a continuous path of growth and learning. In practice this extends an already familiar process through which beginning teachers learn new classroom skills (at first by observing and then emulating). As they progress, it is useful to move their attention to self-control and self-regulation (Task 12.5).

**Task 12.5 Considering the implications of self-regulated learning theory**

- How can beginning teachers and mentors collaboratively set clear, achievable goals for professional growth in teaching modern foreign languages?
- How can beginning teachers and mentors cultivate a mindset of continuous improvement and self-regulation in teaching practices, ensuring sustained professional development?

## Challenges and solutions

Many of us are likely to hold a strong view of what a mentoring relationship entails, shaped by personal experiences with exceptional teachers or mentors, as well as by portrayals in films and literature. The depiction of mentors in 'The Mentoring Manual' by Starr (2021) serves as a useful reminder of how mentoring relationships have influenced us, often through popular media. Starr's examples range from Professor Dumbledore in Harry Potter to Obi-Wan Kenobi in Star Wars, illustrating the powerful and diverse roles mentors can play.

Gallwey, an author and sports coach known for his work in sports psychology, suggests that *performance* is the sum of *potential* minus *interference* (2014). Examples of interference include skill gaps, self-doubt, overthinking, and other obstacles. Embracing this idea can inform your mentoring approach: it encourages us to foster the belief that our beginning teacher has the potential to excel, and our role is to support them by helping to remove interference. One way to do this is to encourage your beginning teacher to reframe obstacles through different lenses. For instance, a 'poorly behaving class' might be due to individual pupil challenges, unclear expectations, teacher-pupil relationships, lack of motivation, environmental factors, or learning difficulties. Gallwey also discusses the 'spotlight' focus on specific skills versus the 'floodlight' broad contextual understanding (Gallwey,

2001). Balancing these two perspectives can enhance your beginning teacher's learning and problem-solving skills.

Adopting the approaches suggested above enables you to offer robust support while also discussing challenges so that your mentee can grow. At the core of the mentor-mentee dynamic should lie your genuine concern for your mentee's success and an earnest commitment to aiding them in achieving their objectives. Your guidance extends through role modelling behaviours and being readily available when challenges arise. Establishing clear communication guidelines in the mentoring relationship is pivotal, especially in navigating obstacles. Equally significant is outlining accountability measures that keep both of you on the path towards your mentee's goals. While you can offer guidance in setting the agenda, encouraging the mentee's active participation in shaping an agenda that is meaningful to their growth is paramount. Your responsibility is to remain fully dedicated to their success, acknowledging their contributions with genuine care. Simultaneously, you should foster a supportive relationship that allows for constructive challenges to their thinking, as a result contributing positively to their overall progress. This collaborative approach fosters an empowering learning experience for both of you (Task 12.6).

### Task 12.6 Reflecting on the ideas presented by Starr and Gallwey

- Consider the examples of mentors depicted in popular media like Harry Potter and Star Wars. How do these portrayals align with or differ from your own expectations of a mentor, and what insights can you gain from them for your current mentoring relationship?
- Reflect on the idea of *performance* being the sum of *potential* minus *interference* (Gallwey, 2014). How does this idea influence your mentoring philosophy, and how could you apply it in supporting your beginning teacher's growth and development?
- Consider the concept of balancing the 'spotlight' and 'floodlight' perspectives in mentoring, as discussed by Gallwey (2001). How do you strike a balance between focusing on specific skills and fostering a broader understanding in your mentoring sessions, and how does this contribute to your mentee's learning and problem-solving abilities?

## Building effective relationships

Effective mentoring relationships are not accidental; they are intentionally developed and represent a mutual learning journey. Such relationships require a commitment to continuous improvement, a non-judgemental mindset, and the willingness to engage in open, honest conversations to assess their effectiveness. Additionally, it is crucial to foster a high-quality connection where the mentee feels supported and the mentor can see the tangible impact they are making. In my experience, there is so much more to a thriving mentor relationship than just the process of supporting someone through their first few years of teaching. If you allow time for the mentee to learn their craft, to explore and decide on who they want to be as a teacher, they will be able to grow into that role. Ultimately, it is the responsibility of the mentee to become the best teacher they can be. If both sides stay committed, mentoring can create a space where this skill can evolve and grow. There are valuable lessons to be gleaned from coaching that can be transferred to mentoring practice. Mentoring in education provides value to both sides, the mentee, and the mentor, and this will ultimately benefit the pupils—and that is what really counts.

During an introduction to a coaching course I taught to adult learners, my pupils found a particular analogy enlightening in understanding key coaching principles. I encouraged them to visualise themselves at eye level with their clients. I introduced the German phrase 'Auf Augenhöhe sein', which directly translates to 'being at eye level'. However, this phrase carries deeper meaning in German beyond its literal translation. It embodies concepts of equality, mutual respect, and fostering relationships where individuals communicate on equal ground, valuing each other's perspectives with fairness and dignity. As a fellow language teacher, you are probably familiar with encountering these 'untranslatable' idiomatic expressions, rich in nuanced meanings that don't always carry over in translation. Visualise yourself seated across or beside your beginning teacher, aiming to see the conversation through their eyes. Extend genuine acknowledgement by treating them as equals, demonstrating authentic respect and careful consideration for their perspective. This approach fosters an environment of mutual respect and empathy, laying the groundwork for transparent communication which can form an exceptional foundation for nurturing a strong and thriving mentoring relationship.

Stone and Heen (2015, p. 8) remind us that 'receiving feedback sits at the intersection of [...] two needs—our drive to learn and our longing for acceptance'. Openly acknowledging these two needs may help mentors and their mentees to better understand what need they have right now. It is worth taking a bit of time agreeing on what might be useful for your mentee or necessary to discuss. The foundation for this to work, however, is trust. It is worth considering that 'trust is not a light switch'. This is an expression coined by Granger in her leadership podcast (Granger, 2020) that really got me thinking. Just because we are in a mentoring relationship, we cannot assume that we have unconditional trust. To foster trust, it is vital to have clarity over what both of you do with confidentially shared information. Building trust and psychological safety (Edmondson, 1999), also opens the possibility for the mentee to share genuine concerns without them being worried that this is going to be discussed with other parties at the school. However, if there is a need to share a specific concern more widely, you might find it more impactful to communicate transparently the rationale to your mentee, fostering mutual understanding and respect.

When building trust with your beginning teacher, you may find it valuable to visualise the concept of 'holding the space', where we create an environment conducive to reflection and exploration without the pressure of immediate solutions. Reflecting on my own teaching journey, I encountered the Michel Thomas Method, which emphasised the importance of 'thinking time' through deliberate pauses and prompts. This approach encouraged learners to engage deeply with the material, echoing the idea of 'holding the space' for learners in mentoring relationships with the aim to create a supportive and non-judgemental environment where mentees feel safe to explore their thoughts, emotions, and experiences (Task 12.7).

> **Task 12.7 Reflect on how to build trust in your mentor-mentee relationship**
>
> - In light of the analogy 'Auf Augenhöhe sein' (being at eye level) and its deeper connotations, how can you envision positioning yourself across or beside your beginning teacher to promote an environment of equality, mutual respect, and transparent communication? What would be the first concrete step that you could take towards this stance in your next mentor meeting?
> - How can you incorporate the concept of 'holding the space' into your mentoring practice to create an environment conducive to reflection and exploration for your beginning teachers?

## Practical applications and techniques

To accelerate your mentee's learning, you could recommend actions or point them toward useful resources, teaching materials, or technological tools. For instance, you might suggest a book like Dix's *When the Adults Change, Everything Changes: Seismic Shifts in School Behaviour* (2017). However, this might not be what the beginning teacher needs at the moment. If you feel compelled to offer a recommendation or share an insight, ask them if they would like to hear your suggestion and let them decide whether to use it. By seeking permission, you empower the beginning teacher to make their own decisions, reinforcing their responsibility and autonomy in their learning journey.

Another valuable coaching tool applicable to mentoring is Stanier's AWE Question, where 'AWE' stands for 'And What Else?' Stanier confidently calls this the 'Best Coaching Question in the World' (2016, p. 56), and for good reason. When assisting a beginning teacher in generating solutions, for example, for addressing a behaviour management challenge, ask 'And what else?' several times (perhaps three to four times). This prompts deeper reflection and generates additional ideas. Instead of worrying about what you will say next, stay in the mindset of 'being at eye level' to give the beginning teacher space to develop their thoughts.

For example, the mentee might initially suggest changing the seating plan. By continuing to ask 'And what else?' they might then consider observing a more experienced teacher, reaching out to a colleague for advice, having a conversation with the pupils to understand their needs, or reflecting on each lesson to identify and avoid challenges in the future. This repetitive questioning fosters deeper exploration and a more comprehensive problem-solving approach. It aligns with adult learning models that challenge existing assumptions and promote self-directed learning. Although it might feel unnatural or clumsy at first, try it out—both you and your beginning teacher can benefit from this technique.

Even with our best intentions to actively listen, we may inadvertently start formulating responses before fully grasping our mentee's perspective. Experienced mentors often struggle with the impulse to provide solutions rather than fostering genuine understanding. Bungay Stanier first introduced the concept of the 'advice monster' (2016) to highlight the instinct many coaches and mentors have to offer unsolicited advice. He later expanded this metaphor by identifying three distinct 'advice monsters' (2020), each representing a different impulse that can disrupt productive coaching conversations. These include: the Tell-It Monster, which compels us to offer immediate solutions and answers; the Save-It Monster, which pushes us to rescue others from their difficulties; and the Control-It Monster, which drives us to take charge and dictate the direction of the conversation. We all tend to have our preferred way of giving advice, so we may lean towards one particular monster over the others. However, all three of these tendencies can undermine the mentee's autonomy and hinder their growth. By recognising and taming these impulses, coaches and mentors can create a more empowering environment that allows the mentee to engage in self-discovery and make independent decisions. Visualising this tendency helps us recognise when we are slipping into the role of problem-solver rather than simply holding space for the mentee. Stanier also introduces another impactful question: 'What's the real challenge here for you?' (2016, p. 86). Use this question when your mentee seems uncertain about their struggles, aiming to prompt focused reflection rather than jumping to conclusions or making assumptions. Emphasising different words in the question can guide the mentee to generate a list of challenges or prompt deeper introspection. Follow up with phrases like 'Tell me more' or 'What makes this the real problem?' to sustain their reflective mindset. It is crucial to recognise our innate preference to provide advice and counterbalance it by taming our 'advice monsters'. Use powerful questioning techniques like AWE (And What Else?) and focus questions (What's the real challenge here?) to steer conversations toward nurturing the mentee's skills. This approach is not about refraining entirely from sharing knowledge or making suggestions but about creating space for mentee-led exploration. When you do offer advice, seek permission first. This simple strategy reminds both you and your mentee that the ultimate decision-making power lies with the mentee, promoting their autonomy and ownership of their development journey.

## Conclusion

The journey of effective mentoring in languages encapsulates a dynamic interplay of principles, practices, and perspectives. By integrating coaching principles into mentoring relationships, mentors can transcend traditional roles, shifting from mere instructors to empowering guides. Embracing coaching-oriented mentorship enables mentors to move beyond rescuer roles, fostering autonomy and clarity in mentor-mentee dynamics. This transformative approach nurtures the holistic development of beginning teachers, empowering them to navigate challenges with confidence and resilience.

Effective mentoring is a deliberate journey of growth and learning, both for mentors and mentees. By prioritising active listening, probing questions, and unwavering support, mentors create environments where beginning teachers can drive their own advancement. This approach not only ensures enduring professional development but also enhances the quality of mentoring relationships. Through mutual respect, open communication, and trust, mentors and mentees co-create spaces for meaningful development, enriching their professional lives and positively impacting the educational landscape.

Understanding the influence of adult learning theories further enriches the mentoring process. By applying frameworks such as andragogy, transformative learning, and self-regulated learning, mentors empower beginning teachers to take ownership of their learning journey. This facilitates growth, reflection, and professional development, fostering independent practitioners capable of adapting to the evolving demands of language education.

Acknowledging the impact of personal experiences and media portrayals on mentoring relationships deepens mentors' understanding of their role. Drawing insights from figures like Gallwey and reflections on mentorship dynamics fosters effective guidance, empowering growth, and development in both mentors and beginning teachers. As mentors strive to hold space for mentees to explore their thoughts, mentees are encouraged to actively engage in their learning journey, seeking resources, reflecting on their practice, and making informed decisions.

Effective mentoring transcends mere instruction; it is a collaborative journey towards excellence. By counterbalancing the impulse to provide advice with empowering mentee autonomy, mentors facilitate mentee-led exploration and decision-making. As mentors and mentees navigate challenges together, they evolve into confident and self-reliant practitioners, equipped to positively impact pupil learning experiences. Thus, as this chapter concludes, let us remember that effective mentoring is not just a process—it is a transformative journey of mutual growth and learning.

## For discussion

- **For the Mentor:** How can you determine when to offer advice versus allowing the mentee to explore their own solutions? How can you recognise and manage the tendency to become the 'advice monster', focusing on providing solutions rather than fostering genuine understanding?
- **For the Mentee:** How can you approach taking ownership of your learning journey, and what specific steps can you take to ensure you are actively directing your professional development with the support of your mentor?

## Further reading

While I am deeply passionate about bringing coaching to a wider audience, I also believe in the importance of a systemic approach that considers the interconnectedness of individuals and their environments. The following three books provide valuable perspectives on this holistic view and are excellent resources for further exploration.

- Clutterbuck, D. (2022). *Coaching and mentoring: A journey through the models, theories, frameworks and narratives of David Clutterbuck*. Routledge.

    This is a foundational text in the field of coaching, with Clutterbuck regarded as a pivotal figure in its development. I see him as my 'godfather' of coaching, given his extensive contributions to shaping coaching theory and practice. This book explores key models such as Systemic Talent Management and Team Coaching, offering invaluable insights.

- Berger, J. G., & Johnston, K. (2015). *Simple habits for complex times: Powerful practices for leaders.* Stanford University Press.

    In education, the challenges faced by leaders often mirror those in the business world—complex, unpredictable, and constantly shifting. Berger's and Johnston's *Simple Habits for Complex Times* offers practical strategies to navigate this uncertainty. By taking multiple perspectives, asking new questions, and understanding the broader system, educational leaders can better align their actions with the needs of both their teams and pupils.

- Hawkins, P., & Turner, E. (2019). *Systemic coaching: Delivering value beyond the individual.* Routledge.

    Hawkins and Turner argue that coaching should extend its value beyond the coachee, impacting a broader network, including colleagues, leaders, and the wider community. In educational settings, this view encourages an understanding of how each individual's actions are intertwined within a larger system, where changes affect everyone involved.

## References

Association of Coaching. (2012, June). *Coaching competency framework.* https://cdn.ymaws.com/www.associationforcoaching.com/resource/resmgr/Accreditation/Accred_General/Coaching_Competency_Framewor.pdf.

Berne, E. (1966). 'Principles of group treatment.' https://psptraining.com/wp-content/uploads/Berne-E.-1966.-Principles-of-group-treatment.pdf

Berne, E. (1968). *Games people play: The psychology of human relationships.* Penguin UK.

Booton, J., Holloweck, T., & Munro, C. (2023). Mentors who coach-coaches who mentor: Accompaniment and stance as unifying and liberating concepts. *CollectivED Working Papers, 40,* 5.

Department for Education, I. (2024). *Initial teacher training and early career framework (ITTECF).* https://assets.publishing.service.gov.uk/media/661d24ac08c3be25cfbd3e61/Initial_Teacher_Training_and_Early_Career_Framework.pdf

Dix, P. (2017). *When the adults change, everything changes: Seismic shifts in school behaviour.* Crown House Publishing Ltd.

Edmondson, A. (1999). Psychological safety and learning behavior in work teams. *Administrative Science Quarterly, 44*(2), 350–383.

Frager, R., & Maslow, A. H. (1987). 'Motivation and personality', *(No Title).* https://www.holybooks.com/wp-content/uploads/Motivation-and-Personality-Maslow.pdf

Franklin, M. (2019). *The HeART of laser-focused coaching: A revolutionary approach to masterful coaching.* Thomas Noble Books.

Gallwey, W. T. (2001) *The inner game of work: Focus, learning, pleasure, and mobility in the workplace.* Random house trade paperbacks.

Gallwey, W. T. (2014). *The inner game of tennis: The classic guide to the mental side of peak performance.* Macmillan.

Garvey, B., Garvey, R., & Stokes, P. (2021). *Coaching and mentoring: Theory and practice.* Sage.

Granger, K. (2020) *Trust is NOT a Light Switch, Podcast.* Accessed January 4, 2023, from http://grangernetwork.hexcode.ca/season-3-episode-43-trust-is-not-a-light-switch/.

International Coaching Federation. (2019, November). *ICF Core Competencies.* International Coaching Federation. Retrieved from https://coachingfederation.org/credentials-and-standards/core-competencies.

Karpman, S. (1968). *Fairy tales and script drama analysis. Transactional Analysis Bulletin, 7*(26), 39–43.

Kline, N. (1999). *Time to think: Listening to ignite the human mind.* Hachette UK.
Knight, J. (2017). *The impact cycle: What instructional coaches should do to foster powerful improvements in teaching.* Corwin Publications.
Knowles, M. S. (1978). Andragogy: Adult learning theory in perspective. *Community College Review, 5*(3), 9-20.
Lancer, N., Clutterbuck, D., & Megginson, D. (2016). *Techniques for coaching and mentoring.* Routledge.
Latimer, T. (2024). *Coach without models: Non-directive coaching approach.* Profitable Leadership. Retrieved November 17, 2024, from https://www.profitableleadership.com/
Mezirow, J. (1996). Contemporary paradigms of learning. *Adult Education Quarterly, 46*(3), 158-172.
Munro, C. (2020). A continuum of professional learning conversations: Coaching, mentoring and everything in between. *CollectivED, 11,* 37-42.
Munro, C. (2022). Engaging in professional conversations. https://www.researchgate.net/publication/372490876_Engaging_in_Professional_Conversations
Murtagh, L., Dawes, L., Rushton, E., & Ball-Smith, C. (2024). Early career teacher mentoring in England: A case study of compliance and mediation. *Professional Development in Education,* 1-14. https://www.tandfonline.com/doi/full/10.1080/19415257.2023.2291357
Oberholzer, L., & Boyle, D. (2023). *Mentoring and coaching in education: A guide to coaching and mentoring teachers at every stage of their careers.* Bloomsbury Publishing.
Quiney, A. (2022). *Who do you think you are?: A leader's guide to what the mirror doesn't show you.* Evergrowth Coaching.
Schunk, D. H., & Zimmerman, B. J. (1997). Social origins of self-regulatory competence. *Educational Psychologist, 32*(4), 195-208.
Stanier, M. B. (2016). *The coaching habit: Say less, ask more & change the way you lead forever.* Box of Crayons Press.
Stanier, M. B. (2020). *The advice trap: Be humble, stay curious & change the way you lead forever.* Box of Crayons Press.
Starr, J. (2021). *The mentoring manual.* Pearson UK.
Stone, D., & Heen, S. (2015) *Thanks for the feedback: The science and art of receiving feedback well.* Penguin. https://coachingforleaders.com/podcast/143/.
West, C. (2020). *The Karpman Drama Triangle explained...: A guide for coaches, managers, trainers, therapists-and everybody else.* CWTK Publications.

# SECTION 4

# Providing effective support for beginning languages teachers' well-being

# 13 Managing well-being and workload with beginning languages teachers

*Juliette Claro and Anna Lise Gordon*

## Objectives

At the end of this chapter, you will have:

- considered professional well-being and what it means for a beginning languages teacher
- reflected on potential challenges to well-being and workload of languages teachers
- identified effective ways to support beginning languages teachers with well-being and workload (Task 13.1)

---

### Task 13.1 Pause for thought

'(T)eacher wellbeing may be defined as an individual sense of personal professional fulfilment, satisfaction, purposefulness and happiness, constructed in a collaborative process with colleagues and students' (Acton & Glasgow, 2015, p. 102).

Before reading on, pause for a moment to consider your own well-being as a teacher and as a mentor. Do you agree with Acton and Glasgow's statement? How do *you* define well-being? Is well-being an individual concept or is it bound up with your school context and the broader educational landscape? Which approaches and strategies do you draw on to manage your own well-being? Where are the pressure points?

---

## Introduction

One beginning languages teacher described the initial teacher education (ITE) experience as follows:

> … it's the image of a rollercoaster ride at the fairground, with its peaks and troughs, and moments of sheer exhilaration, followed by others of fear and despondency.

Almost all beginning teachers will share the highs and lows that are an inevitable part of learning to teach. This turbulent experience is vividly described by Johnson et al. (2014, p. 531) as 'transition trauma', recognising that preconceived notions of the role of the teacher may not match the reality or practice in schools. For this reason, the support, guidance and encouragement that the beginning teacher receives from mentors and others will be an essential part of their early professional journey. Teacher well-being is a growing global concern with some researchers exploring teacher well-being in ITE in European contexts in particular, including Thompson et al. (2020). Thoughtful mentoring on well-being and workload may serve as a springboard for longevity in the career (Gordon, 2020; Jones & Gordon, 2019) as we seek to avoid the devastating pattern among beginning teachers of 'recruit-burnout-replace' identified by Allen and Sims (2018, p. 20) and Turner and Braine (2016).

The extensive literature around teacher well-being must be considered alongside relevant policy documents (Briner & Dewberry, 2007; McCallum & Price, 2010). In England, for example, there have been a number of well-being-related initiatives by the Department for Education (DfE) in the last decade. A quick 'teacher well-being' search on the internet will reveal a plethora of DfE policy and practice documents, some of which are updated on a regular basis – Workload Challenge (2014), Addressing workload in initial teacher education (2018), Reducing School Workload (2018), School Workload Reduction Toolkit (2018), Teacher Recruitment and Retention Strategy (2019), The Education Staff Wellbeing Charter (2021), to name just a few. All these initiatives aim to address growing concerns about excessive workload and other pressures on teacher well-being. However, in spite of such efforts, the annual Teacher Wellbeing Index, published by Education Support, does not make encouraging reading, The current Teachers' Standards (DfE, 2011) do not refer explicitly to teacher well-being, but more recent policy documents (DfE, 2019a, 2019b) and the initial teacher training and early career framework (ITTECF) (DfE, 2024a), aimed specifically at beginning teachers, include the expectation that they will learn, for example, how to manage workload and well-being, including 'protecting time for rest and recovery' (DfE, 2019a, p. 31).

## Teacher well-being

As global concerns around teacher recruitment and retention abound (UNESCO, 2017), discussions around teacher well-being have increased (Hascher & Waber, 2021). There is no doubt that teachers with a clear understanding of how to navigate the challenges of their role are more likely to experience greater job satisfaction. Teachers at every stage in their career need to be alert to the changing and diverse needs of learners, as well as responding to constantly changing policies, examination requirements, technological advances and so on. Although the term 'well-being' is frequently used in the profession, its meaning is not always clearly defined or understood. Stated simply, one person's well-being may not be the same as another person's well-being, and the multi-layered and multi-factorial complexity increases as we consider the full scope of teacher well-being where a focus on professional well-being demands attention to be given to individual, organisational and systemic level considerations (Gu & Day, 2013). This can make the role of a mentor particularly complex when working with a beginning languages teacher.

In the same way as employing schools have a duty of care for their teachers, so ITE providers and their partnership schools must ensure that beginning teachers are equipped and supported in their work with young people. In spite of frequent discussions about teacher well-being, there is a lack of agreed definition, perhaps due to the many factors which might affect a teacher (Dodge et al., 2012; Fox et al., 2023) (Task 13.2).

> ### Task 13.2 A reflective and pro-active approach to well-being
>
> Make a list of factors which might have a negative effect on the well-being of a beginning languages teacher. You might like to discuss with others in your department who will also be working with your mentee. It might also be useful to ask your mentee to make a list and compare notes.
>    For example:
>
> - Less secure subject knowledge in one language
> - Underdeveloped understanding of the academic literature around second language acquisition
> - Lack of familiarity with UK school system if beginning teacher grew up elsewhere
> - Long commute to placement school
> - Lack of confidence in how to correct errors in pupils' written work
> - Huge amount of time spent on lesson planning
> - Contradictory lesson feedback from teachers across the department
> - 'Temporary' nature of an ITE school placement
> - Uncertainty about how to challenge negative/xenophobic discourses around the value of language learning from pupils/parents/colleagues?
>
> Which variables are within your control or sphere of influence as mentor? Are there variables which you cannot influence or which lie beyond your responsibilities as mentor?
>    Now make a list of factors which might have a positive effect on the well-being of a beginning languages teacher. As you read the rest of the chapter, you will hopefully be able to add to this 'protective factor' list.

Viac and Fraser (2020) identify four key components of teachers' occupational well-being:

- cognitive well-being e.g. knowledge and skills, decision making and problem-solving abilities, levels of resilience
- subjective well-being e.g. feelings of self-efficacy, sense of job satisfaction and purpose
- mental and physical well-being e.g. symptoms of stress and tiredness
- social well-being e.g. quality of professional relationships, support from mentor, ability to manage challenging situations with pupils, communities of practice (see Chapter 6 in this volume) (Task 13.3).

> ### Task 13.3 Components of teacher well-being
>
> Based on Viac and Fraser's components of teacher well-being, read back through the list of factors you identified in the previous task. Are all four components represented? Where might additional attention be needed?

The extent to which our cognitive, subjective, physical, mental, and social well-being are held in equilibrium as teachers will have a significant impact on our sense of professional satisfaction. Where there is inconsistency or lack of cohesion in one aspect, there is a potential challenge for well-being. For example, working conditions are often cited as a key factor in teacher stress, not least as they might lead to an unwelcome loss of autonomy and agency (Gordon, 2023).

Many mentors have extensive skills in supporting the emotional well-being of their mentees, knowing precisely when to offer a cup of tea and a chat for example, but it is worth pausing for a moment to consider the aspects of cognitive well-being in a little more detail. The mentor's role in this regard is to encourage professional dialogue so that the mentee gains confidence in engaging with pedagogical issues, wrestling with complex issues such as effective questioning in the target language or managing challenging pupil behaviour, and helping the mentee to reflect deeply (see Chapter 3) on the relationship between theory and practice and its impact on their own teaching. For the mentor, this will require a willingness to engage with the literature and current debates in the languages world, as well as a commitment to knowing the academic requirements of the mentee's ITE programme. A focus on the cognitive well-being of the beginning languages teacher will minimise the risk of a mentoring relationship with a reductionist tick-box approach to weekly tasks and favour instead a longer-lasting, fruitful focus on professional identity and growth.

## Challenges and protective factors

In the opening activity, you reflected on some of the variables which may pose a challenge to the well-being of a beginning languages teachers. Although there appears to be a desire to address some of the issues at a policy level, the impact of such initiatives is less clear and a key role of mentors must be to develop protective factors with their mentee. As Furlong and Maynard stated many years ago: 'the quality of the next generation of teachers will, in large part, depend on the quality of the mentoring they are given' (1995, p. 195).

There are occasions when the beginning languages teacher may become overwhelmed by professional and personal issues which will inevitably have a negative impact on their progress and efficacy as beginning teachers. In this situation, it is important to acknowledge that you are not expected to solve all the problems that arise when working with a mentee; the mentor's role involves enlisting the support of other colleagues as appropriate or it may be simply to listen and signpost the mentee to other sources of external support e.g. the charity, Education Support: https://www.educationsupport.org.uk/. Ultimately, taking responsibility for well-being and workload lies in the hands of the beginning teacher, but the mentor plays a vital role in establishing positive patterns at the start of the professional journey (Black et al., 2017). If you feel overwhelmed at any stage in your work with the mentee, you should also seek support from others, including the ITE provider where appropriate. The role of mentor can be challenging on occasions, and you are not expected to manage the situation alone. Your well-being and workload matter, too!

Having considered some of the literature and policy context around teacher well-being, we will now move to focus on the practice of working with a beginning languages teacher in the school practice context. Above all, the emphasis must be on establishing good habits early, laying secure foundations for workload and well-being to promote a long and enjoyable career as a languages teacher. In their work with mentors, developing so-called protective factors may be the key to success and a long career for beginning languages teachers. Protective factors are simply characteristics or strategies associated with a lower likelihood of a negative outcome or, expressed another way, more likelihood of positive and successful outcomes. A simple example to illustrate the point might be the mentor who encourages the beginning teacher to get a good night's sleep rather than lesson planning late into the night. Even with a less developed plan, the quality of teaching is likely to be higher from a teacher who is well rested and alert.

In the next sections of this chapter, an experienced mentor shares valuable insights into the role of working with beginning teachers over many years.

## Mentoring and managing well-being – reflections of an experienced mentor

You have been paired with a beginning teacher in your languages department. There is often an apprehension in mentoring beginning teachers: Will they be any good? Will they manage the workload? The behaviour? Will they fit in? School leaders may have agreed the placement with you or maybe you have been told you are mentoring a beginning teacher without much input on the decision. In some instances, you may have interviewed the beginning teacher yourself and watched them teach already, as may be the case for specific routes into teaching such as school-centred initial teacher training (SCITT) or apprenticeship options. In other cases you may have just been told that the new beginning teacher is coming, and you do not yet know much about them.

Mentoring a trainee in languages has the potential to add value beyond bringing new ideas to your department and an extra linguist to work with your pupils. Generally speaking, beginning teachers in languages have not only committed to learn about languages and culture and developed cognitive empathy along the way, but they have often lived abroad or are native speakers. This adds an extra layer of resilience and self-management – key components of well-being – which is always helpful. Although these attributes may be an asset for some, it may also come with some difficulties in adapting to a new education system for the native speakers or international pupils (see Chapter 14).

There is, after all, alarming research published in 2018 by the DfE showing that the percentage of teachers still in service after five years post training was the lowest in languages, with 56% compared to data close to 70% in Art, Design, or Music and 75% in Physical Education. Although new policy documents discussed earlier in this chapter are designed to support beginning teachers with their ongoing development and retention, mentors have a vital role to play in nurturing the resilience and the healthy workload habits of beginning teachers during their placement in our care.

The most important thing is to recognise that your experience and expertise as a mentor will not only enrich the career of a beginning teacher of languages (and each one is much needed in our current education climate) but will probably enrich your whole team and of course the learning experience of the pupils in your setting as your trainee develops their own skills and expertise throughout their placement in your department. Put simply, there is the potential to enhance the well-being of everyone in the school setting when working effectively with beginning teachers.

## The mentor's role: whose responsibility is it anyway?

Whether they come from Core PGCE training, SCITT, or Apprenticeship routes, beginning teachers will benefit from working with a range of teachers in the department and it is never the sole responsibility of the mentor to support them in their practice. The role of the mentor will be to meet with the beginning teacher weekly, reviewing progress, and setting SMART (specific, measurable, achievable, realistic, and timed) targets through each phase of their development. However, it is important to remember that the more exposure to expert teaching a beginning teacher will have, the wider the range of pedagogical skills they will gain. It is therefore important to allow beginning teachers to observe and take on lessons of other expert colleagues in the department where possible in order to forge their own teaching identity but also find different approaches. This approach will also afford opportunities for the beginning teacher to discuss workload and well-being with a range of colleagues.

A skilled mentor reflects back on her initial teacher education experience:

> I remember myself as a PGCE student being full of admiration for my mentor who had the ability not only to engage his classes in a full-on sing-along of the endings of the imperfect tense, accompanied with his acoustic guitar which was always at his side, but also make jokes in French which all students enjoyed and took part in using target language! My goal was to become as good as him.

The mentor identifies two slight shortcomings that prevented her from rising to this challenge – an inability to sing, and no instrumental skills other than playing the maracas and the recorder! The well-being of the beginning teacher, a French native speaker, was further challenged by her relative youth, just four of five years older than some of the sixth form pupils. This made the mentor a tough act to follow.

Thankfully, the mentor allowed the beginning teacher to work closely with other young female teachers who enabled her to find her place and identity in the classroom that did not require a guitar to encourage pupils to conjugate verbs. The beginning teacher learnt to develop behaviour management skills, a confident presence in the classroom and pedagogical skills teaching the classes of four or five different teachers, including those of the mentor. Working closely with another native female teacher helped the beginning teacher to develop greater understanding of phonics and grammar but also behaviour management dealing with older male pupils. Supporting the Drama department in clubs at lunch time taught the beginning teacher to project her voice and bring more creativity into her teaching practice. Two decades later, the beginning teacher, now an experienced mentor, is still to learn how to play the guitar, and remembers in awe her first mentor. She says: 'Teaching conjugations while playing the guitar remains my ultimate teacher goal! Maybe one day…'.

The anecdote above highlights the importance of building supportive relationships with colleagues, the wider department, and the whole school professional learning communities. Beginning teachers may also benefit from working closely with expert colleagues in the special educational needs and disability (SEND) team, supporting pupils with SEND in lessons, being a teaching assistant or helping with reading for pupils with low reading ages. This will help develop cognitive empathy for pupils who struggle to decode phonics or with the pupils who can decode but struggle with reading comprehension in English. Working closely with the SEND co-ordinator will help the beginning teacher to develop strategies to support pupils with learning difficulties in their own practice. For international beginning teachers, it is even more important to involve them in working with a range of colleagues to help them develop their understanding of the education system. This will include consistency in expectations, routines and structures across different members of the school community where they may need to adapt what they have experienced in schools in another country. Building a community of practice around beginning teachers helps to nurture their professional understanding and well-being as they feel better equipped to manage teaching and learning in their classrooms. Taking this approach also enhances the well-being of the mentor who does not have to manage the important task of mentoring alone.

Mentoring and nurturing beginning teachers is a collective responsibility, and the mentor's role in this case is to develop their leadership skills working in partnerships with colleagues in the department but also across the school community and beyond. The mentor cannot solve everything but can unlock potential through developing professional links (Task 13.4).

### Task 13.4 Support for role as mentor

Who in my department or in our school community can support me and my role as a mentor to benefit the development of beginning teachers?

Think about conversations you may have with:

- The Professional Coordinator and/or Lead Mentor
- Expert colleagues
- Wider school professional communities

## Managing workload for myself as a mentor and for the beginning teacher

It can feel as though many plates are spinning all at once for you as a mentor and also for the beginning teachers who are not only planning lessons (often taking hours!), but also writing reflective journals, conducting action research tasks and writing academic assignments, as well as collecting evidence for their portfolios and completing multiple documents for their ITE provider.

There are areas of ITE provision that cannot be avoided or rushed; all too often, 'it is what it is' becomes the common phrase when responding to beginning teachers who are feeling overwhelmed. However, this need not be the case if we focus on important areas outlined below where we can work more efficiently and avoid unnecessary workload.

### Planning lessons

Almost every teacher will recognise the challenge of lesson planning in the early stages of a teaching career. Perhaps you remember spending three hours planning a year 7 lesson on pets or family, finding resources and attractive pictures to drill the vocabulary, searching for the right listening activity, creating a gap fill task, designing extension work, making the PowerPoint etc.? From a teacher well-being perspective, this approach is not sustainable.

162  *Mentoring Languages Teachers in the Secondary School*

The reality is that beginning teachers should use a school's schemes of work and shared resources, but part of their training is to plan sequences of lessons themselves so that they understand the logical progression of the components for the pupils to make progress over time (Black et al., 2017). Learning how to plan lessons is part and parcel of the ITE course, however there are ways we can make things simpler and quicker. The Language Show online seminar on YouTube (see Further Reading and Resources) may provide more help but here are the headlines of useful strategies which build the protective factors for the beginning teacher:

- Step 1: Ask the beginning teacher to create a template slide deck aligned with your department or school's teaching and learning expectations. This is likely to be a maximum of six or seven slides with the key activities such as the DO NOW or STARTER, the main activities in target language (leemos, escuchamos, escribimos, hablamos...) with dual coding, extension boxes, and support boxes. The slides can even have a timer on them if necessary, and may include a plenary and homework slide, depending on your department's practice.
- Step 2: Ensure that the beginning teacher uses the prepared slide template every time as this will save them having to create a new slide deck every time. It will also help them to align with routines, and expectations of the department.
- Step 3: Encourage the beginning teachers to save all their lesson plans/PowerPoints in a shared area which you and other colleagues can access remotely. Careful labelling of their folders (e.g.: Year 7 French: 1.1, 1.2, 1.3, etc.) will allow you and your team to check lessons in advance on demand, as well as amend and comment on them 'live'. When the beginning teacher leaves the school, the department has an extra bank of co-created resources, too.
- Step 4: Share top tips to help the beginning teacher to organise their planning:
  - Plan the next lessons as soon as possible after the previous class; key learning and next steps will be fresh in their minds.
  - Discourage the beginning teacher from saving plans on their own laptop and sending you PowerPoints by email. There is a danger of ending up with multiple and slightly different versions and the wrong one being presented to the pupils. Using a cloud-based shared drive for better collaborative work with your beginning teacher and your department will minimise risks in this regard.
  - Guide them on how to organise their sequence of lesson plans in folders.
  - Help them use a teacher planner, showing them how to use it by writing what they will do (e.g. marking, planning year 12 lesson) in their non-teaching time, etc.
  - Allow beginning teachers to go home early when they need to, especially if they have a long commute and they run clubs for you on certain days. They will thank you for it! (Task 13.5)

### Task 13.5 Top tips for lesson planning

Discuss top tips for efficient lesson planning as a department and collate 'top tips' for beginning teachers. As they grow in confidence, encourage the beginning teachers to add their own reflections and ideas for the next beginning teacher to join the department.

## Marking and feedback for learning

As teacher workload has become one of the key areas of the OFSTED inspection framework, marking and effective feedback are key to be 'meaningful, motivating and manageable' (DfE, 2016, p.8). Mentors need to think about how to develop this practice with beginning teachers by allowing them to experience marking and making effective use of assessments to inform their teaching.

We know from research (Collin & Quigley, n.d.) that careful feedback is powerful for pupils to make progress. We also know that well-crafted verbal feedback is as valuable as written feedback (University College London, 2019), hence the importance of developing effective questioning practice and live feedback. Therefore, enabling beginning teachers to use self or peer assessments effectively, to deploy meaningful questioning strategies and live marking using sampling, visualisers, or mini white boards, will help to reduce workload. Encouraging beginning teachers to circulate around the classroom and look at books at granular level will allow them to mark writing pieces, homework, and check for misconceptions 'on the go' in the classroom, reducing the need to have marathon marking sessions at home for example. This, of course, needs to be aligned to the school policy, but live marking and live feedback encourages beginning teachers to pay more attention in lessons to the quality of the work produced by the pupils. It allows real-time opportunities to address spelling or grammar misconceptions to avoid pupils developing bad habits.

Tests and assessments may be shared with beginning teachers and moderated with the class teachers, for example marking a few together and then splitting the class 50/50 for marking before swapping a few tests afterwards to moderate and see if the beginning teacher has applied the mark schemes correctly. This approach enhances the protective factors for the beginning teacher as they develop confidence and cuts the workload of the teacher and the beginning teacher, as well as building professional confidence in the important area of assessment and feedback. The class teacher is also able to maintain and overview of the progress of the class, while the beginning teacher gains experience in applying mark schemes, and the moderation allows for professional conversations planning future lessons. Overall, it is a win-win for everyone.

## Managing the administrative aspects of mentoring

Ideally, the regular mentor meeting with the beginning teacher should be allocated in the mentor's timetable. However, in spite of a payment to schools for working with a beginning teacher, this protected time allocation is not always the case, and it can sometimes be difficult to find a common time. Current ITE policy (DfE, 2024b) states that beginning teachers are entitled to 1.5 hours of mentoring a week. It is therefore important that mentors check with their Senior Leadership Team in their school that they have been allocated the time on their timetable to undertake this important role.

Being efficient and avoiding duplication is key to managing workload for both the mentor and the beginning teacher. For example, identifying who will take notes of discussion and targets for weekly meeting record sheets is essential.

The mentor should encourage beginning teachers to allocate a specific time in their week to complete their ITE course administrative tasks, taking care to ensure that time in school should be directed towards observing, planning or teaching. Some beginning teachers need very clear guidance on how to manage their time and this is considered in one of the scenarios in Chapter 14.

## Additional support

When necessary, additional support plans are useful to help a struggling beginning teacher to get back on track. As we will see in the case study scenarios (Chapter 14), support plans can be extremely helpful when the targets are very specific, and the timetable is adjusted to allow the trainee to address issues with their progress. This might include paired teaching with the class teacher, reducing timetable before gradually re-building to the expected allocation, and allocating some teaching for parallel classes so that the beginning teacher can re-use lesson plans and resources in a new (but similar) context.

When support plans are necessary, it is important to communicate the rationale in a timely manner with the beginning teacher, the lead mentor and the ITE provider to make sure there is transparency about the process. The beginning teacher needs to understand that the support plan is designed to help them, and it is not a punishment. When a support plan is in place, it is vital to share it with the team of expert colleagues who will work with the beginning teacher in order to support them fully. Collective responsibility is essential so that a consistent approach supports the trainee to get back on track as soon as possible.

## Conclusion

There have been great strides in the study of teacher well-being over recent years. This chapter has shone a spotlight on the challenges of defining well-being as so many complex factors are involved – individually and at a wider organisational and systemic level – but we know that well-being matters for the beginning languages teacher. With the annual Language Trends reports, published by the British Council, highlighting the challenges for languages nationally, more than ever we need beginning teachers to survive and thrive in the profession (Margolis et al., 2014). Working with the mentor, nurturing a strong teacher identity and a range of protective coping strategies, including managing high workload, will be helpful as the beginning languages teacher navigates the inevitable challenges and joys of a teaching career. Negative effects on teacher well-being are well documented, such as increased stress, anxiety and workload, but Wang et al.'s (2015) study also found that teachers who have access to supportive learning environments and mentors reported higher levels of well-being.

As this chapter draws to a close, it is important to remember that more robust research is needed to monitor and evaluate the impact of well-being initiatives and factors associated with burnout and retention in the profession. Such research has the potential to inform policy and practice over time. However, mentors play a valuable role in working with beginning languages teachers to minimise negative factors and to cultivate 'positive aspects of teaching and school life' (Fox et al., 2023, p. 4194).

As individual mentors and mentees, we are part of a wider system of education with institutional variations, some of which are within our control and some without our control. Ultimately, mentors will do their best to nurture the so-called protective factors and support the development needs of the beginning teachers in their care, including a genuine concern for managing their well-being and workload. One beginning teacher noted the importance of her mentor in a haiku poem, cited by Gordon (2023, p. 158), which clearly illustrates the need to be on the rollercoaster ride together:

> Tired, tears and doubt.
> 'You can do it', mentor said.
> Self-belief, vital.

## For discussion

- What or who helped you to build resilience and well-being in your early career and training?
- What can you do to support and grow your mentee's well-being, including their ability to manage workload?
- What are the strengths or potential of your beginning teacher? Always build on the positives!
- How can you help beginning teachers to grow in their career as a languages teacher and potential future leader?

## Further reading

Department for Education. (2021). The Education Staff Wellbeing Charter. https://assets.publishing.service.gov.uk/media/6194eb37d3bf7f0551f2d1a5/DfE_Education_Workforce_Welbeing_Charter_Nov21.pdf

Department for Education. (2018). Addressing Workload in Initial Teacher Education. https://www.gov.uk/government/publications/addressing-workload-in-initial-teacher-education-ite

Education Support – The only UK charity dedicated to supporting the mental health and wellbeing of teachers and education staff in schools, colleges and universities. https://educationsupport.org.uk

Language Show Webinar "Surviving Your PGCE and ECT in MFL" Juliette Claro https://www.youtube.com/watch?v=E7z2rDwOOng

## References

Acton, R., & Glasgow, P. (2015). Teacher wellbeing in neoliberal contexts: A review of the literature. *Australian Journal of Teacher Education*, 40(8), 99–114.

Allen, R., & Sims, S. (2018). *The teacher gap*. Abingdon.

Black, L., Gordon, A. L., Hughes, C., MacArthur, R., & Sandy, S. (2017). *Effective mentoring of trainee teachers*. Association for Language Learning.

Briner, R., & Dewberry, C. (2007). *Staff wellbeing is key to school success*. Worklife Support Ltd.

Collin, J., & Quigley, A. (n.d.). *Teacher feedback to improve pupil learning – Guidance report*. Education Endowment Foundation (EEF).

Department for Education. (2016). *Eliminating unnecessary workload around marking*. https://assets.publishing.service.gov.uk/media/5a75129f40f0b6360e47322f/Eliminating-unnecessary-workload-around-marking.pdf

Department for Education. (2019a). *ITT core content framework*. DfE.

Department for Education. (2019b). *Early career framework*. DfE.

Department for Education, I. (2024a). Initial teacher training and early career framework (ITTECF). https://www.gov.uk/government/publications/initial-teacher-training-and-early-career-framework

Department for Education. (2024b). Initial teacher training (ITT): Criteria and supporting advice. Statutory guidance for accredited ITT providers. Academic year 2024/25. https://www.gov.uk/government/publications/initial-teacher-training-criteria

Dodge, R., Daly, A., Huyton, J., & Sanders, L. (2012). The challenge of defining wellbeing. *International Journal of Wellbeing, 2*(3), 222-235.

Fox, H., Walter, H., & Ball, K. (2023). Methods used to evaluate teacher well-being: A systematic review. *Psychology in Schools, 60*(10), 4177-4198.

Furlong, J., & Maynard, T. (1995). *Mentoring student teachers*. Routledge.

Gordon, A. L. (2020). Educate-mentor-nurture: Improving the transition from initial teacher education to qualified teacher status and beyond. *Journal of Education for Teaching, 46*(5), 664-675.

Gordon, A. L., (2023). Early career teaching and resilience. In R. J. Tierney, F. Rizvi, K. Erkican (Eds.), *International encyclopedia of education* (vol. 5, pp. 153-160). Elsevier.

Gu, Q., & Day, C. (2013). Challenges to teacher resilience: Conditions count. *British Educational Research Journal, 39*(1), 22-44.

Hascher, T., & Waber, J. (2021). Teacher well-being: A systematic review of the research literature from the year 2000-2019. *Educational Research Review, 34*, 100411. https://doi.org/10.1016/j.edurev.2021.100411

Department for Education (2016). Eliminating unnecessary workload around marking. Independent Teacher Workload Review Group, Department for Education.

Johnson, B., Down, B., Le Cornu, R., Peters, J., Sullivan, A., Pearce, J., & Hunter, J. (2014). Promoting early career teacher resilience: A framework for understanding and acting. *Teachers and Teaching: Theory and Practice, 20*(5), 530-546.

Jones, J., & Gordon, A. L. (2019). *MFL teachers who flourish: MFL teachers who choose to stay*. Association for Language Learning.

Margolis, J., Hodge, A., & Alexandrou, A. (2014). The teacher educator's role in promoting institutional versus individual teacher wellbeing. *Journal of Education for Teaching, 40*(4), 391-408.

McCallum, F., & Price, D. (2010). Well teachers, well students. *Journal of Student Wellbeing, 4*(1), 19-34.

Thompson, S., Clarke, E., Quickfall, A., & Glazzard, J. (2020). Averting the crisis in trainee teacher well-being – Learning lessons across European contexts: A comparative study. *Journal of Comparative & International Higher Education, 12*, 38-56.

Turner, S., & Braine, M. (2016). Embedding wellbeing knowledge and practice into teacher education: Building emotional resilience. *Teacher Education Advancement Network Journal, 8*(1), 67-82.

UCL Access and Widening Participation Office. (2019). *UCL verbal feedback project report 2019*. UCL.

United Nations Educational, Scientific and Cultural Organization. (2017). *Moving forward the 2030 agenda for sustainable development*. UNESCO. https://unesdoc.unesco.org/ark:/48223/pf0000247785

Viac, C., & Fraser, P. (OECD) (2020). *Teachers' wellbeing: A framework for data collection and analysis*, OECD Working Paper No. 213, OECD Publishing, Paris.

Wang, H., Hall, N. C., & Rahimi, S. (2015). Self-efficacy and causal attributions in teachers: Effects on burnout, job satisfaction, illness, and quitting intentions. *Teaching and Teacher Education, 47*, 120-130.

# 14 Supporting a beginning languages teacher who is struggling: a range of scenarios*

*Kathryn Broom, Juliette Claro, Adam Lamb, Lisa Panford, Sallie Roberts-Crystal, and Maud Waret*

## Objectives

At the end of this chapter, you should be able to:

- Understand the mentor's role in supporting a beginning languages teacher who is struggling
- Have an awareness of a range of scenarios where a beginning languages teacher might struggle
- Understand possible support mechanisms to encourage a beginning teacher to make expected progress
- Consider how to adapt and apply the approaches described in your own practice

## Introduction

Learning to teach can be a challenge on occasions. However motivated a beginning teacher might be, there are likely to be moments of discomfort, a need to un-learn previous experiences, challenging situations which lead to anxiety, de-motivation and even fear. Some of the challenges might be generic (managing pupil behaviour, for example) and other challenges may be more subject-specific (such as weak subject knowledge). Before reading further, undertake Task 14.1.

---

### Task 14.1 Potential struggles

Why might a beginning languages teacher struggle on occasions? Drawing on your own experience as a teacher and mentor, as well as discussions with colleagues, make a list of possible scenarios. You will return to this list towards the end of the chapter.

For example:

- Lesson planning is too slow so insufficient time for marking etc.
- Clarity of instructions for pupils needs attention.

---

*This chapter has been 'crowd-sourced' by the co-editors from the languages community, including among members of the Association for Language Learning.

## Identifying the concern

You will probably have drawn up quite a list in Task 14.1. As a mentor, your role is to identify concerns in a timely manner through scrutiny of lesson plans, observation of lessons, discussion with other colleagues who are also working closely with the beginning teacher and so on. Once a potential concern has been identified, a clear process of support must be put in place, including an exploration of the cause of the problem, development of a support plan and involvement of other colleagues where appropriate. Other chapters in this book are a source of guidance in this regard.

## Consideration of scenarios

It is relatively easy to identify concerns with a beginning languages teacher who is struggling, but it can be more challenging to get to the root cause of the issue and even harder to support the beginning teacher in moving towards improvement. The rest of the chapter outlines a range of scenarios for consideration.

### *Scenario 1*

A beginning teacher is struggling to build positive relationships in school, both with colleagues and with pupils. Everyone in the languages department has been very kind and encouraging of the beginning teacher, and pupils have been 'sympathetic' to their beginning teachers, but patience begins to wear thin six weeks into the placement when there is still no tangible progress in the beginning teacher's ability to build positive relationships (Task 14.2).

---

**Task 14.2 Building positive relationships**

Before reading on, reflect on these questions:

What factors might you need to consider as a mentor in this scenario?
What approach might be helpful in supporting the beginning languages teacher to make progress?

---

Beginning teachers come into the profession with diverse personalities and life experiences. Some beginning teachers may be very shy (perhaps the case in this scenario) and others may be overconfident (as discussed in a later scenario). Some may have experience of working with large numbers of different people, such as in a school context, whereas others may have been working in a more solitary role, perhaps as a freelance translator for example. Getting to know the beginning teacher well, in a non-judgemental way, is a vital starting point for any mentoring relationship. This will act as the springboard for small but helpful steps to supporting the beginning teacher to build relationships which are at the heart of the teaching profession.

A few simple suggestions for helping the beginning teacher build relationships with colleagues:

- Spend time in a mentor meeting with the beginning teacher to discuss the difference between professional relationships and friendships
- Encourage the beginning teacher to make an effort to greet colleagues (teachers, caretaker, etc.) each morning in a positive way
- Suggest that the beginning teacher offers to help colleagues, perhaps with some photocopying or collecting textbooks from another classroom
- Remind the beginning teacher of the importance of thanking colleagues, for their detailed feedback or for sharing useful resources for teaching for example
- Include the beginning teacher in social activities e.g. Friday staff football, as a way to become more involved
- Encourage colleagues to focus on the positive aspects of the beginning teacher's work, celebrating successes however small with a clear explanation of why the work was successful – key steps to building confidence
- As the mentor, ensure that you exude warmth and genuine concern for the beginning teacher, checking in with them formally and informally throughout the week. Even a small phrase like 'I am looking forward to our mentoring meeting later today' may make a big difference to how a beginning teacher feels about their progress.

A few simple suggestions for helping the beginning teacher build relationships with pupils:

- Spend time in a mentor meeting with the beginning teacher to discuss the importance of professional boundaries, combined with showing an interest in the learners as people
- Encourage the beginning teacher to set clear ground rules for the classroom ... and then stick to them in a firm and fair way. Easier said than done on occasions!
- Arrange for the beginning teacher to observe a wide range of teachers across the school to observe the many different ways in which positive relationships are established between the teacher and learners
- If the beginning teacher is shy or anxious, then time invested in team teaching is worthwhile as you are able to model good practice and gradually increase expectations for involvement by the beginning teacher
- Seek opportunities for the beginning teacher to become more involved in wider school life e.g. helping with props for the drama production, assisting with Duke of Edinburgh activities

## Scenario 2

A beginning teacher is struggling to move on from the very traditional and high attaining (grammar school) way they had learnt languages themselves. They find it hard to engage with a more interactive approach and therefore find classroom management and motivational factors challenging. Their mentors are also struggling with a feeling that they were deliberately not taking on board their feedback (Task 14.3).

> **Task 14.3 Adjusting to school context**
>
> Before reading on, reflect on these questions:
>
> What factors might you need to consider as a mentor in this scenario?
> What approach might be helpful in supporting the beginning languages teacher to make progress?

This scenario is one where the mentor's impressions can contrast significantly with the beginning teacher's views of the same situation. The mentor may realise that, in times of stress, the beginning teacher tends to revert to their pre-conceived idea of how languages should be taught. Of course, their idea was based on their own successful experience as a language learner. This echoes Lortie's (1975) apprenticeship of observation, noting that most teachers have been learners with multiple experiences of a range of teachers. Most beginning languages teachers have been a successful language learner and may find it hard to put themselves into the shoes of learners who did not find languages so easy or enjoyable.

1. It can take time to explore different perceptions and sensitivity is needed. The issue here centres around a mismatch in perceptions between the beginning teacher and the mentor. An experienced practitioner shares a possible plan of action in a situation like this which might include building an understanding of one another's background and context. The beginning teacher and mentor are encouraged to discuss their beliefs and values about effective languages teaching and where these came from. This kind of discussion might benefit from a different setting, for example locating the mentor meeting with a coffee at a local cafe (assuming that school leaders are happy to support this idea, of course). The reason for a different location is simple – it takes the conversation away from the paperwork, lesson planning, logistics, etc. and allows the mentor and beginning teacher to frame the conversation in a different way.
2. Sensitive discussions might lead to a realisation that the beginning teacher is not good at taking notes from lesson feedback and often forgets to implement feedback that they were given or even misunderstands the main focus of this feedback. In the scenario above, this came across as the beginning teacher deliberately ignoring feedback. With guidance, the beginning teacher is set a target to make concise bullet point notes during each informal or formal lesson feedback and double check with the observer to make sure that they have understood the feedback given.
3. A 'student voice' task might be a useful way to give the beginning teacher opportunities to ask the learners about how they learned, what kind of activities they found engaging, helpful, difficult, etc.
4. A particularly effective intervention might be to give the beginning teacher two parallel classes. With one of the classes, they would be responsible for leading and, for the other class, they would have the opportunity to observe/team teach. The two groups are at the

same point in the scheme of work and this allows for some useful opportunities for the beginning teacher to observe a lesson being taught by an experienced teacher and then teach the same content with a similar group or vice versa. The beginning teacher can be encouraged to reflect on the differences in approach, for example when introducing new vocabulary, and identify which approach had the most impact on pupil learning.
5. Another possible approach would be to film all or part of a lesson with the beginning teacher as the basis for post-lesson discussion.

## Scenario 3

The beginning languages teacher is newly arrived from France where they excelled academically and gained some limited work experience in their old secondary school before moving to the United Kingdom. They are struggling to settle – personally and professionally. They seem somewhat bewildered by educational jargon (CCF, ECF, etc.) and, on occasions, are outspoken about how 'bad' the pupils are at French for their age. The beginning teacher is also struggling to understand the importance of the non-French teaching aspects of their role, such as being a pastoral tutor (Task 14.4).

---

**Task 14.4 Adapting to UK school context**

Before reading on, reflect on these questions:

What factors might you need to consider as a mentor in this scenario?
What approach might be helpful in supporting the beginning languages teacher to make progress?

---

In the United Kingdom, schools benefit from beginning languages teachers from all over the world with a variety of backgrounds who add rich cultural and linguistic diversity to the community. Experienced mentors may take their school context and the educational system for granted, and so there may be several reasons why international beginning teachers find it difficult to 'fit in' on occasions. In this scenario, there are so many factors which merit consideration by the mentor. For example:

- Personal situation – homesickness, lack of friends and family as a support network, financial and visa concerns, etc.
- Language barriers – even the most able English speaker may, on occasions, find it challenging to understand colleagues and young people's use of colloquial language, delivered at speed and perhaps in an unfamiliar regional accent
- Cultural differences in teaching approaches – textbook approach versus a more interactive and communicative style of teaching; lack of understanding of some terms e.g. adaptive teaching
- Lack of knowledge of the pastoral role with its focus on safeguarding, Prevent, British values, etc. as well as possible teaching of Personal, Social, and Health Education (PSHE)

- Curriculum and assessment issues – consideration of time allocation for the teaching of languages, optional nature of languages in some schools, as well as variations in examination board specifications
- External factors – inspection (e.g. Ofsted), performance tables etc. may not be fully understood by beginning teachers, especially if less familiar with the UK context

In many ways, a whole school approach is needed to support struggling international teachers as many of the challenges are generic. For example, carefully structured induction – not a 'one off' event, but carefully planned sequence of input over time (Gordon, 2020) – is essential to increase the beginning teacher's understanding of the local and national context.

In the scenario above, frequent conversations about issues as they emerge are essential to understand each other's perspectives, reduce misconceptions and promote an open-minded view to learning to teach. Acknowledging that cultural differences play a significant role in the progress of a beginning teacher from beyond the United Kingdom is an important first step. It may be useful to 'buddy' the beginning teacher with another more experienced international teacher who may be able to empathise with some of the culture shock of learning to teach in a new country.

Other practical strategies to support a struggling international beginning teacher might include:

- Extended opportunities for guided observation and follow-up discussion as part of the 'acclimatisation' process
- More opportunities for carefully planned team teaching as part of the learning journey for the beginning teacher, where the more experienced teacher is able to model and explain the rationale for practice
- Time with a pastoral expert outside the languages department who will take the time to explain important issues e.g. County Lines, attendance monitoring, risk assessments
- If the beginning teacher is attached to a university, a conversation between mentor and tutor may identify additional sources of support for the beginning teacher e.g. University professional and pupil services

### Scenario 4

The beginning teacher loves their placement school and is enjoying the excitement of a new career after a few years of travelling since leaving university. They have a strong classroom presence and use humour to good effect to engage pupils. They are popular with colleagues and pupils. Although they appeared to be taking on advice given by their mentor and other colleagues, it soon became clear that this was not the case. The beginning teacher's lack of organisational skills appeared to be the root of the issue (Task 14.5).

### Task 14.5 Poor organisation

Before reading on, reflect on these questions:

What factors might you need to consider as a mentor in this scenario?
What approach might be helpful in supporting the beginning languages teacher to make progress?

When a beginning teacher struggles with organisation, there may be many reasons. For example, the home life of the beginning teacher may be chaotic – perhaps the beginning teacher is even 'sofa surfing' to make ends meet? The beginning teacher may have positive relationships with colleagues and pupils but this is never a substitute for careful lesson planning and meticulous feedback. Some beginning teachers take much longer than others to grasp the nuances inherent in lesson planning, resource creation, marking and feedback, and so on. Beginning teachers have often been successful at school themselves and are keen to 'please' their new colleagues which may lead to a reluctance to admit that they have not fully understood feedback for example.

Possible actions might include:

- A carefully planned observation schedule to focus on organisational aspects of teaching in particular
- Discussion with mentor about how to make the most effective use of non-teaching time for lesson planning and marking rather than enjoyable chats with colleagues in the staff room
- Requirement for lesson plans and resources to be shared with teachers at least 24 hours in advance to allow time for feedback and adjustments where needed
- Teachers to provide detailed written feedback for the beginning teacher to read and then summarise key action points
- Shadow marking with a more experienced colleague to set expectations clearly
- Meticulous note-taking in mentor meetings with SMART targets each week

## Scenario 5

In spite of induction sessions in the school about the importance of being open-minded while on placement, the beginning teacher is outspoken and quick to judge with opinions on a wide range of matters, including curriculum, assessment, resources, teaching quality, and ability of pupils. This is causing friction within the department and significant tensions in the mentor – beginning teacher relationship (Task 14.6).

### Task 14.6 Overconfident beginning teacher

Before reading on, reflect on these questions:

What factors might you need to consider as a mentor in this scenario?
What approach might be helpful in supporting the beginning languages teacher to make progress?

Beginning teachers come with a huge range of experience – some fresh out of university and some who have had high-flying leadership roles in a previous career. This variety of starting point for the beginning teacher requires sensitivity and a consistent approach by the mentor, including dedicated meeting time, clear communication, and actionable and appropriate targets. Teaching can often feel a time-poor profession but many experienced mentors acknowledge that time is the most precious resource and is usually the key to the good progress of the beginning teachers in their care. Put simply, development takes time, and mentor – beginning teacher relationships are central in this regard.

Possible actions for working with an overconfident beginning teacher:

- All initial teacher education (ITE) providers should have a clear code of conduct and it is essential to establish clear ground rules from the outset. Even in the early stages of working together, the mentor should not hesitate in referring the beginning teacher to the code of conduct when actions might be considered inappropriate.
- Contracting may also be considered a key step in this process. Contracting features in much ITT/ECT provision, whereby the mentor and the beginning teacher meet to discuss the format of mentoring sessions and draw up a set of agreements. Agreeing expectations of one another and rules of engagement are an essential part of the discussion.
- Discussion about the importance of openness and honesty from both parties, including when we make mistakes. In the context of the scenario above, for example, the overconfidence might be an act to mask the beginning teacher's uncertainty as they do not want to be viewed as vulnerable or novice in their new role. When the mentor models being open and honest, it shows a vulnerability, in that the mentor is unlikely to be right all of the time. It is hoped that the beginning teacher is more likely to be vulnerable and open to learning as a result, too.

Table 14.1 provided by an experienced mentor may be useful for mentors and beginning teachers considering their way of working.

If things go wrong in spite of the intentions and processes outlined above, it is important to hold a conversation with the beginning teacher to address any issues. This should be done in a timely manner as, left unchallenged, unresolved issues can create a sentiment of dissonance within a team. This conversation must be carried out tactfully, and it would be wise for the mentor to consult with a more senior colleague in advance for guidance on how best to manage the conversation. Preparation is key and the mentor will need clear and specific examples to hand to illustrate the concerns. Simply saying someone is overconfident can come across as a judgement; having an example, such as criticising or being dismissive to feedback, or citing a specific comment or a reaction, ensures that the discussion is not based on hearsay but on facts.

During the conversation, the mentor must work hard to keep the tone of the meeting positive and solutions-focused. It is important to allow time for the beginning teacher to respond to the concerns expressed, but they should be encouraged to do so in a professional and non-defensive manner. Finally, both parties need to agree on how to move forward – what is going to change, identification of any additional support needs, and a shared understanding of success criteria for progress. Having such conversations is vital to minimise risk of breakdowns in relationships and high levels of friction in teams. They are difficult conversations, but essential for the effectiveness of the team, the beginning teacher and, most importantly, for the pupils in our schools.

*Table 14.1* Ways of working

|  | **Mentor** | **Mentee** |
|---|---|---|
| 1. **Relationship** establishment<br>• How the professional relationship works?<br>• What both parties want to get out of the process?<br>• How do we get to these goals? | Enthusiastic and open about how they are looking forward to working with mentee.<br>Discuss their values – openness, honesty, constructive criticism.<br>Reiterate if their mentee is not happy, to speak up, and be open about why. | Understands that:<br>• they need to communicate and be vulnerable/open to learning.<br>• they should feel appreciated, valued, and supported.<br>• they will receive criticism and that it is not personal, but to improve their effectiveness in the classroom.<br>• they can speak up if the mentoring relationship is not working effectively. |
| 2. **Operations** of the mentor meeting<br>• Time<br>• Location<br>• Place | Clear that meeting is dedicated time for their mentee.<br>Discuss the importance of practicalities e.g. punctuality, prepared paperwork.<br>Discuss the best way to communicate. | Understands that:<br>• this is their undivided time that is set aside for their professional development as a beginning teacher.<br>• they must respect the practical aspects of the meeting to get the most out of sessions.<br>• there is a preferred way for communication to take place. |
| 3. **Expectations** of the meeting<br>• Note-taking<br>• Mobile phones<br>• Engagement | Reiterate that they will be giving undivided attention.<br>They will not have their mobile phone or emails open.<br>They will give their undivided attention to the needs of the beginning teacher. | Understands that:<br>• they should actively engage by taking notes of what their mentor is saying.<br>• they need to be fully present – e.g. no mobile phones.<br>• they should engage fully with activities in the meeting, including deliberate practice if appropriate.<br>• follow up reading and activities to be carried out for appropriate deadlines. |

## Scenario 6

The beginning teacher completed their undergraduate degree in their country of birth, Senegal. Following decades of professional experience in hospitality in the United Kingdom and the completion of an MSc, they chose to train as a languages teacher. They had a successful start to their first school placement, feeling welcomed and supported in the multi-cultural, multi faith, inner-city school which prides itself on its inclusive ethos. The beginning languages teacher was complimented by their mentor for their professional behaviours as well as the positive relationships they had cultivated with her pupils. Problems with progress emerged however, when concerns were raised by their colleagues in relation to subject knowledge. In particular, their language proficiency and grasp of grammar were identified as requiring improvement (Task 14.7).

---

**Task 14.7 Subject knowledge concerns**

Before reading on, reflect on these questions:

What factors might you need to consider as a mentor in this scenario?
What approach might be helpful in supporting the beginning languages teacher to make progress?

---

Subject knowledge can be a challenge of all sorts of reasons, including weaker subject knowledge among beginning languages teachers who may not have benefitted from a year abroad due to the Covid-19 pandemic restrictions for example. Mentors may be understandably concerned by weaker subject knowledge in the beginning languages teacher's second or third language for teaching. Whatever the situation, sensitivity is needed as we seek to nurture the beginning teacher to make necessary progress in all areas of their role.

In this scenario, an experienced languages ITE mentor shared that there was general consensus among colleagues in the department that the phonetic, phonological, lexical, and grammatical differences of the beginning teacher's language were causing considerable confusion to the pupils who had been used to learning 'standard French'. On the other hand, as a native speaker, the beginning languages teacher's proficiency in French could not really be questioned. A plan of action to focus on specific concerns about grammar was agreed:

- The beginning languages teacher identified key grammar teaching points on the school's key stage 3 and 4 curriculum and 'learnt' how these grammar points were presented in textbooks, school resources.
- Their progress in this area was monitored over the next couple of months – with focused observations of their practice and regular review meetings with their mentor and university tutor.
- At the final review meeting, the beginning teacher shared that the additional focus on the grammar points featured in the curriculum had benefited their ability to plan and deliver effective lessons. The beginning teacher was complimented for embracing the process and for their exceptional progress in this area.

Although this might be considered a successful outcome, an alternative view to this scenario might be to problematise the fact that the school colleagues had perceived the beginning teacher's French as inappropriate and requiring intervention. This perspective would also problematise the university tutor's actions which were justified by reference to the statutory frameworks and effectively contributed to the beginning teacher needing to modify their language in order to be perceived as legitimate (Cushing, 2023; Rosa & Flores, 2017). A more adequate and inclusive response would be to appreciate all linguistic varieties, thereby providing space to illuminate the linguistic capital (Yosso, 2005) of our communities of Colour. Mentors who are concerned with anti-racist advancements in our subject domain (including the recruitment and retention of languages teachers of Colour) must remain alert to the many and varied dynamics as they play out in our own institutions/practices, including:

- the privileging of 'Parisian French' (Benaglia & Smith, 2022) and mainland Spanish (Macedo, 2019) within our curricula and our departments which exists in stark contrast with the global context of French and Spanish speakers (Bevan, 2024);
- the pervasive acceptance of terms such as Native Speaker which are associated with white speakers (Benaglia & Smith, 2022; Bevan, 2024);
- the questioning of the expertise and legitimacy of teachers of Colour (Vitanova, 2018) and the requirement of teachers of Colour to modify their language in order to be perceived as legitimate (Cushing, 2023).

In this chapter, we have considered a number of scenarios and potential solutions. Task 14.8 takes you back to your own list which was made at the start of the chapter.

### Task 14.8 Your Scenarios

Refer back to the list of situations that you made in Task 14.1 For each one:

What factors might you need to consider as a mentor in this scenario?
What approach might be helpful in supporting the beginning languages teacher to make progress?
Ideally, share your thinking with a colleague, as a department or, if appropriate, a beginning teacher.

## Conclusion

In this chapter, we have considered a number of scenarios where beginning teachers might be struggling to make the necessary progress. Important principles about the mentor's own openness to learning and trying alternative approaches have emerged throughout. As a mentor, there is an opportunity to learn from every scenario, especially in discussion with other languages colleagues in the department and beyond. Working together, the languages community is strengthened by taking a positive and pro-active approach to challenging scenarios. This requires flexibility and adaptability from the mentor, as well as a consistent focus on ensuring that the beginning teacher makes the required progress so that, in turn, pupils are able to thrive in the languages classroom.

## For discussion

- Which of the scenarios discussed in the chapter most closely resemble your own experiences of mentoring to date? Why might this be?

- How might effective engagement with a range of scenarios over time inform our development as mentors and more broadly as languages teachers?

## Further reading

- Black, L., Gordon, A.L., Hughes, C., MacArthur, R. and Sandy, S. (2017). *Effective mentoring of trainee teachers*. Association for Language Learning.
    This publication also contains some scenarios – problems and solutions – for consideration when working with a beginning languages teacher and may be a useful additional source of guidance to add to the mentor's repertoire.

## References

Benaglia, C., & Smith, M. A. (2022). Multilingual texts and contexts: Inclusive pedagogies in the French foreign language classroom. In S. Bouamer & L. Bourdeau (Eds.), *Diversity and decolonization in French studies: New approaches to teaching* (pp. 17–32). Springer International Publishing.

Bevan, K. (2024). An exploration of student MFL teachers' emerging perceptions of decolonising the MFL curriculum. *Focus on Practice (Wales Journal of Education)*, 1. https://doi.org/10.16922/wje.p6

Cushing, I. (2023). "Miss, can you speak English?": Raciolinguistic ideologies and language oppression in initial teacher education. *British Journal of Sociology of Education*, 44(5), 896-911.

Gordon, A. L. (2020). Educate-mentor-nurture: Improving the transition from initial teacher education to qualified teacher status and beyond. *Journal of Education for Teaching*, 46(5), 664-675.

Lortie, D. (1975). *Schoolteacher: A sociological study*. University of Chicago Press.

Macedo, D., (2019). Rupturing the yoke of colonialism in foreign language education: An introduction. In D. Macedo (Eds.), *Decolonizing foreign language education* (pp. 1–49). Routledge.

Rosa, J., & Flores, N. (2017). Unsettling race and language: Toward a raciolinguistic perspective. *Language in Society*, 46(5), 621-647.

Vitanova, G. (2018). "Just treat me as a teacher!" Mapping language teacher agency through gender, race, and professional discourses. *System*, 79, 28-37.

Yosso, T. J. (2005). Whose culture has capital? A critical race theory discussion of community cultural wealth. *Race Ethnicity and Education*, 8(1), 69-91.

# SECTION 5

# Supporting languages teachers as they progress through later stages of their training and beyond

# 15 Engaging with and in research for classroom practice supporting the beginning languages teacher

*Suzanne Graham*

## Introduction

This chapter considers how mentors can work effectively with their beginning teachers to help them to make their practice more research-informed. It begins by considering the reasons why research-informed practice is desirable. It then goes on to outline and exemplify a set of principles for working with research with your beginning teacher. At the end of this chapter, you should be able to:

- Have a greater understanding of how being research-informed might help your beginning teacher
- Understand some key principles for supporting your beginning teacher to work with research in their practice
- Know some resources to support your beginning teacher in working with research, including where to find research evidence and how to evaluate its claims.

Before reading further, undertake Task 15.1, then read on to compare your thoughts with ours:

---

**Task 15.1 Contribution of research knowledge to teacher development**

Consider the following questions:

- To what extent is your own practice research-informed?
- In what ways might research findings be useful for classroom practice?
- What might be some barriers that make it hard for teachers to engage with research?
- What might be facilitators for engagement with research?

---

It can be hard for a busy teacher to find time to engage with current research, perhaps especially in languages, but working as a mentor provides a wonderful opportunity to do so. Even if research does not feature much or at all in your practice, there are still ways that you can support your beginning teacher in that important area.

## In what ways might research findings be useful for classroom practice?

In order to answer that question, it is useful to consider the place of research in models of initial teacher education (ITE) and indeed in-service teaching across the world. In certain countries, such as Denmark, Finland, Norway, and Sweden, there is quite a heavy emphasis in ITE on gaining research-based knowledge and skills, perhaps more so than is the case in England, although recent reforms to ITE in England, through the core content framework (CCF, Department for Education [DfE], 2019), emphasise more strongly the importance of research. For example, the aim of the CCF is to create a generation of well-trained teachers by embedding 'a "golden thread" of high-quality evidence' (DfE, 2019, p. 5) into their training, including in the early years of their career. This seems to align with the idea that attaching importance to research knowledge in teacher education contributes to high levels of educational attainment in countries such as Finland (Tatto, 2013). The relationship between research and practice is, furthermore, likely to be a reciprocal one: classroom practice can be enhanced through knowledge of research (Parr et al., 2007), and 'research itself can be enriched, through greater insight into the challenges and complexities of educational practice' (Winch et al., 2013, p. 16). Importantly, however, what constitutes 'high quality evidence' (DfE, 2022, p. 5) sounds as if it is beyond dispute, which could be debated, and in any case, it could be argued that all research can and should be viewed with a critical eye. Furthermore, Menter et al. (2010, p. 17) place a strong emphasis on teacher education that develops what they call the 'reflective' or 'transformative' teacher, whereby beginning teachers do not just accept research findings unquestioningly, but rather reflect on what might be most effective in their own particular classrooms and why, use research to transform what goes on in those classrooms, and reflect on the outcomes of any research based principles that they have implemented.

Research-based knowledge can support teachers' ability to make informed pedagogical decisions as well as enhancing their understanding of the learning process (Rankin & Becker, 2006). Contact with research can lead to changes in teachers' beliefs as well as changing their practice, and indeed belief modification may well need to precede practice change (Graham & Santos, 2020). Beginning teachers as well as in-service teachers are very largely influenced by the teaching they have experienced themselves as learners (Lortie, 1975). It may not, however, be particularly helpful to simply teach in the manner that one has experienced oneself either as a learner or an observer during initial training. That may be especially true if the teacher had learner characteristics that are hugely different from the learners they themselves are educating, or the curriculum goals of the setting in which they were educated or trained were very different from those they need to address in their current role. They therefore need more enduring evidence-based principles from which to form decisions. Furthermore, it stands to reason that there needs to be certain modifications in their beliefs about what might be good practice before their practice itself can be modified.

## What might be some barriers to engagement with research?

We thus have some arguments as to why we might want to introduce our beginning teachers to research. Unfortunately we also know that there are barriers to teachers of all kinds engaging with research findings (Marsden & Kasprowicz, 2017). First, research reports can seem inaccessible from a time, location and language perspective: teachers may very simply not have enough time to read about research or to reflect on it, and the style of some research reports can be less than transparent. They may find it difficult to know where and how to access relevant research. Second, the contexts presented in research publications may seem very different from the setting in which the beginning teacher is teaching, leading them to reject the research because they cannot see its relevance for their own classroom. Third, problems can also arise from what we might call result-driven classrooms, where the beginning teacher believes that their prime role is to achieve the best possible examination results; that expectation can be seen as contradictory to incorporating research-based practice (Macaro et al., 2015). Finally, the mistake is often made that it is possible to directly transmit findings from research into practice, and that it is a simple process to do so. Such a view ignores the fact that the research was likely undertaken under quite controlled conditions that may be quite different from those in which the beginning teacher is working. Perhaps the most important point to bear in mind regarding the research-practice relationship is that research cannot provide 'recipes for success' (Macaro et al., 2015, p. 141). Believing it can lead to immediate success is likely to lead to disillusionment. For example, MacDonald et al. (2001) reported that beginning teachers on a pre-service course were found to be intent on that course giving them 'instant panaceas, rigid rules of thumb, clear statements of practice and absolute generalizations' (p. 950). There is the possibility that research findings will be expected to do the same (as is implied, perhaps, by the CCF view of a 'golden thread' of high-quality evidence (DfE, 2019, p. 5). When research evidence is unable to provide instant solutions, teachers may reject it as having nothing useful to contribute to their everyday practice. It is instead more helpful to view research findings as offering 'pedagogic proposals' or 'provisional specifications' (Ellis, 1997, p. 83). In other words, the process needs to be one of 'transformation not transmission' (p. 88). Finally, there is evidence that the imposition of certain ways of teaching on the grounds that they are recommended by research has been shown to run the risk of being counterproductive. Researching teachers in China, Wang and Zhang (2014) argued that implementation of a new curriculum there has been less than successful because it has followed a 'top-down approach by disseminating ideas through "experts" and teacher trainers rather than enabling teachers to take their own initiatives to solve problems at the classroom level' (p. 223).

## What might be facilitators for engagement with research?

For research to be of most use to a beginning teacher, then, they need to be able to transform a finding into something that is appropriate for their particular setting, and to understand and appreciate its relevance for a particular challenge they wish to tackle. The mentor's role is therefore likely to be to help their beginning teacher to extract certain principles from relevant research, then support them in thinking about how the finding might be applied usefully in their particular context, and finally to help them evaluate on how useful the application of the finding in fact was.

In order to illustrate a particular way of proceeding I am going to draw on what we did in the project the Professional Development Consortium in MFL, a collaboration between the Universities of Reading and Oxford and teachers, in which we worked with in-service teachers to help make their practice more research informed. I believe that the principles we used for that work can be extended to mentoring beginning teachers. We argued that research-based teacher development is facilitated if the following happens:

- research findings are presented in an accessible way to teachers, ideally based on studies conducted in contexts similar to their own;
- teachers draw out the relevance of the research for their own contexts;
- teachers see a need for change in their own practice and are given opportunities to reflect on their existing beliefs and practices;
- the initial 'translation' of findings is followed by their 'transformation' by the teachers themselves: i.e. the research is offered as 'provisional specifications' or guiding principles for practice, rather than as 'recipes for success';
- teachers' self-efficacy is developed by allowing them to see similar others successfully implementing the research findings in the classroom (a form of vicarious experience);
- on-going support is given in implementing the research findings themselves (e.g. through peers, external advisors, exemplification materials and collaborative partnerships), offering teachers 'mastery experiences' which further enhance their self-efficacy and seal changes in their beliefs.

(Macaro et al., 2015, p. 141)

In what follows, examples are given of how these might be applied for your work with your beginning teacher. I will however take the above items in a slightly different order, as probably the first step you need to take as a mentor is to help your beginning teacher to identify which aspect of their practice might be most usefully informed by research, and which research could be of the most help.

**Teachers see a need for change in their own practice and are given opportunities to reflect on their existing beliefs and practices.**

The most appropriate starting point for considering which research your beginning teacher might explore is their own practice. For example, are there particular areas where they are experiencing difficulties, or where they feel they need to improve; are there areas of learning that the pupils they are teaching are having the most difficulty with?

Try to begin by helping your beginning teacher to identify language-specific areas that could be targets for exploration. Thus, rather than considering the rather broad area of behaviour management, for example, it might be more sensible to narrow it down to something that could be impacting on behaviour. That might be, for example, language learning engagement or motivation for language learning. Other language specific areas of focus could be particular skills: for example, developing pupils' speaking skills, their reading skills, and their vocabulary knowledge. Therefore, the first step as a mentor is to support your beginning teacher in identifying very precisely which aspects of their practice and or understanding could benefit from possible insights from research.

How might that work in practice? The following might occur: when observing your beginning teacher teach, you noticed that learners were not engaged in the reading activity the beginning teacher set them and they gave up easily. A useful debriefing conversation with your beginning teacher could be to ask them what reasons they could identify for that lack of learner engagement; for instance, was the reading material too difficult? did learners give up because they felt they did not have the necessary reading skills or vocabulary knowledge to make much sense of the text? In other words, did they lack self-efficacy for reading?

Once your beginning teacher has identified one area to investigate (self-efficacy for reading, in this example) it is time to support them in finding appropriate and accessible research, which is our second principle (Task 15.2).

---

**Task 15.2 Planning an initial discussion about research**

Identify an upcoming mentor meeting or classroom observation where you could begin discussions about an area of focus for the beginning teacher's engagement with research.

---

**Research findings are presented in an accessible way to teachers, ideally based on studies conducted in contexts similar to their own.**

These days it is much easier to access free research publications, as UK universities at least have to make the articles their staff write freely available. As a result, one problem might be knowing where to start.

Your beginning teacher's ITE provider has very likely introduced some research in the on-site training sessions it has provided, especially if those sessions are run by or linked to a university provider. Good practice is therefore to ask your beginning teacher in mentor meetings what they have been learning about and to reflect on how they could relate that learning to the needs of their practice. Some providers suggest questions that mentors can pose in mentor meetings to get that sort of conversation started. For example, at the University of Reading, mentors are given what are called 'Mentor Conversations' documents for each placement, consisting of a list of questions that link the discussion back to the core content framework and what has been presented at university. Here is an example that might relate to the beginning teacher's difficulty we are thinking about.

What have you learnt and read about how to develop learners' reading and listening skills alongside their metacognition? Can you use that knowledge to plan a microteach in those areas?

The ITE provider has also probably given beginning teachers reading lists for relevant research. It is a good idea to look at that list with your beginning teacher. Does it give any initial suggestions for research related to the 'problem area' identified? Often it might be helpful to get an overview first of relevant research in that area. There are publications specifically aimed at beginning language teachers that aim to do just that – for example, *Debates in Second Language Education* (Macaro & Woore, 2021). Other overviews can provide an assessment of the 'state of the art' in the field, such as the one provided by Murphy et al. (2020) for the Education Endowment Foundation, that not only looks at research evidence regarding the general benefits of language learning but also at the evidence regarding the effective teaching of MFL. Section 3, *Findings*, provides useful insights into what research says about the effective teaching of vocabulary, grammar and the four skills. Each part of Section 3 ends with a summary of key points of evidence for the skill or knowledge area in question.

The advantage of EEF reviews such as Murphy et al. (2020) is that they are very transparent about the criteria applied for the inclusion of the research they cite, and also take steps to evaluate the strength of the evidence provided by different studies. A very important skill for teachers to develop is how to evaluate the strength of claims made by research studies and indeed by summaries of research evidence. In their discussion of the *Curriculum Research Review for Languages* published by England's Office for Standards in Education (OFSTED, 2021), Woore et al. (2022) highlight the potential danger of presenting claims from research with no or very few supporting citations, and the importance of research reviews outlining in detail exactly how and why certain studies have been included. If beginning teachers read the original research themselves, they should reflect on the methods employed in the research, identifying who was involved (for example, what age were the learners, in what sort of context were they learning), how many learners were being investigated, what sort of evidence was gathered, and to what extent are the conclusions supported by the data gathered. For example, if an article on teacher use of the target language claims that the more the teacher spoke the target language, the greater the impact on learners' own speaking skills, we should probably expect some measure of learners' spoken skills to have been taken, as well as information about how the extent of the teacher's target language use was identified. We would also expect to be told how the data from that measure were analysed, and how the comparisons between teacher target language use and learner data were made. If such details are absent, then we might question the strength of the claims being made.

Where the research is published can also give an indication of its quality. Is it in an international peer-reviewed journal or just part of a blog? Higher quality journals that may contain research relevant to your beginning teacher include *The Language Learning Journal*, *Language Teaching Research*, and *System*, as well as several others. Is it from a research-based organisation, like the EEF? Such publications are a likely indication of quality. Overviews such as Murphy et al. (2020) are a good starting point because they give your beginning teacher a reliable and trustworthy insight into what research has been conducted and what some research-based principles might be for the particular area of practice that they are interested in. They may, however, still be a little inaccessible conceptually and also not give too many details about what was actually done in the studies they include. To get round that, your beginning teacher can turn to a resource that we are fortunate to have in languages education: the Oasis Database, accessible at: https://oasis-database.org. It provides accessible summaries of very relevant and recent research studies, all of which are drawn from peer-reviewed journals.

Your beginning teacher can perform searches in the Oasis database in different ways. Let's assume, by way of example, that as a first step to addressing their problem area, your beginning teacher is interested in finding out more about how to improve reading self-efficacy. They can enter 'self-efficacy' as a search term on the top right-hand corner of the Oasis website and then filter the results by categories, some of which are listed below:

- Language being learned
- Participant type
- Age of learner
- First language of learners

- Proficiency of learners
- Feature being learned
- Of likely interest to
- Country
- Context of language use
- Gender of learners

Typing 'self-efficacy' into the search box gives 354 hits at the time of writing (Figure 15.1), far too many to make much sense of, and also probably including areas that are of little interest to your beginning teacher.

If we refined our search further, by, for example, clicking on 'Area of research', we would get these 354 hits broken down into more useful categories (Figure 15.2).

Selecting the area our beginning teacher is interested in, reading (34 hits), we can then narrow things down further, by, for example, clicking on 'Age of learner' and selecting 'Adolescents' and also 'Context of Language Use' to 'School language instruction only'. That would then give us a much more manageable and relevant list of five summaries of potential relevance to a beginning teacher placed in a secondary school (Figure 15.3).

Your beginning teacher might then need some support in understanding the summaries located, even though they are written in accessible language. They should read the whole summary (one page), but then focus in on certain sections. The following order might be helpful to suggest, with the beginning teacher doing the reading and highlighting of key points prior to a meeting with you to discuss.

A useful section of the summary to start with is entitled 'What this research was about and why it is important'. Reading this opening section closely will help the beginning teacher gain a sense of how relevant the research is for the issue they themselves wish to tackle. Encourage them to look for parallels between the research context and their own, even if these are not immediately apparent. For example, taking the second summary listed in

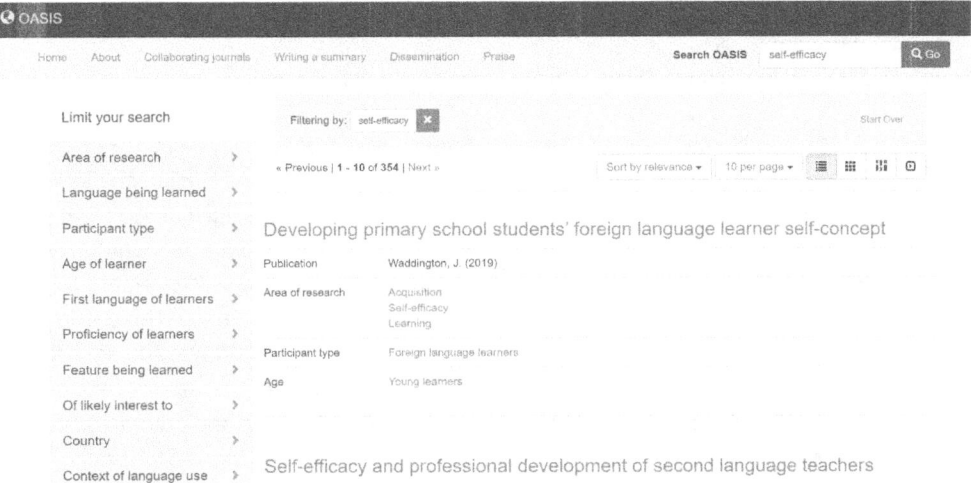

*Figure 15.1* Example of hits for 'self-efficacy' in https://www.oasis-database.org.

| Area of research | |
|---|---|
| Learning | 124 |
| Other | 114 |
| Production | 71 |
| Learner attitudes | 69 |
| Speaking | 68 |
| Teaching methods (style, approach, technique) | 63 |
| Writing | 50 |
| Comprehension | 50 |
| Motivation | 47 |
| Effectiveness of teaching | 46 |
| Learner strategies | 46 |
| Identity | 44 |
| Proficiency | 41 |
| Multilingualism | 40 |
| Teacher cognition | 37 |
| Grammar | 36 |
| Vocabulary | 35 |
| Reading | 34 |
| Computer-assisted language learning | 33 |
| Cultural identity | 32 |

*Figure 15.2* Areas of research filter in https://www.oasis-database.org.

Figure 15.3, the study participants, Chinese English-as-a-foreign-language (EFL) readers in a high-stakes testing environment in Years 11-12, might face very similar challenges to learners aged 15-16 sitting public examinations in a range of contexts, including Year 11 pupils in England. The section should also help the beginning teacher understand why the factor they are interested in (in this case self-efficacy) is important and how it is related to other factors they might not have considered before (such as reading strategies). The section usually ends with a concise statement of what the main findings for the study were, again giving the beginning teacher something precise to note down or highlight.

The sections 'What the researchers found' and 'Things to consider' should then be re-read next. The latter is particularly helpful for again giving the beginning teacher a concise 'takeaway' from the summary, but also sometimes some caveats – for example, that the approach used in the research was more successful with some learners than with others.

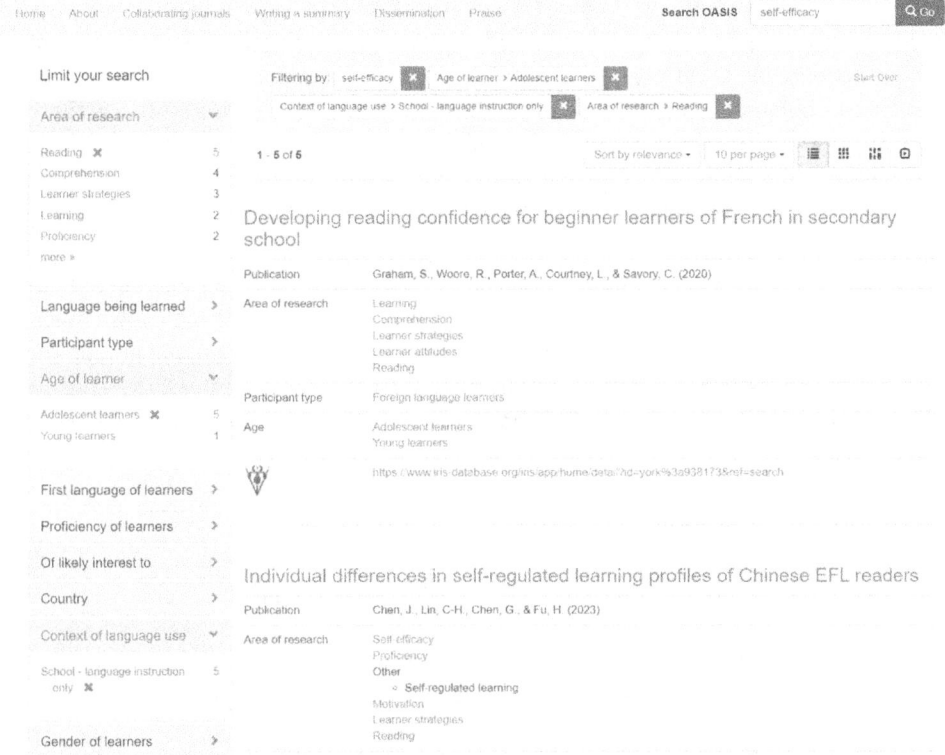

*Figure 15.3* Example returns from a narrower search in https://www.oasis-database.org.

Arguably, the middle section 'What the researchers did' could be read last: while it gives important details of, for example who the participants were, its main importance is explaining what the research involved. Gaining insights into that may well be easier once the beginning teacher has a broader overview from the other sections. Then, the precise details of what was done in the research could usefully be discussed in a further separate meeting, where the beginning teacher tries to incorporate some of the findings into their own research – which takes us to our next heading (Task 15.3).

### Task 15.3 Familiarise yourself with accessible summaries

Have a look at the Oasis database (oasisdatabase.org). Using either an area of language learning on which you yourself would like to have research insights, or one that you think would be relevant to your beginning teacher, explore the search and filter functions. This will prepare you for supporting your beginning teacher in their own explorations. You might like to share some of the findings in a languages department meeting, as other colleagues will also be working with the beginning teacher. It then becomes an opportunity to spread enthusiasm for research-informed practice.

**The initial 'translation' of findings is followed by their 'transformation' by the teachers themselves: i.e. the research is offered as 'provisional specifications' or guiding principles for practice, rather than as 'recipes for success'.**

This is the point at which the beginning teacher tries to put into practice teaching approaches that the research they have read suggests might be effective. Returning to our Oasis summary document, your beginning teacher should re-read the section 'What the researchers did'. That will give an overview of the approach implemented. It is likely however that not a great deal of detail will be included, and if they can, your beginning teacher might be advised to look at the original publication on which the Oasis summary is based, turning to the *Methodology* section. For classroom interventions, where innovative practices are tried out, that section should include more detail on what the researchers did in the classroom. Some research projects do provide access to the materials the researchers used – for example, in the FLEUR French reading project where improving reading self-efficacy was a goal (Woore et al., 2018), the team made many resources available at https://research.reading.ac.uk/pdc-in-mfl (see FLEUR under 'Projects').

Regardless of the level of detail provided, what the researchers implemented might need a bit of interpreting and adapting to fit the context in which the beginning teacher is working, and also so that they take ownership of what they are doing. We probably have all experienced trying to teach using someone else's materials, which can seem rather incomprehensible compared with something we have created ourselves. So, trying to adapt what the researchers did can be a good idea, and is also essential to the process of 'transformation' our guiding principle refers to. To help with that process, you could ask your beginning teacher to write bullet-points outlining the different intervention steps implemented by the researchers, and then writing a second version that is modified to show what those steps might look like in their own classroom. That modification might involve things like altering the order of different elements of the intervention, simplifying certain activities, and so on.

As an example, in the Professional Development Consortium in MFL project (pdcinmfl) (Macaro et al., 2015), we worked with one teacher, Florence. We gave her a framework for teaching listening strategies, based on what we had ourselves implemented in Graham and Macaro (2008), as well as on other scholars' work (e.g. Vandergrift, 2003). We also gave her an outline for an actual lesson that we created to fit in with a textbook passage and some possible resources – for example, a prediction grid. We left Florence to work with these materials and to make sense of them for herself so that she could actually implement them with her own learners. The resulting lesson differed from what we had suggested, in that there was no deliberate and explicit modelling of strategies by the teacher, rather a more implicit approach in which learners discussed and verified predictions about what they would hear, and also the strategies they had themselves used when listening. Florence then commented on those strategies, adding in a more explicit element, drawing up a list at the end rather than at the start of the lesson as we had done in our own study. Importantly, at the start of the lesson she emphasised to learners that they would develop tools for dealing with challenge, and at the end, drew their attention to the link between the strategies they had used and their success on the task. Florence's teaching thus very much aligned with the main outcome we had intended, namely improved listening comprehension and listening self-efficacy through strategy instruction, but she had transformed our 'guiding principles for practice' into her own approach while preserving the underlying principles of what our research had indicated to be important.

**On-going support is given in implementing the research findings themselves (e.g. through peers, external advisors, exemplification materials and collaborative partnerships), offering teachers 'mastery experiences' which further enhance their self-efficacy and seal changes in their beliefs.**

As well as implementing suggestions from research into their practice, your beginning teacher will also benefit from evaluating what impact it has on learners' outcomes. Teacher self-efficacy, their confidence in their ability to bring about desired learning outcomes, can be enhanced if they can experience 'success' that stems from something they themselves have done ('mastery experience', Bandura, 1997, p. 80). They are more likely to experience that success with support from you and others.

Evaluation needs to follow certain guidelines too. In the above example, Florence was likely responding to what she knew about her learners when modifying the research guidelines. Indeed, when implementing research findings in the classroom, it is important that your beginning teacher values pupil perspectives. For example, if the teaching approach suggested by researchers is one that your beginning teacher suspects will be too challenging for learners, it would be appropriate for them to try out a modified version on a small scale first, as a kind of pilot. Likewise, if your beginning teacher is implementing research findings as part of an academic assignment they are writing, perhaps as part of their ITE programme or a masters module, then it is important that they adhere to the university's requirements in terms of research ethics. For example, should they be asking learners and parents to actively express consent/assent to the use of their data in any write-up of what they have tried with learners? Requirements will vary according to the nature of the assignment, but it is essential that the beginning teacher follows the requirements closely.

In preparation for following those procedures, your beginning teacher needs to be clear about data collection, that is, how will they assess what impact there is on learning from any research-informed teaching they have implemented? This will require careful planning and you can make a useful contribution to the formulation of those plans. First, make sure your beginning teacher has a clear focus, as we have discussed, and encourage them to turn it into a question to be answered. The latter needs to be as precise as possible, including some indication of the success criteria to be applied.

Here are some examples of precise questions (there are of course many others):

**Speaking:**
If I teach beginner learners *strategies to use when faced with communication difficulties*, what impact does it have on their ability to keep going when speaking in the target language?

**Listening and reading:**
What impact does teaching some grapheme-phoneme (sound-spelling) rules have on learners' ability to understand detail in reading or listening passages?

**Writing:**
If I teach learners how to create a plan for a longer piece of writing, how far does it help them to make their writing more coherent and complex?

**Vocabulary:**
Is it more effective to teach learners new vocabulary as chunks or individual words, in terms of their ability to use the vocabulary in their written work?

Having considered some examples of precise questions, consider Task 15.4.

> **Task 15.4 Developing a precise question**
>
> Take an area of practice that either your beginning teacher or you yourself would like to improve with the help of some guiding principles from research. Using the above examples, try to formulate a precise question that you or your beginning teacher could try to answer.

Subsequently, your beginning teacher needs to identify the kind of information or 'data' they could collect to assess what impact their intervention has had. How 'scientific' and 'rigorous' your beginning teacher's evaluation is will depend on how much time they have available. Ideally, before starting the implementation it would be useful for them to gain a baseline understanding of what usually happens in class, of how pupils' learning usually develops. We could take one of our example questions above as an example of how that might work:

**Speaking:**

If I teach beginner learners *strategies to use when faced with communication difficulties*, what impact does it have on their ability to keep going when speaking in the target language?

The beginning teacher could set the class in question off on a pair work task that includes an open-ended element for each speaker. They select a few pairs and listen in. If they can, it would be ideal to try to time the length of 'utterance' from each partner and note it down. Or, they could observe the class being taught by someone else, and note down some of the following:

- When the teacher asks a question in the target language, how long and complex are typical responses?
- Are they one-word answers, simple nouns or adjectives, or do the responses contain a verb?

The beginning teacher would then implement a small intervention. That might include measures such as teaching learners filler phrases (for example, target language versions of *Well, I mean, First of all*, and so on). Learners could listen to recordings or live modelling of conversations using such phrases, to raise their awareness of how fillers can help keep a conversation going because they give the speaker thinking time. The beginning teacher could then give learners a prompt sheet for use in pair work activities, where they could tick off phrases used. Other strategies could include modelling for learners how to use paraphrase and repair strategies like repetition to minimise breakdowns in communication, and then giving them practice opportunities to try them out. After the intervention, the beginning teacher could repeat the initial exercise and note any improvements in length of pupil responses.

After implementing the research principles themselves and evaluating their impact, it would not only be useful for your beginning teacher to discuss with you what they have found out in a mentor meeting, but also share their findings with the rest of the department. This brings us to our final principle.

**Teachers' self-efficacy is developed by allowing them to see similar others successfully implementing research findings in the classroom (a form of vicarious experience).**

If engaging with research is to become a permanent part of your beginning teacher's development, that is, something that they maintain beyond the ITE phase, then they need to observe and collaborate with other teachers who share that engagement. Participating in an evidence-informed community of practice is an important part of that maintenance. Some schools might offer that kind of community in the form of research-focused after-school meetings. There are also external organisations that bring teachers from different disciplines together, such as ResearchEd in the United Kingdom. Some universities run subject-specific research support groups for teachers, where members can discuss research and share their experiences with implementing aspects of it. Subject associations, like the Association for Language Learning in the United Kingdom, SCILT in Scotland, and so on, also offer opportunities to be part of an evidence-informed community of practice, through online events, in-person meetings, conferences and publications. The best way to encourage your beginning teacher to participate in such communities is to do so yourself!

## Conclusion

Engaging with research as a busy teacher is challenging, as is developing that capacity in someone else. In this chapter, we have considered:

- how being research-informed might help your beginning teacher, emphasising how it can support teachers' ability to make informed pedagogical decisions as well as enhancing their understanding of the learning process.
- some key principles for supporting your beginning teacher to work with research in their practice, including helping them find a focus for their research-based reflections and to make sense of any research reports they read.
- the importance of beginning teachers relating research to their own practice and implementing aspects of it in a meaningful way, and the mentor's role in offering advice and support on evaluating their experimentations.
- some resources to support your beginning teacher in working with research, including where to find research evidence and how to evaluate its claims.
- and, finally, showing interest and enthusiasm yourself about engaging with research is a vital part of inspiring your beginning teacher to do likewise.

## For discussion

After reading this chapter, how has your understanding of how teachers might engage with research changed? What impact will that have on your practice as a mentor?

Can you identify any additional resources your beginning teacher could draw upon for finding out about and trying out some ideas from research?

## Further reading

https://ripl.uk/

Research in Primary Languages (RiPL) provides free, easy access to and summaries of research in relation to young learners, that are also of relevance to secondary school learners. Beginning teachers and mentors can gain useful overviews on topics such as primary to secondary transition, cultural competence, and intercultural understanding, and so on.

research.reading.ac.uk/pdcinmfl

The Professional Development Consortium in MFL website provides a set of research-based principles, together with materials and video clips exemplifying their use in classrooms. It also includes links to materials from research projects conducted by members of the Consortium. Beginning teachers could use some of these as a basis for their own small projects.

Language Driven Pedagogy: https://ldpedagogy.org/resources/research-informed-resources/

This site, as well as providing classroom resources, provides research-based rationales for the approaches used in the resources. There is also a link to the Oasis database.

## References

Bandura, A. (1997). Self-efficacy: Towards a unifying theory of behavioural change. *Psychological Review*, 84, 191-215. https://doi.org/10.1037/0033-295x.84.2.191

Department for Education. (2019) *ITT core content framework*. Accessed January 15, 2024, from https://www.gov.uk/government/publications/initial-teacher-training-itt-core-content-framework.

Department for Education. (2022). *Delivering world class teacher development*. Accessed January 15, 2024, https://assets.publishing.service.gov.uk/government/uploads/system/uploads/attachment_data/file/1076587/Delivering_world_class_teacher_development_policy_paper.pdf

Ellis, R. (1997). SLA and language pedagogy: An educational perspective. *Studies in Second Language Acquisition*, 20, 69-92.

Graham, S., & Macaro, E. (2008). Strategy instruction in listening for lower-intermediate learners of French. *Language Learning*, 58(4), 747-783.

Graham, S., & Santos, D. (2020). The 'good' teacher of listening. In C. Griffiths (Ed.), *The good language teacher* (pp. 246-259). Cambridge University Press.

Lortie, D. C. (1975). *Schoolteacher: A sociological study*. University of Chicago Press.

Macaro, E., Graham, S., & Woore, R. (2015). *Improving foreign language education: A research-based approach*. Routledge.

Macaro, E., & Woore, R. (2021). *Debates in second language education*. Routledge.

MacDonald, M., Badger, R., & White, G. (2001). Changing values: What use are theories of language learning and teaching? *Teaching and Teacher Education*, 17, 1949-963.

Marsden, E., & Kasprowicz, R. (2017). Foreign language educators' exposure to research: Reported experiences, exposure via citations, and a proposal for action. *The Modern Language Journal*, 101, 613-642.

Menter, I., Hulme, M., Elliot, D., & Lewin, J. (2010). *Literature review on teacher education in the 21st century*. The Scottish Government.

Murphy, V., Arndt, H., Briggs Baffoe-Djan, J., Chalmers, H., Macaro, E., Rose, H., Vanderplank, R., & Woore, R. (2020). *Foreign language learning and its impact on wider academic outcomes: A rapid evidence assessment*. Education Endowment Foundation. Accessed January 15, 2024, from https://ora.ox.ac.uk/objects/uuid:4e6f26ba-44b3-452c-b959-18150b9d4093

Office for Standards in Education (2021). *Curriculum research review for languages.* Accessed January 15, 2024, from https://www.gov.uk/government/publications/curriculum-research-review-series-languages.

Parr, J., Timperley, H., Reddish, P., Jesson, R., & Adams, R. (2007). *Literacy professional development project: Identifying effective teaching and professional development practices for enhanced student learning. Report to the ministry of education.* School of Education, University of Auckland.

Rankin, J., & Becker, F. (2006). Does reading the research make a difference? A case study of teacher growth in FL German. *The Modern Language Journal, 90,* 353–372.

Tatto, M. T. (2013). *The role of research in international policy and practice in teacher education.* Accessed January 15, 2024, from https://www.bera.ac.uk/project/research-and-teacher-education.

Vandergrift, L. (2003). Orchestrating strategy use: Toward a model of the skilled second language listener. *Language Learning, 53*(3), 463–496.

Wang, Q., & Zhang, H. (2014). Promoting teacher autonomy through university-school collaborative action. *Language Teaching Research, 18,* 222–241.

Winch, C., Orchard, J., & Oancea, A. (2013). *The contribution of educational research to teachers' professional learning – Philosophical understandings.* BERA.

Woore, R., Graham, S., Porter, A., Courtney, L., & Savory, C. (2018). *Foreign language education: Unlocking Reading (FLEUR) – A study into the teaching of Reading to beginner learners of French in secondary school.* Nuffield Foundation. https://ora.ox.ac.uk/objects/uuid:4b0cb239-72f0-49e4-8f32-3672625884f0

Woore, R., Molway, L., & Macaro, E. (2022). Keeping sight of the big picture: A critical response to Ofsted's 2021 curriculum research review for languages. *The Language Learning Journal, 50,* 146–155. https://doi.org/10.1080/09571736.2022.2045677

# 16 Developing the wider professional role of the beginning languages teacher

*Rob Bown*

## Introduction

This chapter will consider how mentors can help beginning languages teachers to develop in their wider professional role. To help your beginning teacher understand what is meant by the wider professional role, it is useful to consider the questions below with them. Many of these refer to ideas mentioned in the Teachers' Standards (Department for Education [DfE], 2012) including in *Part Two: Personal and professional conduct*. These ideas are discussed through the chapter.

- Do you have a clear understanding of how UK schools are organised and your place in this organisation? (This is particularly important for beginning teachers who were not educated in a UK school.)
- What are languages teachers' roles in school above and beyond the delivery of language lessons?
- How can you develop your ability to have a positive influence on behaviour around the school site?
- How can you promote high standards of literacy, articulacy and the correct use of standard English in language lessons?
- How can you contribute to the wider life and ethos of the school?
- What impact can your contact with parents/carers, pastoral, and SEND teams have on your classroom interaction with individual pupils?
- What is your role as a tutor and how can you develop in this role?
- What does it mean to have effective professional relationships?
- How can you demonstrate high standards of personal and professional conduct?

At the end of this chapter, these questions will have been considered and you should be able to:

- Demonstrate a clear understanding of what a teacher's wider professional role involves for the beginning teacher
- Identify practical steps that a beginning teacher can take to develop in this aspect of their role.

## Being a professional

What does it mean to be a professional in the realm of teaching? Hickman (2019, p. 142) identifies a number of authors who argue that the impact of state intervention on the teaching profession over the last 30 years has been to create a profession in which individual teachers are 'compliant in and accountable for delivery, rather than conceptualisation, of a centralised curriculum'. This corresponds with a change in expectations of beginning teachers. Thirty years ago, it was common to expect beginning teachers to plan a large number of lessons and create their own resources: worksheets or overhead transparencies for the department filing cabinet. Nowadays, new arrivals to languages departments are often presented with a set of pre-prepared slides and other resources which they are expected to deliver. There has been a 'deskilling of the teaching profession' (Pachler & Field, 2001, p. 15) when it comes to curriculum design but it can be argued that expectations of teachers as professionals have increased in those areas above and beyond the delivery of subject lessons. For example, our commitment as tutors to meeting the needs of our pupils has had to increase as schools have become responsible for a much broader range of pupil needs. It is in our non-teaching roles – when we communicate with parents, contribute to the wider life and ethos of the school, draw on advice from colleagues, and take responsibility for our own development – that we display other key characteristics of professionalism such as autonomy, creativity, reflection, and engagement with complexity.

## Understanding how UK schools are organised and your place in this organisation

Most UK teachers were educated within its school system but this does not mean that they understand life on the other side of the teacher's desk. When beginning teachers first arrive in schools in their new role as teachers, they need guidance on how schools are structured and the different roles within the academic and pastoral structures. For colleagues joining the UK education system from overseas, it is important to note some of the defining features of being a teacher in the United Kingdom, especially where these differ from many other countries. Even when we look to our nearest European neighbours, there are significant differences: The number of school weeks per year is largely similar across France, Germany, Spain, and the United Kingdom but the United Kingdom suffers from a long hours' culture. According to recent research, in England 'a quarter of teachers work more than 60 hours per week during term time, 40% report that they usually work in the evening and around 10% during the weekend' (Allen et al., 2021, p. 1). According to surveys conducted in the past 20 years, a teacher in England works eight hours a week on average more than the Organisation for Economic Co-operation and Development (OECD) average and the majority feel their workload is unmanageable (Maisuria et al., 2023). Class sizes are also likely to be larger. In 2020 in UK secondary schools the average class size was 17.7 pupils which is higher than all but a handful of OECD countries, albeit only slightly higher than the OECD average of 13.4 (OECD, 2023). In England, teachers are more likely to work in classes with at least 10% of pupils with special needs (41% compared to an OECD average of 27%) and in classes with at least 10% of pupils whose first language is different from the language of instruction (27% compared to an OECD average of 18%) (TALIS, 2018). Beginning teachers who were educated abroad or teachers who are new to the United Kingdom will benefit from understanding the context for teaching in the United Kingdom.

## Languages teachers' roles above and beyond the delivery of language lessons

To help beginning teachers consider their different roles in school, it is useful to ask them to consider the purpose of schools. Is it to prepare pupils for the world of work, to help them gain the best possible qualifications, to build their character or to prepare them to be good citizens and parents? A useful starting point for reading on this point would be Claxton's book, *What's The Point of School?* There are arguments for all of these suggestions and a beginning teacher should be able to respond to each of them. They will, for example, make little headway in a conversation with a pupil about poor uniform if they can only explain schools as facilitators of qualifications. Hickman (2019, p. 149) describes another purpose of schools: 'as a form of social justice to address disadvantage and inequality'. She goes on to suggest that reflection on this and other definitions of the purpose of education is central to 'the development of the ethical practice of a professional teacher'. In considering these competing definitions, a teacher is required to demonstrate a further key characteristic of professionalism: reflection on our own values and beliefs. In terms of the ethos of the school, Task 16.1 should help you and your beginning teacher identify what is meant by ethos in your context and how you can both contribute to it.

---

**Task 16.1 What's the point of school? Questions to discuss with a beginning teacher.**

- What are the purposes of education or of this school?
- How can each of these be justified?
- When are each of these most pertinent?
- What values underpin each of these?
- What are your values in this context?

---

A consideration of the questions listed above should lead beginning teachers to consider the many roles that they will perform and also the many specialist roles that exist within schools. Hudson (2012) highlights the advantages of involving a wide range of staff in the development of beginning teachers so that a wide spectrum of expertise is shared. A greater range of input will also help where individual mentor-mentee relationships are not optimal. A good professional studies programme could bring together presentations from leaders in special educational needs and disabilities (SEND), pastoral care, behaviour management, attendance, safeguarding, equality, and diversity among others. See Hickman (2019, pp. 144-145) for a thorough consideration of what constitutes a good professional studies programme.

## Promoting high standards of literacy, articulacy, and the correct use of standard English in language lessons

The third Teachers' Standard (DfE, 2012) challenges all teachers to contribute to high standards of numeracy and literacy. Language teachers have a clear role to play in the latter in particular. Drawing attention to the differences in spelling of cognates in English and the target language helps pupils avoid spelling mistakes in both languages and appreciate the differences in each language's phonetic system. In schools, there is often a belief that learning a foreign language will hinder the progress of pupils with SEND in other areas of the curriculum. Howard (2023, p. 154) suggests that 'learning new languages is, on the whole, possible–and perhaps hugely beneficial–for children with developmental differences and learning difficulties'. This is just one example of on-going professional debates and, as discussed below, beginning teachers need to be aware and ready to engage with the issues.

## Contribution to the wider life and ethos of the school

As a mentor, you may have spent little time thinking about this or take your own contributions for granted. However, the expansion of the previous one year Newly Qualified Teacher induction to the current two-year Early Career Teacher induction has placed greater demands on mentoring capacity in schools and, as a result, teachers with less experience may be asked to mentor beginning teachers.

The wider life of the school can be considered as all interactions outside of the classroom. This includes a teacher's behaviour management around the school site which will be addressed below. The wider life of the school also refers to the extracurricular clubs and activities offered by a school. This has been an area of focus in recent years as schools have tried to build back their extracurricular programmes to pre-pandemic levels and as these programmes have become part of what the Office for Standards in Education, Children's Services and Skills (OFSTED) considers when they inspect a school's personal development curriculum. The Social Mobility Commission's report, *An Unequal Playing Field: Extra-Curricular Activities, Soft Skills and Social Mobility* (Social Mobility Commission, 2019, pp. 1-3), makes it clear that 'extracurricular activities are important in developing soft (especially social) skills as well as being associated with a range of other positive outcomes (e.g. achievement, attendance at school)'. In addition, it found that 'children from the poorest households were much less likely to take part in any extracurricular activity'. It is clear, therefore, that beginning teachers who value schools as institutions which develop skills and address social disadvantage should consider involvement in extracurricular activities. This is all the more true for beginning language teachers who have the possibility of running enrichment sessions, as well as visits to restaurants and, crucially, trips abroad. There is a dearth of research into the impact of such trips but a school-led experience in a target-language country clearly provides the immersive experience we try to provide our pupils in the classroom. What evidence there is suggests that language trips have a 'valuable impact on one's memory and learning process' (Sprachcaffe, 2017, p. 9).

## Impact of contact with parents, pastoral, and SEND teams on interactions in the classroom

All classroom teachers have access to information about individual pupils: prior achievement, SEND information and strategies, behaviour logs, relevant information about home circumstances etc. However, speaking to the tutor, SEND or pastoral leader who deals most closely with an individual pupil will provide further insights. Furthermore, in their early years in the profession, beginning teachers are more likely to encounter poor behaviour but there will always be someone in the school in whose classroom individual (and sometimes challenging) pupils meet expectations. Speaking to and observing these colleagues in action with the pupil in question can be very helpful.

Parents and carers can also be valuable allies in the struggle to improve the behaviour or achievement of a pupil. However, contacting home can be a daunting prospect for a beginning teacher. Mentors can help beginning teachers build experience with contacting home by prompting them to start with positive emails or postcards. They could then move on to positive home contact before observing you, their mentor, making a more challenging phone call. Finally a mentor could offer to stay in the room with the beginning teacher as they make their first solo call. Task 16.2 could be used to prepare for such a call.

> **Task 16.2 Preparing to contact parents/carer. Questions to consider with your beginning teacher.**
>
> - Have you spoken to the pastoral/SEND team to see whether there are any issues which you should be aware of and how your call is likely to be received?
> - Have you prepared a brief plan for the conversations? This should include:
>
>   - Introducing yourself (name, school, role)
>   - Checking whether they have time to speak at this moment
>   - Something positive that you can say about their child
>   - What it is that you would like parents/carers to understand
>   - What it is that you would like them to do
>   - What it is that you are going to do (e.g. next contact point)
>   - Why/How you think this will lead to a positive outcome

Another unsettling task for beginning teachers can be their first parents' evening. These often extend an already long day into an evening of quick-fire meetings which can sometimes be challenging. Here again, preparation is the key (Task 16.3).

> **Task 16.3 Preparing for parents' evening. Questions to discuss with a beginning teacher.**
>
> - What will you need to hand? E.g. your mark book, pupils' exercise books
> - Have you got all key information to hand? E.g. SEND data, previous attainment profiles
> - What might parents/carers of this child be anxious about? E.g. SEND provision for a child who has recently moved from primary to secondary school
> - Have you prepared a brief plan for each conversation? This could be:
>
>   - Introduction, including your plan to structure the conversation in the time available
>   - What you have covered in lessons so far and what you will be covering in the near future
>   - Your opinion of the pupil's progress
>   - The key thing that you would like parents/carers to know or do
>   - A question to ask the pupil to get them involved (if they are in attendance)
>   - Time for the parents/carers to ask you any questions

## Positive influence on behaviour around the school

As Hudson (2012) points out, a key predictor of teacher burnout is lack of appreciation by pupils and this often manifests itself in the form of poor behaviour in the classroom and beyond. Beginning teachers are often adept at managing behaviour in a classroom setting long before they develop an ability to challenge poor behaviour in the corridors or playground. Observation of experienced staff on duty can help this development. Mentors could plan a joint break or lunchtime duty from the first week of induction or training. As mentioned above, managing behaviour around the site can be seen as a contribution to the wider life and ethos of the school. OFSTED will certainly be looking at interactions between lessons, and at break and lunch times, as part of their evaluation of behaviour and attitudes. Behaviour management in this context is different to what one practises in the classroom. Pupils are not usually engaged in teacher-directed, organised activities at break and lunch time and have a lot more freedom to decide what is appropriate behaviour and what is not. Beginning teachers need to be clear about expectations outside of lessons. If they are not, pupils will fill this void. Once they have clear expectations, beginning teachers need to consider how to challenge pupils who are not meeting these expectations outside of lessons. To some degree, the same principles apply as in the classroom. Dix (2017) offers some helpful guidelines, stating that interventions should be calm, planned, consistent across all staff and, as much as possible, conducted away from the eyes and ears of others. In the context of managing behaviour out of lessons, Dix's concept of 'deliberate botheredness' (p. 37) is particularly useful. Where time or the context does not allow for a thorough engagement with poor behaviour, staff can still make it clear that they have noticed a problem and reiterate expectations. What beginning teachers need to avoid is being the weak link in the chain which allows poor behaviour to gain a foothold. The maxim that 'you promote what you permit' applies here (Task 16.4).

---

### Task 16.4 Behaviour management outside of lessons. Questions to discuss with a beginning teacher.

- What opportunities to build relationships are available to you when doing break/lunch duties and other activities outside of the classroom?
- What types of poor behaviour are you likely to encounter between lessons and at break/lunch?
- What are the school's rules and expectations with regard to behaviour in these non-classroom situations?
- What would be an appropriate reaction to each of these? What exactly will you say? What will you do if your intervention is ignored?

---

## Form tutor role

This is a role that beginning teachers who are unfamiliar with the English education system may need some help to understand. A starting point could be reading Marland and Rogers'

(2004) book which provides a helpful and realistic guide. Beginning teachers should also have opportunities to observe different form tutors. During their initial teacher training, beginning teachers will observe many different classroom teachers but observing a range of form tutors is also important. Can you create an observation schedule of different tutors for your beginning teacher such that they observe a number of different tutors with different year groups? It can also be helpful to consider what is specific to the tutor role and how it is different to the classroom teacher role (Task 16.5).

---

**Task 16.5 Being a super tutor. Questions to discuss with a beginning teacher.**

- What is the purpose of tutor time? E.g. setting the tone for the day
- How is your role as a tutor different to your classroom teaching role? You may see your pupils every day for several years, so how might this help you to notice changes/problems?
- How can you build rapport, and create a sense of belonging for all?
- Who are your high-profile pupils? How can you champion and challenge them?

---

Tutor time is also often the setting in which personal, social, health, and economic (PSHE) lessons are delivered. PSHE includes statutory content known as relationships, sex, and health education (RSHE) (DfE, 2013). These lessons address issues which are of key importance to young people: healthy relationships, sex education, addiction, economic well-being and careers, online safety, and much more. Beginning teachers should ensure they are as well prepared to deliver these lessons as they are to teach their subject-specific lessons. Delivering PSHE lessons is an excellent opportunity for a tutor to demonstrate their concern for the well-being of pupils.

## What does it mean to have *effective professional relationships*?

Mentoring a beginning teacher is often a teacher's first leadership role. You lead a department of one and your role is to help your new colleague develop as a professional and enter the professional community with confidence. The first step here is to help your beginning teacher find their voice by orchestrating opportunities for them to present at departmental meetings or in other more formal settings. Even a small contribution in the form of a new resource or website can build confidence. These professional conversations also take place outside of school and online. Black (2017, p. 23) lists the many benefits of joining the Association for Language Learning and points out useful online communities such as #mfltwitterati on X. Joining these networks will allow your beginning teacher to follow and contribute to national debates about languages policy and education in general. Knowledge of such debates is another characteristic of professionalism. As Smalley (2023, p. 231) points out, following these debates is also part of your role as mentor or 'the knowledgeable other'.

Communication within the school is another area in which beginning teachers will need careful and sensitive guidance. They need to understand the dangers of addressing difficult issues with colleagues and parents via email and why a conversation face-to-face or over the phone is preferable in such cases. They should also consider the timing of difficult conversations and do their best to avoid Friday afternoon, as everyone is tired, and a poorly chosen phrase can lead to a weekend of worry. A lot of the stress of difficult conversations can be removed for all teachers by sharing some guidelines on how to prepare for them:

- Choose a moment when each of you has time and a place with some privacy
- Be clear about your concern, why it is important and your desired outcome
- Ask the other person for their point of view and listen with an open mind
- Keep the conversation focused and go over agreed next steps at the end

Taking on advice is particularly relevant to the professional relationship between beginning teachers and their mentors. However, as Smalley (2023, pp. 234-235) points out, although initial conversations with beginning teachers might be 'filled with advice', over time advice should give way to probing questions which require the beginning teacher to justify decisions. Blair (2021, p. 70) also recommends a move away from 'judgementoring' and towards self-regulation. She recommends that mentors encourage beginning teachers to be 'intentional learners' who 'make their own decisions, innovate, take risks and experiment' so that they can exercise their judgement. Blair (2021) highlights that there is a balance to be struck here as innovation and experimentation can come into conflict with the accountability agenda. Ideally, beginning teachers will be experimenting with well-tested practices which are all effective but involve different strengths and weaknesses. It is the mentor's duty, particularly with beginning teachers, to ensure that only this type of responsible experimentation is what takes place and that the pupil experience is not adversely affected.

When discussing the relationship between mentor and beginning teacher, it is important to point out how much impact the mentor can have on the resilience of someone new to teaching. This is all the more relevant as the profession struggles to retain beginning teachers. Hudson (2019) suggests several questions which can be asked of beginning teachers in order to help them identify and develop resilience strategies. The questions below reflect Hudson's ideas and can help beginning teachers identify sources of support. They can also help beginning teachers pin down what has given them a sense of success and achievement and what threatens those positive feelings. Hudson recommends gathering written answers and then discussing them in groups. This could be particularly productive with the first question about achievements. In the discussion, a mentor could provide a list of possible answers (see Hudson, p.75) to provoke further thought. They could then analyse answers to help the beginning teacher to see what they hold to be valuable in their teaching role. How do they define their own self-worth? What are the benefits and drawbacks to these judgements? Is the beginning teacher building their sense of confidence on firm ground? For example, many teachers feel great pride in being able to reach very challenging pupils but such interactions are unpredictable and a teacher who defines their value in terms of doing this successfully is likely to feel inadequate a lot of the time (Task 16.6).

### Task 16.6 Resilience-building survey

Looking back on the academic year (or since the start of your placement):

- What are your greatest achievements?
- What have been your greatest challenges?
- Do you have a teacher in your classroom or 'next door' to whom you can turn for help mid-lesson?
- Which members of staff have been most supportive to you? In what ways?
- Have you been made to feel part of the school teaching team? How?
- Do you feel appreciated by pupils? How? Why?
- Do you feel appreciated by parents/carers?
- Have you developed a good work-life balance? How?
- Do you have a clear idea of what you need to learn?
- What have been your key learning points? How did you learn these things? Was the learning planned or unplanned?

The mentor has a profound influence on the shape of learning conversations and the opportunities for learning. Hudson (2012) and Blair (2021) refer to a number of mentor practices which will help the beginning teacher get the most out of their relationship with the mentor. These range from listening to concerns and talking about teaching and learning to modelling effective teaching and setting targets. The survey below collates these ideas and could also be used by mentors as a self-audit tool and checklist. Managed sensitively, the survey could be given to beginning teachers by the mentor's line manager or lead professional mentor in the school. Respondents should answer using a five-point Likert scale of agreement. Results could be discussed with the mentor but also with the beginning teacher as the survey will draw attention to key learning processes and can be a starting point for a conversation about how effective they have been and how they could be improved (Task 16.7).

### Task 16.7 Survey of mentoring practices

- Does your mentor listen to your concerns?
- In meetings, do you and your mentor have equal shares of the talking?
- Do you feel able to take risks and 'give things a go'?
- Is your mentor open to exploring new practices in the classroom?
- Is your mentor positive about what you do well and your ability to improve?
- Is your mentor comfortable talking about teaching and learning?
- Does your mentor make you feel more confident in your ability to teach?

- Does your mentor help you to plan lessons and review lesson plans?
- Does your mentor discuss the objectives of specific lesson activities?
- Does your mentor help you plan for assessment and feedback?
- Does your mentor model effective teaching and positive relationships with pupils?
- Does your mentor model and discuss effective behaviour management strategies?
- Does your mentor help you to reflect on the efficacy of teaching practices?
- Does your mentor explains school policies when relevant?
- Does your mentor help you to feel positive about the pupils that you teach?
- Does your mentor help you to achieve an overview of your subject curriculum?
- Does your mentor give you written feedback on your teaching, related to ITTECF framework and Teachers' Standards as appropriate?
- Does your mentor devise SMART (specific, measurable, achievable, realistic, and time-related) targets with you?
- Do you have opportunities to talk to your mentor throughout the day/week?

## High standards of personal and professional conduct

The final section of the Teachers' Standards (DfE, 2012) refers to a number of concepts which can be difficult to define, such as tolerance and British values. A beginning language teacher, for example, could ask themselves whether they are actively embracing diversity by reviewing their resources for teaching. Do the resources reflect the UK's diverse population? When teaching pupils how to describe physical appearance in a language lesson, does the beginning teacher teach language related to different ethnicities? Within a form tutor context, a beginning teacher may be asked to discuss politically sensitive issues. Maintaining and signposting impartiality is recommended and can be done by using the following sentence starters: Some believe ... Others believe ... My own personal opinion is that ... What do you think? The mentor should facilitate opportunities for the beginning teacher to observe experienced teachers who are particularly skilful in facilitating challenging conversations in an appropriate manner.

## Conclusion

As noted earlier, there may have been a 'deskilling of the teaching profession' when it comes to curriculum design and it can be argued that expectations of teachers as professionals have increased in those areas beyond the delivery of subject lessons. Mentors should help beginning teachers understand:

- how UK schools are structured (particularly if they were educated overseas)
- how to express the purpose(s) of education
- the relationship between teaching literacy, phonics and languages
- the scope for language teachers to provide extracurricular activities
- how to communicate effectively with colleagues and parents
- how to have a positive influence on behaviour around the school

- the purpose of a form tutor and how to be an effective form tutor
- how to develop effective professional relationships by contributing to discussions and taking on advice
- how to become 'intentional learners' who take risks and experiment
- how to develop their resilience by identifying sources of support
- how they can demonstrate tolerance and British values.

## For discussion

Take some time, with trusted colleagues and/or your beginning teacher, to consider the questions outlined in the introduction to this chapter. Where do you feel more or less confident? Are there other questions that you might add to the list for discussion?

## Further reading

Claxton, G. (2008). *What's the Point of School?: Rediscovering the Heart of Education*. One World Publications.

This book explores the assumptions that underpin what we do every day in schools. It explores different ideas about the purpose of education and we might change our education system to better meet the needs of our pupils.

Dix, P. (2017). *When the adults change, everything changes: Seismic shifts in school behaviour*. Crown House Publishing.

Dix offers expert advice on how to manage behaviour not only on a whole school level but also as an individual teacher. He explains both what does not work and why it is counterproductive and also what does work and why. There are many practical takeaways including helpful microscripts to use in challenging situations.

Marland, M., & Rogers, R. (2004). *How to be a successful form tutor*. Continuum.

This guide covers topics such as managing tutor periods, contact with families, dealing with bullying, and getting to know your pupils. The book is particularly good at describing how tutors can help their pupils understand their academic progress across subjects and how to improve their study skills, their classroom performance and their interaction with subject teachers.

## References

Allen, R., Benhenda, A., & Jerrim, J. (2021). New evidence on teachers' working hours in England: An empirical analysis of four datasets. *Research Papers in Education*, 36(6), 657–681.

Black, L. (2017). Nurturing the professional journey. In L. Black, A. L. Gordon, C. Hughes, R. MacArthur, & S. Sandy, *Effective mentoring of trainee teachers*. Association for Language Learning.

Blair, T. (2021). How can we support beginning teachers to be deliberative, engaging in self-regulation as they learn teaching. *Impact*, Autumn (13). The Chartered College of Teaching. https://my.chartered.college/impact_article/how-can-we-support-beginning-teachers-to-be-deliberative-engaging-in-self-regulation-as-they-learn-teaching/

Claxton, G. (2008). *What's the point of school?: Rediscovering the heart of education*. One World Publications.

Department for Education. (2012). Teachers' Standards. https://assets.publishing.service.gov.uk/media/61b73d6c8fa8f50384489c9a/Teachers__Standards_Dec_2021.pdf

Department for Education. (2013). *Personal, social, health and economic (PSHE) education* [online]. https://www.gov.uk/government/publications/personal-social-health-and-economic-education-pshe

Dix, P. (2017). *When the adults change, everything changes: Seismic shifts in school behaviour*. Crown House Publishing.

Hickman, D. (2019). Developing the wider, professional role of the teacher. In D. Hickman (Ed.), *Mentoring English teachers in the secondary school*. Routledge.

Howard, K. B. (2023). Supporting learners with special educational needs and disabilities in the foreign languages classroom. *Support for Learning* [online]. Accessed June 8, 2024, https://doi.org/10.1111/1467-9604.12449.

Hudson, P. (2012). How can schools support beginning teachers? A call for timely induction and mentoring for effective teaching. *Australian Journal of Teacher Education, 37*(7), 71–84. http://ro.ecu.edu.au/ajte/vol37/iss7/6

Maisuria, A., Roberts, N., Long, R., & Danechi, S. (2023). *Teacher recruitment and retention in England*. House of Commons Library.

Marland, M., & Rogers, R. (2004). *How to be a successful form tutor*. Continuum.

OECD. (2023). *Teachers – Students per teaching staff – OECD Data* [online]. Accessed June 8, 2024, from https://data.oecd.org/teachers/students-per-teaching-staff.htm.

Pachler, N., & Field, K. (2001). From mentor to co-tutor: Reconceptualising secondary modern foreign languages initial teacher education. *The Language Learning Journal, 23*(1), 15–25.

Smalley, P. (2023). Helping beginning religious education teachers develop their professional practice. In H. Sheehan (Ed.), *Mentoring religious education teachers in the secondary school*. Routledge.

Social Mobility Commission. (2019). *An unequal playing field: Extra-curricular activities, soft skills and social mobility*. London. https://www.gov.uk/government/publications/extra-curricular-activities-soft-skills-and-social-mobility/an-unequal-playing-field-extra-curricular-activities-soft-skills-and-social-mobility#contents

Sprachcaffe. (2017). The Language Learning Sustainability Project [online]. https://www.sprachcaffe.com/fileadmin/Redaktion/img/_sprachcaffe/specials/Sustainability_Survey/ENG_The_language_learning_sustainability_project_2017.pdf

TALIS. (2018). *England (UK) – Country Note – TALIS 2018 Results* [online]. Accessed June 8, 2024, from https://www.oecd.org/education/talis/TALIS2018_CN_ENG_Vol_II_extended.pdf.

# 17 Continuing to mentor beginning languages teachers beyond their initial teacher training

*Elizabeth Cundick, Anselm Fisher, and Emily Thornton*

## Introduction

In this chapter, we examine the changing nature and focus of mentor support for early career teachers (ECTs) during their transition from initial teacher education (ITE) through the early career framework (ECF) and beyond. We explore scenarios that can arise when balancing the career interests and aspirations of the beginning teacher with institutional needs, priorities and professional responsibilities. We consider issues of agency and autonomy in early career development, promoting a healthy work-life balance for career longevity, and the importance of navigating the challenges of high-stakes accountability. We advocate for a formative approach to lesson observations and propose a bespoke professional conversation framework, termed SCRIPTS, designed to support ECTs with their languages-specific pedagogical and professional development. At the end of this chapter, you should be able to:

- Understand how the needs of beginning teachers change over time and how the mentor relationship can grow to accommodate these needs
- Access and use a range of tools to support your mentoring of beginning languages teachers beyond their initial training year

## Possible approaches to ECT mentoring

At this juncture, it is important to consider what is meant by the term 'mentor' in the context of ECT, as this is likely to look quite different from the mentoring role in ITE. Whereas the ITE mentor has to wear two hats, one of support and one of assessment, in the current English context we argue that the role of the ECT mentor is primarily one of guidance and support. The question is no longer about the ECT being ready to work independently; rather, to work interdependently as a member of a team. Whilst a teacher who has gained qualified teacher status (QTS) may still want or need direction at the beginning of the year, the mentor should also allow the ECT to have agency in their own professional and career development, to have a say in the work of the department and to be valued as an equal. To achieve this, mentors have often been encouraged to adopt an increasingly 'coaching' style; yet, this can still create an unhelpful power dynamic and can foster a sense of dependence. Instead, we advocate that ECT development should be situated within a wider framework of professional encounters, both internal and external to the place of employment, as per Table 17.1.

DOI: 10.4324/9781003495468-23

Table 17.1 Varying mentor relationships within a school setting. Adapted from Marcdante and Simpson (2018)

| | Mentor | Coach | Critical friend/ knowledgeable other | 'Accidental' expert | External Expert |
|---|---|---|---|---|---|
| Example | Member of the languages department | Often designated by school's system | Contemporary (ECT buddy) or colleague, one or so years' additional experience | Colleague with no formalised link to ECT | Subject expert; exam board trainer; university link |
| Area of expertise | Languages specialist. Not necessarily expert in the same languages as their mentee | Not necessarily subject expert. Proven 'good' teacher | Often not subject expert. Knowledge of school, of ECT and comparable current experience | Teaching within this particular school setting | Subject expert (often) |
| Initiator | School/department | School/ECT | Head of Department / Mentor /ECT | Incidental interaction – perhaps in staffroom before morning briefing | ECT – perhaps after attending a course run by the external expert |
| Sphere of influence | Languages pedagogy and practice | An area of practical pedagogy: often general | Direct application of theory to lived early teaching experience | Pedagogical 'troubleshooting' – often very practical | Isolated question/issue |
| Interaction with ECT | 1:1 – regular | 1:1 – semi-regular | 1:1/small group | 1:1 | Group level |
| Style of input | Regulated, pre-ordained weekly/fortnightly, building a professional relationship | Regular, targeted 'drop-ins' with follow-up. Often adhering to pre-written structure | Relational | Relational and often drawing on the broader school context beyond the languages department | Single input session (e.g. subject-specific continuing professional development) |
| Lesson observation | Whole lesson or regular lesson observation and feedback | A few targeted observations of segments of lessons | None | None | None |
| Communication style | In person, formalised record | In person session with short summary email | Regular, free-flowing, unregulated conversation | Shorter conversation ± summary email | ECT might reach out (possibly at mentor's suggestion) |

## How can we adapt our feedback?

As demonstrated in Table 17.1, the role of the mentor needs careful consideration at different stages. Work with the mentor is the most formalised and regular of interactions amongst many that an ECT will experience. As an example, let us consider lesson observation and feedback: the ECT who is in their second induction year requires a different, but specific, level of statutory mentorship, as set out in the ECF (Department for Education [DfE], 2024), meaning that we need to develop a different mode of feedback to that which we would use for an ECT in their first induction year. Where the first-year feedback may have focused on building the individual ECT's pedagogical framework, or schema, within the practical demands of the school setting, the second year affords more chances to be flexible, reflective, and creative within the professional relationship.

Of course, the needs of the ECT at the beginning of the first year of teaching will be vastly different to that of an ECT in their second year of teaching. And differences between individual ECTs notwithstanding, the *purpose* and *direction* of mentor feedback need to reflect that change. Reframing feed*back* as feed*forward* is the first useful step towards differentiating the purpose of the exercise. Feedforward discussions do not spend a long time recapitulating lesson content, sequencing and pedagogical choices. They can be done with a few open questions in discussion, pointing the ECT back to relevant research and giving them the chance to control the narrative about what could/should/might/ought to have happened at particular moments in the observed lesson segment. Feedforward discussions have a broader perspective. They point to a 'future horizon' (Sadler et al., 2022, p. 2) and thus inherently require more reflective application by the ECT so that they (not the mentor) can use these targets towards their own career ends.

In this chapter, we argue that undergoing formalised processes of professional reflection together can create this future-focused impetus, and we provide examples and a proforma at the end for mentors who are interested in trying this out.

Table 17.2 reflects how a 'feedforward' discussion might seem in comparison to the feedback of the first year as an ECT.

Although the ECT brings a variety of knowledge, skills, and experience to their role, there will still be occasions when mentoring skills are required and the mentor needs to take a more directive role. The summer holidays may make some ECTs feel rusty and nervous, others over-confident. For some, it may have been a time of reading, reflection, perhaps (depending on

*Table 17.2* Feedback to feedforward over time

| Feedback/forward | First year | Second year – first half | Second year – second half |
| --- | --- | --- | --- |
| Lesson observation | Full lessons, regular | Segments, sporadic | Very few |
| Target setting | Mentor's direction | Mutual agreement | ECT initiative |
| Relationship to department targets, priorities and pedagogies | Loosely linked | More aware | Affording the ECT the chance to show criticality/creativity towards the status quo |
| Relationship to school priorities | Closely linked | Remaining linked | As above – accountability offered but autonomy respected |
| Work-life balance | Directive targets if needed | Awareness shown in targets if needed | Conversations and delegation where needed – rarely written |
| Career interests | Nascent | Purposeful | Led by ECT |

the ITE course) academic work, and so each teacher will enter the second teaching year with a different mindset – perhaps energised, perhaps energy-sapped – by all such experiences and endeavours. If you are working with an ECT who you mentored previously, remember to take time to find out how they are feeling and the type of support they may need, even if you feel you have a well-established mentorship formula that worked in your ECT's first year of training. With a new mentoring relationship, it is particularly important to spend time getting to know your ECT and their experiences in the first year in the profession. Across the ECT years you are looking to gradually feed into the ECT's growing autonomy as a teaching professional whilst also monitoring their well-being and ensuring, as far as you can, that they retain healthy attitudes to their workload, for example having a sustainable pattern of work with space to maintain their own interests. In mentor meetings, you are providing the sounding board for them to test and work through their career aspirations. All these elements feed forward in the way you interact with your ECT, record your discussions and frame their development. Over time, the ECT should be becoming the main driver of these conversations about the way in which they see their career developing (Task 17.1).

### Task 17.1 Mentor reflection

Here are six key questions to ask yourself as you prepare for each interaction point with your ECT over the year. Being mindful of your evolving role in the trajectory of the ECT's development should help ensure these answers do not remain stagnant from one interaction to the next:

- What is my role in relation to the ECT (see Table 17.1 for definitions) here? How can I ensure I maintain that role when discussing their practice?
- What extra knowledge or experience am I bringing to the table? How will I share this?
- How might the ECT's targets be framed in a way that values their autonomy as a fellow professional and individual practitioner?
- How do I open up the discussion? Which open-ended questions are most pertinent here? How would I use a reflective model to better drive the discussion?
- What would be of most use to the ECT's personal career trajectory, whilst aligning with both school and department targets?
- What can I learn from the ECT in relation to this particular question? What about my practice could be addressed as a result of this interaction?

Being an ECT mentor requires an awareness of larger issues than simply keeping a beginning teacher afloat early in their new career. The concurrent pressures of the ECF and the school/multi-academy trust priorities, coupled with the ECT's own reaction to school life and desire to progress in their career, are all elements that require you to be both delicate and hard-nosed on occasions. Here are some of the tensions you might encounter:

## High stakes accountability

This phrase is used to refer to the phenomenon whereby excessive scrutiny and oversight of the work of schools and teachers can lead to a culture of fear and a heavy burden of responsibility.

212  *Mentoring Languages Teachers in the Secondary School*

The knowledge that one's work is being observed, evaluated, compared, then used as evidence for judgements going far beyond one's own classroom, is a formidable challenge. It may be that beginning teachers have not experienced such scrutiny before and therefore may need some support in navigating the situation. As expectations on teachers evolve and expand, so their accountability to a hierarchy of interested parties increases (as in Figure 17.1), leading to a culture of 'performativity' (Ball, 2003, p. 215). Figure 17.1 also illustrates how different sources can exert contrasting, competing and sometimes contradictory pressures on an ECT at any given point. ECTs can often find themselves conflicted between what they perceive quality teaching to be and the official requirements of a 'quality teacher' within a specific policy context (Sullivan et al., 2020, p. 398), so they should be encouraged to problematise and discuss with their mentor in an open and non-judgemental manner.

School leaders, including those who mentor, are in a powerful position to adjust policies and expectations in order to avoid creating the situation in which a beginning teacher bears

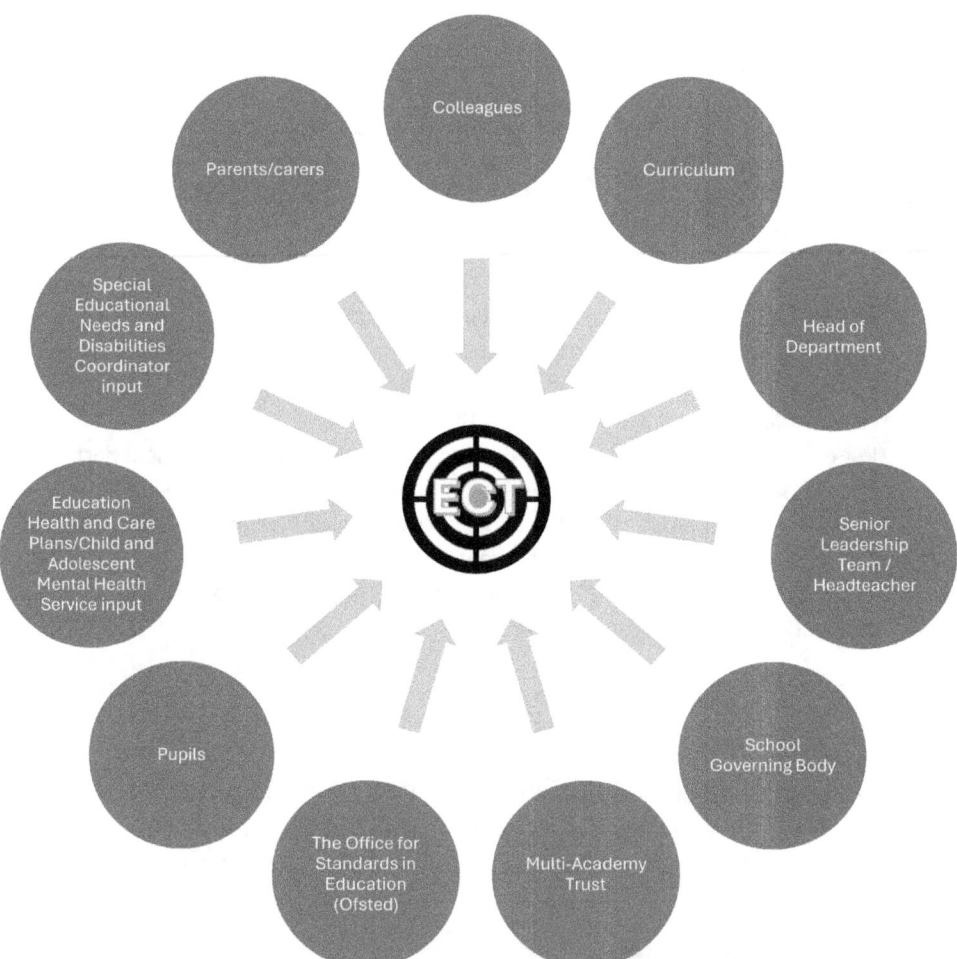

*Figure 17.1* The many potential pressures on a beginning teacher.

the responsibility for achieving certain goals, without the autonomy and authority to make an impact (Pearson & Moomaw, 2005).

Of course, one way in which mentors can protect their ECTs from being in the stressful position of bearing responsibility without autonomy or authority is to encourage collaborative ways of working. Feeling part of a team can alleviate that burden of responsibility, so an important element of a mentor's role is to ensure that systems and expectations allow for teamwork. An in-depth exploration of the differences between cooperation, collaboration, and co-teaching is beyond the scope of this chapter and it is important to acknowledge that the smaller the languages department, the narrower the scope for any sort of sharing of responsibilities, but it may be worth considering the approaches as laid out in Table 17.3.

*Table 17.3* Team or individual approaches to professional challenges

| Professional challenge | Individual approach | Team approach |
| --- | --- | --- |
| Schemes of work (SoW) need to be updated in the light of revised GCSE vocabulary lists. | Head of Department (HoD) sets aside time in October half term to rewrite Y7 SoW with plans to do the same for Y8 over Christmas, Year 9 in February etc., then gives updated schemes to department, including ECT and instructs them to start using the updated scheme. | HoD uses department meeting time for members of the department, including ECT, to rewrite Y7 SoW, then allocates a year group SoW to department members, including ECT, for them to re-write. |
| A newly introduced unit of work lacks teaching materials. | Each member of the department, including ECT prepares their own slides, handouts, worksheets etc. OR HoD prepares slides, handouts, worksheets etc. and expects them to be used by all members of the department, including ECT. | At a department meeting, members of the department, including the ECT, decide on which resources are going to be created by whom and by when. If possible, time is set aside for colleagues to work in pairs. |
| Senior Leadership Team (SLT) is unwilling to allow pupils preparing for GCSE exams to take time out of other subjects in order to do a mock speaking exam. | HoD requests a meeting in which they explain the importance of giving pupils the opportunity for a mock exam and try to convince SLT that the disruption to normal lessons will be minimal. | The department, including the ECT, drafts a document for SLT acknowledging the potential disruption, but also outlining the benefits of running mock speaking exams and proposing ways in which disruption can be minimised. |
| A parent has made a complaint that their child's languages teacher (ECT) is confusing their child by speaking in the Target Language (TL) instead of English. | The ECT writes an email explaining the philosophy behind using TL as the primary means of communication in a languages classroom and copies in the HoD. | The department, including the ECT, prepares a statement to add to the existing information on the school website, explaining the department policy on use of TL and the philosophy behind it. They invite the parent in to school to observe a lesson and see the policy in practice. |

Some potential professional challenges are cited in Table 17.3, and it is always important to consider relevance and applicability in one's own context (Task 17.2).

> **Task 17.2 Considering a team approach**
>
> After considering the examples in Table 17.3, can you think of a professional challenge specific to your current context where you might be able to coordinate a team approach including your ECT(s) in collaborative problem solving?

## Maintaining a healthy work/life balance

'Workload remains the most important factor influencing teachers' decisions to leave the profession and most suggested solutions to addressing retention were linked to workload in some way' (DfE, 2018a, p. 6).

Given that one of the reasons most cited by teachers for leaving the profession is the overwhelming workload, it is of great importance that beginning teachers are supported in trying to manage the competing demands on their time and expertise from the start. Excessive workload can lead to poor mental health and side-effects can manifest themselves in the form of a loss of confidence, absence from work, poor relationships, and an inability to feel empathy. As a mentor it is important to acknowledge that approaches to working practices are as many and varied as there are personality types and that we should therefore avoid the 'do as I do' axiom. What follows is a selection of tips or recommendations which the mentor could use to keep the ECT on track, none of which are presented as a panacea to an unhealthy work/life balance, but all of which are deemed to be helpful to some teachers, some of the time.

- Keep a diary for a week or two and note your work patterns – can any of these be changed?
- Set boundaries or goals such as aiming to finish work by a certain time every day or separating home and work by keeping books and marking in school.
- Give up on perfection! Planning and delivering good lessons consistently is more valuable than planning and delivering the occasional outstanding lesson.
- Be aware of and advocate the use of time-management resources such as those collated by the DfE (2023) to identify the areas which are most problematic and put together a plan to change ways of working which may be causing problems.
- Prioritise your tasks. Ordering your to-do-list according to the Eisenhower Matrix (Figure 17.2), for example, can streamline what might seem overwhelming into clear, visual, ordered tasks.

Above all, remember that it is incumbent upon us as mentor to try and model the sort of behaviours that we would want to encourage in our beginning teachers.

*Figure 17.2* The Eisenhower Matrix. This version adapted from https://slab.com/blog/eisenhower-matrix/ (retrieved January 2024).

## Developing and promoting positive career aspirations in our ECTs

Before focusing on the mentor's role in supporting the career aspirations of ECTs, it is important to pause and reflect on one's own experiences in this regard (Task 17.3).

---

**Task 17.3 Mentor reflection on career development**

Take a moment to consider the development of your own career in the first two or three years of teaching. What opportunities arose for you? How did you find out about these and was there anyone who you can recall supporting you in formulating and taking steps towards your career goals? Was there any support that you would have valued but did not receive?

---

In their second year of teaching, the increase in timetabled responsibilities and duties can, on occasions, seem to swamp the ECT. However, this initial shock soon dissipates as rhythms and routines set in. Your ECT might seem extremely self-motivated and ambitious, or lack evidence of professional self-confidence, or be somewhere in between. Here is your chance to help them discover who they could be as a teacher by getting to know them as a person and seeing where their strengths and passions could take them within the institution where you both work and more broadly. Relationship is key. We acknowledge that there may be interpersonal tensions between mentor and ECT, leading to some difficulties in the professional relationship, but part of the responsibility of a mentor in these circumstances is ensuring that the ECT has regular chances to speak with critical friends/knowledgeable others. Table 17.1 at the start of the chapter gives a possible framework for this purpose.

Here are some examples of positive career paths you might want to encourage your ECT to consider:

- Taking greater pastoral responsibility

    Liaising with the Head of Year/House – how are they faring as a tutor and what further opportunities are there?
- Taking responsibility for a school trip/visit

    Shadowing someone currently running a trip, walking them through the institutional requirements as well as with the travel company. What passions does the ECT bring to the department that could be demonstrated in a trip? This could be to a local exhibition, play or film, as well as a foreign trip. Start small!
- Taking on extra-curricular responsibility

    Could the ECT start a conversation club? A film club? A passion project (such as a group dedicated to exploring politics, discussing climate action, playing board games in the target language (TL; L2), listening to and discussing L2 music, history, fashion) for a specific group of learners? If you have the benefit of employing a Language Assistant, could they join forces to start something new? Equally, this does not have to be languages-specific and Outdoor Education is often a suitable place to start to explore added responsibilities. Use your contacts within school, and/or your experiences in other schools to explore opportunities for your ECT as appropriate.
- Contributing to academic leadership within the department

    Is there a SoW that could be refreshed and led by the ECT? Could the ECT attend an external training course on behalf of the department and report back? Could they take a termly slot in departmental meetings to report back on reading/a recent pedagogical innovation?
- Developing an awareness of possible career paths

    Encourage your ECT to observe a more senior colleague from your own or another department, and meet with them afterwards to discuss middle/senior management experience and sensible first steps towards this end.
- Developing expertise in supporting learners with English as an additional language (EAL)

    What training is on offer? Could you devise a new role (e.g. 'EAL champion') to raise the profile of EAL in languages? What provision does your school offer and, through the ECT, how could languages better join in with this?
- Developing expertise in supporting pupils with special educational needs and disabilities (SEND)

    Encourage your ECT to attend courses/read and implement ideas working alongside the SEND coordinator. Encourage regular meetings to develop the ECT's profile in this area in the school.

## The professional conversation toolkit

Time is not a luxury when mentoring in school, and so we would encourage you to focus on two elements when planning for high-quality, meaningful interactions with your ECT. These are feedforwards and reflections. Spending a little time at the beginning of the year intentionally planning the overarching rationale and structure of these interactions will prevent them from becoming ad hoc and, as is often with school life, somewhat chaotic. This section aims to support this work for you.

## How might we reframe lesson observations to look *forward*?

As discussed throughout this chapter and wider book, there are key issues within languages pedagogy which, without specialist subject knowledge and experience, can be very difficult to tease out. These elements will transcend particular schools' common practices, cultures and methodologies. They will feed *forward* into the ECT's development into an independent practitioner of languages pedagogy, expertly drawing on a number of sources, influences and research angles. As the languages expert, you could be one of a number of colleagues observing the ECT, but the only subject specialist. How can you make your feedback count in this context?

In order to help you retain a focus on elements of lessons that are unique to languages, chapter co-author, Emily Thornton, has devised the following **SCRIPTS** framework to be followed in the order most appropriate to your situation and context. Evidently, not all elements of **SCRIPTS** will be visible every lesson and often it may be useful to discuss the ECT's rationale for leaving some elements *out*. We strongly suggest you keep this acronym in mind as you seek to report on the subject-specific nature of the lesson you observed.

**Sequencing.** How clear is it to the pupils from the presentation of the concepts and activities than this leads on from the previous learning? How much is recapitulated and built on from previous years/topics at the appropriate next higher level (spiral curriculum)? This section could dovetail neatly with the ECF (DfE, 2024).

**Cultural input.** How much of the lesson is grounded in the reality of the countries and cultures in which this language is spoken? Is there enough reference made to the background context of this topic?

**Relevance and accessibility (adaptive teaching).** What has the ECT done to apply the context to the range of pupils in front of them? Is the content and context framed in a way to be accessible and motivational? Refer to the ECF (DfE, 2024) in your comments.

**Individuality.** Is this an 'off the peg' lesson? How much of the passions and interests of the ECT are on display in the presentation, execution, adaptation, and resources provided in the lesson?

**Pillars.** Which foundational language knowledge is covered in the lesson? Grammar/vocabulary/phonics/a combination? Are there elements that needed further consolidation or reference back to previous learning?

**TL Use.** What is the ECT's rationale behind their TL use and where did you notice it be particularly effective? Instructions? Routines? Board work? Displays?

**Skills.** Was the focus on input/output? Was it varied enough? Were there measurable outcomes from a skills perspective regardless of the overall aim of the lesson?

218  *Mentoring Languages Teachers in the Secondary School*

As we have discussed, professional conversations with your ECT and colleague need to be different at this stage in their professional journey. An easy way of encouraging dialogic feedback and avoiding didactic interaction is by ensuring you encourage, model and share good professional reflective practice, retaining a languages focus through the aforementioned SCRIPTS lenses.

## Why is reflection beneficial to mentors and ECTs?

Professional reflective practice is a well-established tool for educators to deepen their understanding of their personal and professional philosophies, their specific subject discipline and the complexities of the learning environment (Robins et al., 2003). Applying reflective models to teaching practice has gained increasing traction in the literature and practice of ITE to evidence professional development, expose biases, normalise issues of accountability, and strive towards excellence. From the authors' experience, reflective models, when used well, are a powerful and efficient method of improving longer term and in-the-moment decision making and can helpfully structure discussions. If you have not encountered reflective models before, they are not to be feared. They are simply a helpful and sensible way of systematising thoughts, and it is likely that you have worked through professional incidents in this way before, just not necessarily known you were using a reflective model.

Being familiar with one or more reflective models, as a mentor, should not be an onerous task, and will help you as you prepare to meet with the ECT. It is a valuable exercise for your own teaching as well as your mentorship, so we urge you to try out the framework we have laid out in Figure 17.3. Engaging in structured reflection as part of your meetings will encourage professional autonomy in your ECT and hopefully lead you to reexamine some of your own professional assumptions and opinions, which is always healthy, if not always easy.

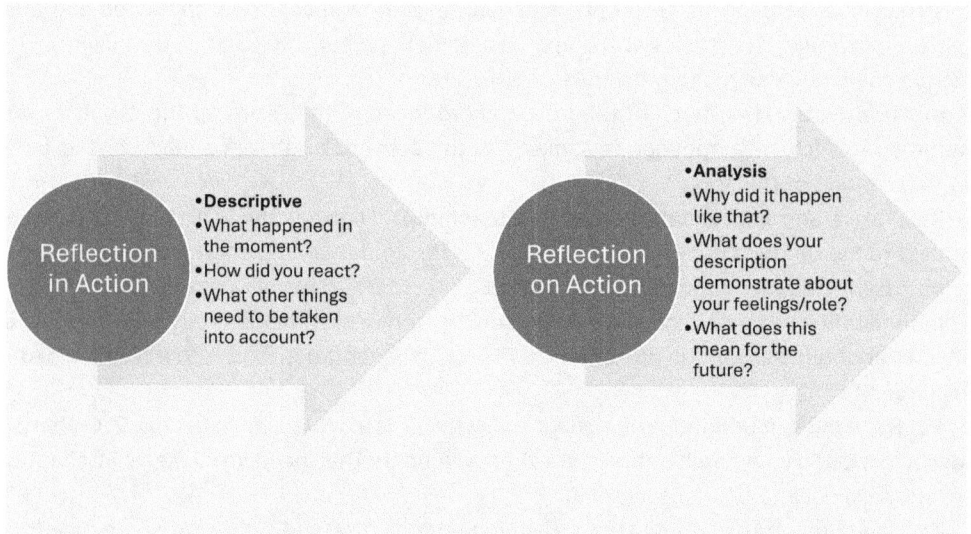

*Figure 17.3* Schön's (1983) model of reflection, making tacit knowledge explicit through the process of reflection.

One of the reasons that structured reflection with their mentor may be helpful for beginning teachers is that it helps the ECT to access their mentor's **tacit knowledge**. This is the knowledge and expertise that you display without consciously thinking or trying: the 'layers of knowledge which presuppose explicit skills, competencies and the ability to reason' (Engel, 2008, p. 184). How often do you look back on a lesson, go through each decision you made and work out why you did what you did? When did you last watch a recording of yourself teaching? As a mentor you will be required to activate the processes behind your decisions more often than a classroom teacher without this coaching role. This is called **explicit knowledge.** You will need to tease apart what comes naturally and through experience. One theorist who works with the idea of tacit and explicit knowledge is Schön (1983), who calls it 'knowing-in-action', where we do not always know why we take the decisions we do. Schön's theories encourage professionals to become 'reflective practitioners', and his structured reflective model (Figure 17.3) is one we recommend to structure interactions with your ECT, with our adaptations. Please see the end of this chapter for more resources on reflection and pointers to other models.

Concretely, 'reflection-on-action' might mean considering in detail questions such as: why did you switch to English at this point in the lesson? Why did you spontaneously decide to go back to previous learning on a different topic for this grammar point? Why did you stop the listening task two questions before the end and move on to the next element of the lesson?

As soon as you begin to think about these decisions, your *knowing-in-action* becomes *knowledge-in-action*. Why does this matter? Breaking down this whole process is an act of professional reflection, and it is useful to label each stage in turn. Some decisions will take on the significance of a 'critical incident', namely 'the interpretation of the significance of an event' (Tripp, 1994, p. 8). Before we apply these concepts to your role as a mentor, take a moment to work through Task 17.4 as a way of moving your own tacit knowledge to the domain of the explicit and seeing how you might conceptualise a 'critical incident'.

### Task 17.4 Exploring tacit knowledge

Bring to mind a recent scenario (pedagogical, interpersonal, or a mixture of both) in your teaching: this could be one where something you did worked really well, or one where something went wrong. Ideally, this would be fresh in your mind from the last couple of days. We suggest you jot this exercise down on a piece of paper as it is in two parts.

Firstly, describe the event as you remember it. Sketch it out chronologically.

- what was the context?
- what led you to act in the way you acted? What previous experience(s) did you draw on?
- what happened?
- what was your role? What were others'?
- how much did your action differ from a similar situation previously?
- what was the outcome?
- how did you feel after the situation?

> Now go and have a cup of tea (or plan tomorrow's lessons!) and leave these ideas to brew. When you return, re-read your notes and ask yourself these follow-up questions:
>
> 1. Is there a particular theme or emotional tone that I can see in my writing? Has this affected my interpretation of the event?
> 2. Was my role as I had described? Was my first description skewed in any way? Why might this be?
> 3. When I reconsider the situation, what would I keep the same?
> 4. What would I change?
> 5. What input/help would I need to improve a similar situation?
>
> How has this process changed your analysis of your role as mentor when considering tacit knowledge, if at all?

We suggest that the process of reflection described in Task 17.4 could form the backbone of your formalised interactions with your ECT over the whole year, with frequent reference to the ECF (DfE, 2024) to root reflections in statutory expectations. Using Schön's (1983) model, supported by the suggested questions in Figure 17.4, will provide a structure for your individual interactions and help to sequence and frame them over the course of the year, with the aim of empowering the ECT to embed these tools of professional reflection in their practice in the formative stages of their career. The elements for reflection can be chosen by the mentor or ECT, with an increasing degree of agency given to the ECT over the course of their induction years.

Adding the element of 'Reflection *before* action', as we have done in Figure 17.4, gives Schön's model a helpful tripartite structure to bookend your discussions. The questions in three parts should prove more than enough for a mentor session. Aim to spend the most time on the final segment, but as Task 17.4 has hopefully demonstrated, this section is most useful when

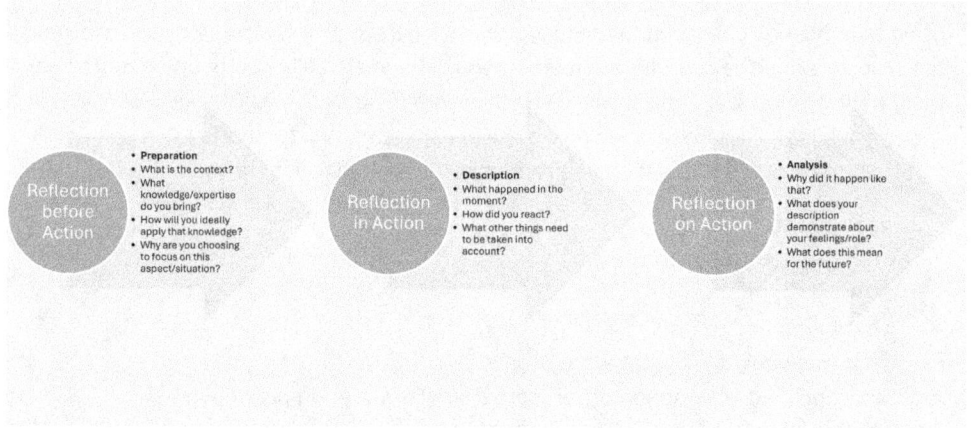

*Figure 17.4* Adaptation of Schön's (1983) reflective model to provide structure for meaningful and forward-looking interactions over the ECT year(s).

*Continuing to mentor beginning languages teachers* 221

the reflection *in* action has been discussed fully. It is necessary for previous conversations, experiences and events in the ECT's recent teaching to feed into the focus for the next observation, as well as elements pre-determined by the ECF (DfE, 2024). Using the elements of **SCRIPTS** from your previous interaction/observation, consider together (by email if needed) what your next focus should be, and link this in with the ECF. By following this approach, you should find you need to direct your ECT less and less as the year progresses. Further, the ECT will be empowered to 'rewrite the script' to best serve their own professional and career goals (Task 17.5). See Appendix 2 for a proforma to support your structured reflections with your mentee.

### Task 17.5 Scenarios

Having read the above, how would you react in these scenarios? How might your ECT react? These scenarios could form the basis for a discussion between the mentor and other colleagues as well as the ECT to promote departmental consistency. Please see Appendix 3 for some possible responses to these scenarios.

- Scenario 1
    It is the end of October, and you are starting the second half of the Autumn Term. You are continuing to mentor a beginning teacher who has successfully completed their first year as an ECT at your school. Your ECT is conscientious and competent and has built positive relationships with their pupils. You have scheduled fortnightly meetings during which you have discussed basics such as time management and prioritising tasks. At the most recent meeting you suggested your ECT could contribute to the work of the department by creating a resource such as a text for reading comprehension which all members of the department could use. This is something encouraged in your department as there is a philosophy of sharing resources. Since then, you get the impression that your ECT has been avoiding you and you have heard from another colleague that they have been unhappy at being given what they perceive to be an additional task which they should not be obliged to do. Your next meeting is tomorrow. How would you proceed?

- Scenario 2
    It is early September and you have been asked to mentor a new member of staff who has successfully completed their PGCE year and is embarking on their first teaching job as an ECT. This member of staff is a French national, a native speaker of French who came to the UK to train as a teacher. Your first impressions are that your ECT is enthusiastic, energetic, and keen to adopt the working practices of the department. During an informal 'pop in' to a Year 10 class you observe that a rather high number of pupils are off task, and it becomes clear they have not understood the task they have been given. Rather than this being a one-off, you realise that your ECT has adopted the department's policy of using maximum TL so enthusiastically with all classes that their lessons are conducted almost exclusively in

French. As time goes on your ECT expresses frustration at what they perceive to be non-cooperation amongst their pupils, while the pupils express frustration at not understanding important parts of their lessons. How would you proceed?

- Scenario 3

    It is February and your ECT is progressing well. They enjoy positive relationships with both pupils and colleagues and their lessons are well planned and delivered. They now want to take on a new challenge and have expressed the desire to plan and run a residential trip to Spain for Year 8 pupils in the summer term of this year. Your school has not run any overseas trips for a while and the colleague who used to run a similar trip has since left the school. Your ECT is full of enthusiasm for this trip and talks excitedly about how much their pupils will enjoy visiting a country where the language they are learning is spoken. You are concerned that this plan is rather ambitious and that your ECT does not fully appreciate the time scale, the bureaucracy and the negotiations involved. How would you proceed?

- Scenario 4

    You have been asked to 'buddy' a new member of staff who is in their third year of teaching, having joined your languages team from a much smaller school where they completed their two ECT years. Your colleague is independent and self-sufficient and rarely initiates discussions about departmental policy or ways of working. You are aware that before and after school hours, as well as lunchtime, your new colleague prefers not to join the rest of the team in the languages office, remaining in their classroom to prepare lessons and mark pupil work. Your suggestion that they might like to work in the office has been rejected on the grounds that the atmosphere in the office would not be as conducive to work. You feel your 'buddy' would benefit from being part of the many informal discussions taking place in the office and you suspect they may be feeling overwhelmed by the workload. How would you proceed?

## Conclusion

In this chapter we considered how school-based mentors can support a beginning teacher as they develop from being newly qualified to being an experienced member of staff. We acknowledge that there is no one way to fulfil the role of mentor but advocate a dialogic and reciprocal approach.

The evolving role of the mentor, linked to the emerging independence of the ECT, was explored and suggestions were made about how this changing relationship might be navigated. We highlighted the sorts of tensions a mentor might experience, such as the phenomenon of 'high stakes accountability' and the importance of maintaining a healthy work/life balance. Possible solutions were offered, while emphasising that there is no 'one size fits all' way of doing things. Consideration was given to the promotion of career aspirations for the beginning teacher.

The acronym **SCRIPTS** (**S**equencing, **C**ultural input, **R**elevance and accessibility, **I**ndividuality, **P**illars, **T**L, **S**kills) was presented as a possible feedback framework, so that professional conversations remain languages-focused and have maximum impact.

Schön's (1983) model for reflection was presented and its benefits to both mentors and ECTs were explained. The chapter finished with some scenarios one might encounter as a mentor to an ECT, inviting the reader to consider how they would proceed, having read and digested the content of this chapter.

## For discussion

After reading this chapter, mentors may benefit from reflecting on the following questions:

- Am I giving my ECT the opportunities they need to forge their path from dependence to independence?
- Have I played my part in ensuring that my ECT's sense of accountability is not overwhelming?
- Is my feedback framed as *feedforward*, pointing towards a 'future horizon'?
- Is my ECT starting to set themselves some next steps towards their career aspirations?
- Am I making best use of the **SCRIPTS** acronym in my professional conversations with my mentee?
- How systematic is my own professional reflection? Am I modelling how to use reflective frameworks effectively?

## Further reading

Language teacher retention, in the first five years of entering the profession, is a matter of concern not just for nations of the United Kingdom (DfE, 2018a) but internationally too. We recommend reading this open-access article, which explores a multitude of different factors contributing to ECT' decisions as to whether to remain or to leave. You may find this information helpful when supporting ECTs with their career development, promotion or relocation decisions.

- Sulis, G., Babic, S., Mairitsch, A., Mercer, S., Jin, J., & King, J. (2022). Retention and attrition in early-career foreign language teachers in Austria and the United Kingdom. *The Modern Language Journal, 106*(1), 155–171.

    We consider that effective mentoring for the retention of ECT should be regarded as a critical investment for schools, particularly in 'shortage subjects' such as languages. This e-book explores the factors that not only encourage languages teachers to remain in the profession but also enable them to thrive.

- Jones, J., & Gordon, A. L. (2020). *Teachers who flourish: Why MFL teachers stay in the classroom.* https://www.all-languages.org.uk/product/teachers-who-flourish-why-mfl-teachers-stay-in-the-classroom-by-jane-jones-and-anna-lise-gordon/

## References

Ball, S. (2003). The teacher's soul and the terrors of performativity. *Journal of Education Policy, 18*(2), 215–228.

Department for Education. (2018a). *Factors affecting teacher retention: Qualitative investigation.* https://assets.publishing.service.gov.uk/media/5aa15d24e5274a53c0b29341/Factors_affecting_teacher_retention_-_qualitative_investigation.pdf

Department for Education. (2018b). *Reducing school workload.* [online] GOV.UK. https://www.gov.uk/government/collections/reducing-school-workload

Department for Education. (2024). *Initial Teacher Training and Early Career Framework.* https://www.gov.uk/government/publications/initial-teacher-training-and-early-career-framework.

Heiberg Engel, P. J. (2008). Tacit knowledge and visual expertise in medical diagnostic reasoning: Implications for medical education. *Medical Teacher, 30*(7), e184-e188. https://doi.org/10.1080/01421590802144260.

Marcdante, K., & Simpson, D. (2018). Choosing when to advise, coach, or mentor. *Journal of Graduate Medical Education, 10*(2), 227-228. https://doi.org/10.4300/jgme-d-18-00111.1.

Pearson, L., & Moomaw, W. (2005). *The relationship between teacher autonomy and stress, work satisfaction, empowerment, and professionalism.* [online]. https://files.eric.ed.gov/fulltext/EJ718115.pdf

Robins, A., Ashbaker, B., Enriquez, J., & Morgan, J. (2003). *Learning to reflect: Professional practice for Professionals and paraprofessionals. International Journal of Learning, 10,* 2555-2565.

Sadler, I., Reimann, N., & Sambell, K. (2022). Feedforward practices: A systematic review of the literature. *Assessment & Evaluation in Higher Education, 48*(3), 1-16. https://doi.org/10.1080/02602938.2022.2073434.

Schön, D. (1983). *The reflective practitioner: How professionals think in action.* TempleSmith.

Sullivan, A., Johnson, B., Simons, M., & Tippett, N. (2020). When performativity meets agency: How early career teachers struggle to reconcile competing agendas to become 'quality' teachers. *Teachers and Teaching,* 1-16. https://doi.org/10.1080/13540602.2020.1806050.

Tripp, D. (1994). Teachers' lives, critical incidents and professional practice. *International Journal of Qualitative Studies in Education, 7*(1), 65-76. https://doi.org/10.1080/0951839940070105

# 18 Supporting expert languages teachers: educative mentoring for success

*Bernadette Holmes, Judith Rifeser, and Caroline Conlon*

## Introduction

In this chapter we will explore the relevance of peer mentoring to experienced teachers of languages. Our aim is that, taken together with Chapter 5 in this volume, we will illustrate the concept of mentoring as an evolutionary process, which by its nature changes over time and sustains its value. We invite you to reflect on key areas and consider the answers to some reflexive questions to support action planning. The process intends to engage readers (existing or prospective mentors) in developing a shared understanding of how mentoring can bring about constructive change as part of a carefully planned programme of professional learning across the teacher's career.

At the end of this chapter, you should be able to:

- Define and clarify the role of peer mentoring for established practitioners.
- Identify the benefits of the mentoring process for professional learning and continuous improvement at all stages of the teacher's career.
- Understand how the mentoring process can refresh and deepen professional knowledge, valorise subject experience and expertise, and sustain teacher motivation.

## The national context for professional learning and system-leadership

In defining and clarifying the role of peer mentoring for established practitioners, it will be helpful to explore the ecology of professional learning and how the current national context in teacher development appears to conceptualise professional learning as a central part of system leadership. The environment for professional learning in England has changed considerably over recent years. There is now significant emphasis on providing guidance on how to build common understandings across the sector regarding what constitutes effective professional learning and system-leadership. The Department for Education (DfE), working with a range of sector organisations, has developed a suite of frameworks and national professional qualifications (NPQs) to support professional development at different stages of the teacher's career. There is a clear trajectory from initial teacher training to middle leadership and onward through to senior leadership and executive headship (DfE, 2020). The new frameworks have been endorsed by the Education Endowment Foundation (EEF) following an independent review of the former suite of NPQs which they now supersede.

The intentions behind these frameworks and qualifications merit some closer attention, as we explore the status and position of mentoring within this changing and dynamic ecosystem. The DfE policy paper *Delivering world-class teacher development* sets out a range of reforms to England's teacher development system (DfE, 2022). This publication appeared on the back of the *Teacher Recruitment and Retention Strategy* (DfE, 2019) and the government response to the *Initial Teacher Training (ITT) Market Review* (DfE, 2021). The policy paper outlines the government's explicit intentions to provide world-class teacher development by transforming the system and defining a route map of support, guidance, and professional learning from trainee teacher to beginning teacher, to experienced teachers and middle leaders to senior leaders, heads, and executive leaders. The reforms propose major changes not only in how professional development is made available and to whom but also in what we consider to constitute professional learning. There is commonality between the expectations and foundational principles underpinning each of the frameworks. It is intended that one framework leads onto the next providing a coherent pathway of teacher development. As teachers reach each milestone in their career, they are signposted in the direction of the next. The NPQs are voluntary and accredited and at the time of writing, they are fully funded by the DfE for teachers who are working in state-funded settings or in contexts where they engage with vulnerable or disadvantaged youth (Task 18.1).

---

**Task 18.1 Reflect on System-leadership and professional learning**

What do you understand by the term system leadership and how does this relate to professional learning?

---

## Understanding the golden thread

This suite of policy initiatives for England explicitly sets outs to connect each phase of the teacher's career through nationwide system-leadership reform. The focus of the frameworks moves away from external evaluation of teaching standards to greater self-efficacy and 'continuous improvement' through professional development. It can be argued that the DfE frameworks have learned much from the world of business where performance frameworks are often used developmentally, aligning goals, vision and values to organisational systems and processes and most importantly with the people, who will deliver them. The theory of the golden thread (familiar to the world of business) has been applied to education.

The theory of the golden thread in a business context is all about improving performance across the operational system to achieve specific goals. The Chartered Management Institute (CMI) provides a clear definition and an explanation of how the golden thread theory works in practice within business. It is described as:

> a performance model that aligns business goals to measures of success. The Golden Thread is the link between vision, analysis, systems, and people, amounting to a shared understanding of how the vision, goals and values of the organisation relate to daily work. The alignment to organisational goals is essential if performance is to improve on a sustainable basis.
>
> (CMI, 2024)

In the educational context, the intentions of the golden thread appear to be very similar to those of the business context, namely, to achieve national goals by strengthening the quality of system-leadership. The golden thread in business (CMI, 2018, 2021) draws explicit attention to the often overlooked middle and operational management activities that are key to linking an organisation's strategy to its goals, ensuring that the contribution of individuals across the system are in alignment. Within the educational context, recognition of the centrality of the middle manager in bringing about organisational success is highly salient, particularly relating to the potential of the mentoring process in promoting and sustaining meaningful change.

The intended processes and outcomes of the NPQ qualifications aspire to develop common expectations, professional values, and behaviours. They are informed by a common vision and intent to build a world class education system providing equity for every child by levelling up opportunities and strengthening the quality of leadership, teaching, and learning. 'These qualifications complete the golden thread: a curriculum, sequenced over time, for teaching and leading in schools from initial training to executive leadership' (Hood, 2021, para 7) (Task 18.2).

---

**Task 18.2 Understanding the golden thread**

What is your understanding of the golden thread? How can the dolden thread improve the quality of education and contribute to meeting national goals?

---

## Relating the golden thread to 'Best bets'

The Frameworks draw on evidence from across the United Kingdom and overseas and references reviews, syntheses, and metanalyses of best practice. Building on this evidence, the concept of 'best bets' has been developed. These relate to content, methods, and pedagogical approaches which are judged to be the most effective in closing the attainment gap. Summarised in the Education Endowment Foundation's Toolkit (EEF 2021) these 'best bets' are intended to support teachers and teacher leaders in making decisions about the curriculum and teaching and learning. The content of the toolkits is evidence-based and is underpinned by foundational principles. Each approach or method is evaluated and scored in relation to the extent of progress in learning outcomes that it generates. The impact is calculated and expressed in notional additional months of progress made by the average child who experiences this form of teaching or intervention.

The EEF justifies the concept behind 'best bets' explaining that because the toolkits are based on real life data garnered from schools, they provide evidence of what has worked in real classrooms over time. While the toolkits provide high quality information about what is likely to be beneficial based on existing evidence, this does not obviate the need for professional judgement and the essential role of teachers in testing out methods and approaches within the crucible of the classroom and making informed decisions about what will work most effectively in their context. In this sense, teachers explore the extent to which *best bets* are the *best fit* for their learners.

Various kinds of activities, methods and interventions constitute 'best bets' and are generic in nature, for example, the use of low stakes quizzing, sequencing the curriculum, learning about cognitive load theory, and developing metacognition and self-regulated learning, said to result in seven months of additional progress for the average child (EEF, 2021). For any or all of these 'best bets' to be effective, there needs to be a conversion of the generic principles to the subject specific. This process requires situated-inquiry, criticality, and evaluation of the impact on learning outcomes. 'Ultimately, for a judgement about whether teaching is effective, to be seen as trustworthy, it must be checked against the progress being made by students' (Coe et al., 2014). We can assume that to bring about constructive change in how we teach with the intention of improving learning outcomes, individuals and teams of teachers will need to engage in learning conversations, peer observation, and co-planning. The role of the mentor will be central in supporting this process and in making connections between theory and practice that will be adaptive and reflective of the needs and interests of the learners in each context.

A national study from New Zealand (Timperley et al., 2007) describes a teacher 'knowledge-building cycle' that forms a feedback loop for teachers that is closely associated with improved pupil outcomes. The knowledge building cycle develops over time involving teachers in a continuing process of inquiry and reflection, based on evidence from their own context and experience, and evaluated against the learning experiences and outcomes of their pupils. The full title of the study can be seen to encapsulate the processes involved in this evidence-informed approach to professional learning. The Teacher Professional Learning and Development Best Evidence Synthesis (BES) Iteration (Timperley et al., 2007) includes a synthesis of relevant research literature identifying what is known about effective professional learning and what remains to be explored further. The study acknowledges that there are no quick fixes, and that professional learning is iterative and requires teachers to invest in a longer-term commitment to bring about constructive change.

The New Zealand study (Timperley et al., 2007) wisely recognises that experienced teachers need to be convinced that there can be benefit in doing things differently. While more traditional approaches to continuing professional development have tended to rely on an individual teacher attending a training course and then adapting or adopting the recommendations or methods put forward, the BES approach requires greater engagement from the teacher in the short and longer-term. The knowledge building loop requires a two-stage inquiry and evaluation process. The first stage involves the teacher in reflecting on their own experience and practice taking account of their own context and evaluating the impact of their teaching on the learning outcomes of their pupils. The second inquiry stage involves teachers in accessing and reflecting on knowledge and research from other valid and reliable sources. They are then encouraged to test out new approaches and to develop and use new pedagogical understandings in their teaching. The priority always lies in monitoring the impact of teaching approaches to improving learning outcomes.

For processes such as these to work effectively, they should be developed, coordinated, and led by specialist mentors. To be sustainable, such processes should be supported by school leaders and should become system wide, as we know system-leadership is a complex business. Organisational structures, systems, and processes need to combine to weave the golden thread across the career span of the teacher. Through such approaches to professional learning, every teacher can be an agent of change, but to facilitate the process, maximise impact, and foster the culture of continuous development, it is the pivotal role of the mentor that should be recognised and supported (Task 18.3).

### Task 18.3 Relating the golden thread to system leadership

How would you describe the role of the mentor in relation to golden thread theory and system leadership?

## Parameters and purposes of the peer mentoring model for experienced teachers

As we read in Chapter 5, the established and familiar parameters and purposes of mentoring normally (but not always) involve a mentee of less experience benefiting from regular contact with a more experienced mentor. This has become standard practice in initial teacher education and forms an essential part of most if not all routes into teaching. As we consider the value of mentoring and explore how the benefits of the mentoring process can be carried over into peer-to-peer mentoring at different stages of a teacher's career, it will be helpful to look more closely at the evolving nature of mentoring and the different kinds of relationships that can be included in the definition of mentorship.

There is much to be learned from international and interdisciplinary perspectives on mentorship, particularly from STEMM (Science, Technology, Engineering, Maths, and Medicine) in the United States. An impressive example of the priority given to the importance of mentorship to optimising the potential of the future STEMM workforce in the United States, the National Academies of Sciences, Engineering and Medicine, otherwise known as the National Academies, chose to focus their Consensus Study Report (2019) on mentorship. The National Academies in the US liaise directly with the Office of Congressional and Government Affairs (OCGA) and influence policy and legislation. It is significant that the Academies recognised that mentorship could be a catalyst for developing participation in STEMM subjects and a means of improving the training environment and developmental spaces for future specialists of STEMM. Acknowledging that practice in mentorship varied in range and quality in higher education, the National Academies sought to codify, develop and strengthen mentoring across STEMM, leaving nothing to chance. The report is available online and provides a comprehensive definition of mentorship.

> The committee defines mentorship as a professional, working alliance in which individuals work together over time to support the personal and professional growth, development, and success of the relational partners through the provision of career and psychosocial support. The committee uses the term mentorship to connote that mentoring occurs via a process based on reciprocal activities in mentoring relationships.
> 
> (NASEM Consensus Study Report 2019, footnote p. x)

The key characteristics of this definition would seem to be relevant to individuals in most professional contexts and to most disciplines. The purposes outlined span both personal and professional dimensions, emphasising the interrelationship of psychosocial support and professional career development. It is salient that the committee understands the mentoring process to be reciprocal implying that mentors and mentees are equal beneficiaries of the process itself.

The focus on psychosocial support within the definition is of particular interest as we know that the well-being of our early career teachers is crucial if we are to retain teachers long-term in our profession. Successful mentorship can be assumed to involve relational understanding based on trust, confidentiality, and empathy as well as professional credibility, constructive criticality, and subject knowledge. It can be argued that understanding the psychosocial needs of teachers should take precedence as the parameters of the mentoring structure are agreed and put in place. It is widely understood that the needs of good mental health include a sense of safety, autonomy, relatedness, competence, and self-esteem. These also form the essential components of self-efficacy and self-determination theory (Ryan & Deci, 2000).

In developing the NASEM Consensus Report 2019, several theories were considered in thinking about mentorship. Of particular interest was Social Cognitive Career Theory (SCCT) developed largely from the seminal work of Bandura (1986) on social cognitive theory. The underpinning rationale rested on the theory that the beliefs and behaviours of individuals and the career choices that they make are socially constructed. They rely on positive learning experiences and a sense of making progress, self-efficacy, and expectation of successful learning outcomes. Career choices can therefore be shaped by the training environment and influenced by effective or ineffective mentoring.

Logic would suggest that the influence of the training environment and effective or ineffective mentoring is likely to have similar impact and outcomes in languages education and the recruitment and retention of teachers as it exerts in STEMM.

If we consider and apply the NASEM definition (2019) as a working model for mentorship in schools, there are implications for how schools provide optimal conditions for mentorship to be effectively developed and sustained. The importance of the development of *a working alliance over time* is of particular importance. Mentoring structures that are time poor are unlikely to yield fruitful benefits to either the mentee(s) or the mentor(s) (Task 18.4).

### Task 18.4 Exploring the peer mentoring model

How can schools provide optimal conditions for peer-to-peer mentoring?

The NASEM Consensus Report (2019) draws attention to the differences between formal, semi-formal, and informal mentoring structures:

> Mentoring relationships can occur in formal, structured, and intentional settings or as informal, organically developed relationships—sometimes structured, sometimes not— that a mentee develops with a more experienced individual with whom the mentee has regular contact.
>
> (Inzer & Crawford, 2005, Box 2-1, p. 37)

Taking their analysis from the world of STEMM, Inzer and Crawford (2005) categorise a variety of mentoring relationship structures with different degrees of formality that can include the following:

i. *A single mentor working with a single mentee in a classic dyadic relationship.*
ii. *A group of mentors sharing their collective wisdom with one mentee.*
iii. *One mentor working with multiple mentees.*
iv. *Peer and near-peer mentoring structure.*
v. *Online peer communities.*
vi. *Programmatic mentoring.*
vii. *Mentoring experiences delivered through carefully constructed short-term seminars, workshops, or presentations.*

The NASEM Consensus report (2019, p. 37) observes that:

> although this last format [vii] challenges the idea of mentoring relationships involving personal interaction between individuals, a mentee can see it as being equivalent to or sometimes superior to what can be obtained in an individual, dyadic relationship.

If we consider these categories in relation to mentorship of future languages teachers, almost all the categories defined can be applied to our discipline and to our educational contexts. Lessons from the pandemic have shown us how to use technology effectively to teach, to give feedback and to evaluate. Now, in healthier times, we can benefit from the affordances of technology and our heightened understanding of their flexibility and potential to create a new hybrid environment for professional learning and mentoring. We can widen access to more individuals and to a greater range of contexts through learning conversations between mentors and mentees and between peers in-person and on-line. We can continue to experience classroom teaching through direct observation in-person, but we now have the capability through video technology systems to develop the use of video observation and coaching in teacher development (EEF, 2017). Teachers are now able to record lessons, edit and comment on teaching and learning individually or in groups. Through dialogue and feedback from peers either on a one-to-one or collaborative small group basis, teachers can strengthen their subject knowledge and widen their professional skills using evidence of pupils' learning garnered directly from current classrooms. The opportunities for expanding the modalities for our professional development synchronously and asynchronously through technology are increasing rapidly (EEF, 2020) (Task 18.5).

---

**Task 18.5 Rethinking the modalities for professional learning**

Thinking about your own recent experiences of professional learning or networking, how was this structured? Consider the degree of formality, the professional relationship of participants involved, and how knowledge was shared and developed. If technology supported the process, how was this organised and what were the advantages/disadvantages of its use?

Whether in-person or at distance through virtual connections, the relationship between participants in the mentoring process is crucial. There are several factors that can affect the success or otherwise of the mentoring structure. The status of those involved in the mentorship process matters as it can compromise the level of candour between participants and the extent to which each party is willing to be open and transparent. The more asymmetrical the relationship, the more it may tend towards an expert versus apprentice model. Other important factors may include the degree of formality and accountability; whether the arrangement is chosen or imposed; the choice of who works with whom and how this decision is made, internally or externally; and the stage of each person's career.

There are ways to optimise the benefits of mentoring and to mitigate against any negative reactions and reluctance to participate. From the inception of the mentoring process, it is helpful to:

- Agree upon a definition of mentorship.
- Develop a collective understanding of the rationale for the mentoring process.
- Set out clear parameters and purposes.
- Discuss and agree ethical principles that can inform a Code of Conduct for mentoring.
- Decide on the length of time that the mentoring process will be in place.
- Agree on intended outcomes and what success will look like.

Introducing peer-to-peer or near-peer mentoring requires fresh thinking and a re-definition of the mentor-mentee relationship. The process can be voluntary or imposed by senior leadership, but the essential feature is usually that there is a set purpose with specific outcomes in mind which galvanises the approach and gives a steer as to the expected outcomes of the process. Peer-to-peer or near-peer mentoring can be introduced short or longer-term for different purposes:

- As a form of professional development for individuals.
- To enhance team building.
- To support innovation in a particular curriculum area.
- To implement school policy.
- To bring about specific changes to instigate school improvement.

A further key feature of successful mentoring is that it is not static. The mentoring process is dynamic and developmental. It has continued relevance and value at every stage of the teacher's career.

## Developing, deepening, and co-constructing professional knowledge through the mentoring process

Peer and near-peer mentoring structures have attracted significant attention in recent years both in the United Kingdom and in the United States through approaches like Instructional Coaching (Knight, 2007; Knight & van Nieuwerburgh, 2012) and Educative Mentoring (Stanulis et al., 2019; White and Mackintosh, 2022). It will be helpful to briefly reflect on the similarities and differences in these approaches as we consider how to develop and deepen professional knowledge and skills for more experienced teachers through the mentoring process.

According to Knight and van Nieuwerburgh (2012), instructional coaching was primarily designed for more experienced teachers rather than beginning teachers. Instructional coaching *a priori* sets out to change current pedagogical practice through the introduction of techniques and strategies which are intended to achieve specific outcomes. It involves coaching, modelling and goal setting and normally intends to bring about mastery of a particular technique or strategy in a short timeframe. Some instructional coaching models can include step-by-step analysis of how to teach following a particular pedagogical approach (Sims, 2019). The coach provides support, and the training is often repeated until the trainee has met the goal. It can be argued that the step-by-step specificity and repeated modelling can reduce the cognitive load required to understand and implement the pedagogical technique being introduced. The risk of this approach is that it can be prescriptive and transactional, reliant on a transmission model underpinned by an expert to apprentice conceptual framework. While this may be time-efficient and effective in some contexts, it can lead to an overdependence on external support (White & Mackintosh, 2022) and is maybe less likely to develop the self-efficacy and independence of the mentee.

As we read from the New Zealand study (Timperley et al., 2007), the reciprocal benefits of the mentoring process must be apparent to both participants. This is particularly important regarding peer-to-peer mentorship. Educative mentoring assumes a constructivist approach that takes account of the professional knowledge and skills of mentor and mentee and builds on these. It is relational and its success depends on trust, mutual respect and criticality. According to White and Mackintosh (2022, para 4): 'educative mentoring can be understood as a form of situated inquiry embedded in practice'. In a peer-to-peer mentoring arrangement, this approach can be very effective as it can become a routine part of individual and departmental professional learning processes.

There are commonalities between educative mentoring and instructional coaching in that both approaches involve discussion between the mentor and mentee, observation and planning. The approaches differ in that educative mentoring has a broader and longer-term impact of developing teacher agency, helping teachers to understand theoretical principles and how these relate to pedagogy and practice within their own setting. It is less about training teachers to perform better by adopting a particular teaching strategy or to implement a national directive, and more about developing a broader understanding of teaching and learning based on inquiry, reflection and willingness to adapt to meet the needs of learners in context. It is cyclical and iterative encouraging teachers to foster a collegial culture of critical thinking, co-planning and development.

> The advantage of using educative mentoring as an underpinning approach rather than instructional coaching is that educative mentoring focuses more widely than just developing different teaching strategies. It is a holistic and emotionally intelligent approach to professional development.
>
> (White & Mackintosh, 2022, para 12)

There are several processes which characterise educative mentoring that have the potential to reset teacher behaviours, attitudes, and beliefs and can lead to positive change in how teacher knowledge can be developed, co-constructed and shared. The 'think aloud technique' where a teacher talks through their thought processes with a colleague or colleagues as they are teaching, analysing what they are doing and reflecting on why they are doing it, has proved very successful in developing a shared understanding of the rationale for decisions relating to lesson planning and pedagogical approaches. Modelling practice can be of value to teachers at any stage of their career and should be an essential element of professional learning. Modelling must be accompanied by the learning conversation that follows the observation stage. Peer-to-peer or mentor and mentee(s) should ensure planned time for reflection and analysis discussing the thought processes that informed the choice of teaching methods and relating these to a reference point that either reflects a particular theory or previous experience (Polombo & Daly, 2022). In situations where experienced teachers are working collaboratively to develop a consistent approach to teaching across a subject team through peer-to-peer mentoring, paired or peer observation can be transformative.

The National Consortium for Languages (NCLE – https://ncle-language-hubs.ucl.ac.uk) has introduced paired/peer observation and peer-to-peer mentoring via its lead hubs and their partner schools to reinvigorate language teaching and learning across the government regions in England. The notion of professional and social reciprocity has become a foundational principle underpinning peer-to-peer mentoring within our conceptualisation of the mentorship process and informs our rationale for how specialist teachers from our lead hub schools work collaboratively, collegially and creatively with our partner schools. Through peer-to-peer mentoring we intend to foster a culture of continuous professional learning by establishing social and work-related norms of positive behaviours responding to positive actions and rewarding constructive change.

NCLE has developed a creative use of peer observation as part of situated classroom inquiry. Teachers identify a key area for inquiry and agree key questions for exploration. For example, a group of two or three teachers decide their focus will be on assessment for learning. They agree to observe each other's lessons over a set period such as a half-term. Their questions for exploration are as follows:

- How does assessment for learning develop metacognition and improve pupil confidence and independent learning behaviours?
- What small changes can teachers make through including assessment for learning in their lesson planning that optimise independent learning habits?

Working as a pair or a three, each teacher will have the opportunity to alternate roles in the peer-to-peer observation/mentoring process. In a group of three, teacher 1 delivers the lesson. Teacher 2 observes the lesson focusing on what the teacher is doing at each stage of the lesson. Teacher 3 observes the learners and experiences the lesson through the learners' lens. If teachers are working in a pair, they can change the lens of their observation across a series of lessons and vary between the teacher lens and the learner lens. Before the observation(s), teachers develop a collaborative lesson observation schedule (CLOSCH) where they elaborate prompts and questions to guide their observations. During the lesson, the observer(s) will make notes and record key observations of what is taking place at each stage of the lesson. Following the lesson, the teachers meet to discuss and triangulate what they have observed. Using evidence from the learners' responses and their learning outcomes, the teachers co-plan the next lesson or series of lessons, making small modifications to the teaching to improve the learning experience. Depending on the ethos of the department and the school as a whole other processes can accompany the peer mentoring and lesson observation process such as pupil focus groups and book looks.

The systematic use of peer observation and the co-planning of the CLOSCH can make a significant contribution to implementing constructive change. The process combines theory and practical experience and involves reflective and reflexive practice. In this way, teaching approaches and interventions can be tested inside the classroom and decisions can be made based on evidence of success. The peer-to-peer co-construction of the CLOSCH develops a shared purpose and clear understanding of the nature of the changes that teachers are seeking to make. The learning conversations provide rich opportunities for teachers to develop a common language to describe the intervention(s) that they have decided to implement. This can lead to greater fidelity to principles or approaches that are being introduced and can avoid misconceptions. Interventions can be introduced at an appropriate pace and scale and can be embedded and sustained more successfully across groups of teachers in schools and across networks of schools within hubs. In this way, professional learning supports the resetting and co-construction of teacher knowledge and the embedding of evidence-based practice. Professional learning and the educative mentoring process can be seen to contribute to the development of system leadership across the sector.

Bringing about constructive change in pedagogy among established practitioners can be challenging and uncomfortable. We are being asked to question our epistemological beliefs: how do we know what we know and why do we believe that what we do works? Through educative mentoring, we can address these challenges collegially as a part of our professional learning. Using processes such as peer observation and co-constructing a bespoke CLOSCH we can bring about long-term, sustainable change in pedagogical approaches, leading to improved learning outcomes (Task 18.6).

---

### Task 18.6 Developing, deepening, and co-constructing professional knowledge

How can we work collaboratively, collegially, and creatively to reinvigorate our teaching and foster a shared ethos of continuous improvement?

---

Constructive change comes about through iterative reflection and the evaluation of one's own and other colleagues' teaching practice. Criticality is key (Barnett, 1997) and the first step to continuous improvement is made by being aware of essential knowledge and belief systems that can influence decision-making. For continuous improvement to take place there needs to be a shared readiness to explore and challenge robust beliefs about teaching and learning and take account of new research as well as revisiting and engaging with established principles. The role of theory is instrumental in supporting criticality and enabling changes to be made in our conceptual understanding of why particular approaches may be effective in the classroom. However, knowledge of theory in isolation from classroom experience and evidence-based practice is less helpful. Generic theories from cognitive science must be understood within the context of specific subject disciplines if they are to strengthen practice and inform longer-term change.

## Conclusion

In this chapter, we have considered the conditions necessary to bring about a culture of continuous improvement. There are clear professional gains in developing the concept of mentoring as an evolutionary process where both mentor and mentee are beneficiaries and where colleagues at any stage of their career can voluntarily set up peer-to-peer mentoring processes to refresh and improve classroom practice. We have seen that mentorship is neither one-dimensional nor static. The interplay between expert and neophyte is complex, and the mentor-mentee relationship can be asymmetrical where the mentor is more experienced than the mentee in one context with a reversal of roles in another context. Peer and near-peer mentoring among experienced teachers facing new challenges together is an example of this.

Peer-to-peer mentoring across a department or community of practice enables us as a collective to notice, analyse, and evaluate what is working well and less well. Through co-planning and co-construction, we can develop interventions and introduce innovations that we can test in our classrooms supported by our peers in a safe space (EEF, 2018). One of the central purposes of peer observation is to identify critical incidents, analyse what is happening in the learning and why, plan and test out new approaches, and observe their effects (Tripp, 1993). Through the range of mentoring strategies and techniques available to us we can systematise knowledge to create conceptual frameworks that facilitate critical evaluation and support us to adapt teaching practice. Thinking through what we observe enables us to develop and agree evidence-based principled practice to improve learning outcomes. The classroom becomes a knowing, doing and adaptive environment with the mentor becoming the catalyst for change.

## For discussion

Having read this chapter, find here three points to help you develop the mentoring process:

1. Consider with the members of your department, how you evaluate your own practice, learning from what works.
2. How do you ensure equity for all learners by providing consistent high-quality teaching and learning?
3. How can you introduce the peer-to-peer mentoring process to co-construct pedagogy in your department?

## Further reading

- White, E. & Mackintosh, J. (2022). Educative mentoring versus instructional coaching: What approaches enables mentors to support student-teacher learning, 6(1). https://www.herts.ac.uk/link/volume-6,-issue-1,-april-2022/educative-mentoring-versus-instructional-coaching-what-approach-enables-mentors-to-support-student-teacher-learning

In recent years there has been a focus on instructional coaching and a perception of dualism between this and educative mentoring. In this article, White and Mackintosh provide an extensive overview of the two approaches of mentoring. Consider the advantages of both processes, recognising their commonalities and how particular aspects of these processes can complement each other in developing strong and flexible mentorship to suit different contexts.

## References

Bandura, A. (1986). *Social foundations of thought and action: A social cognitive theory*. Prentice-Hall.

Barnett, R. (1997). *Higher education: A critical business*. Open University Press.

Chartered Management Institute. (2018). *Pathways to Management and Leadership Unit 515: Creating and Delivering Operation Plans* [online]. https://www.managers.org.uk/wp-content/uploads/2020/03/L5-Management-Leadership-Syllabus-1.pdf

Chartered Management Institute. (2021). *Pathways to Management and Leadership Level 5 RQF Syllabus*. Version 9 [online]. https://www.managers.org.uk/wp-content/uploads/2020/03/L5-Management-Leadership-Syllabus-1_20210705-11-24-58.pdf

Chartered Management Institute. (2024). *Golden Thread Theory: Aligning Vision, Goals, and Performance in Strategic Management and Planning* [online]. https://www.managers.org.uk/~/media/Files/Qualifications/Level-5-in-Management-and-Leadership/Pathways-Workbook/Unit-515.pdf

Coe, R., Aloisi, C., Higgins, S. & Elliot Major, L (2014). *What makes great teaching?* The Sutton Trust [online]. https://www.suttontrust.com/our-research/great-teaching/

Department for Education. (2019). *Teacher recruitment and retention strategy: Policy paper* [online]. https://www.gov.uk/government/publications/teacher-recruitment-and-retention-strategy

Department for Education. (2020). *National Professional Qualification NPQ Leading Teacher Development* [online]. https://assets.publishing.service.gov.uk/government/uploads/system/uploads/attachment_data/file/925511/NPQ_Leading_Teacher_Development.pdf

Department for Education. (2021). *Initial teacher training (ITT) market review report* [online]. https://www.gov.uk/government/publications/initial-teacher-training-itt-market-review-report

Department for Education. (2022). *Delivering world-class teacher development: Policy paper* [online] https://assets.publishing.service.gov.uk/media/62850bddd3bf7f1f433ae149/Delivering_world_class_teacher_development_policy_paper.pdf

Education Endowment Foundation. (2017). *IRIS Connect: Developing classroom dialogue and feedback through collective video reflection*. Whole Education and Iris Connect [online]. Available at: https://educationendowmentfoundation.org.uk/projects-and-evaluation/projects/iris-connect

Education and Endowment Foundation. (2018). *Putting evidence to work – A school's guide to implementation* [online]. https://educationendowmentfoundation.org.uk/education-evidence/guidance-reports/implementation

Education Endowment Foundation. (2020). *Remote Professional Development* [online]. Available at: https://educationendowmentfoundation.org.uk/education-evidence/evidence-reviews/remote-professional-development

Education Endowment Foundation. (2021). *Teaching and learning toolkit: An accessible summary of education evidence* [online]. https://educationendowmentfoundation.org.uk/education-evidence/teaching-learning-toolkit

Hardman, M., Taylor, B., & Daly, C. (2023). An inquiry into teacher agency and professional development: The introduction of the early career framework in England. In I. Menter (Ed.), *The Palgrave handbook of teacher education research* (Vol. 1, pp. 477–502). Palgrave Macmillan.

Hood, M. (2021). New NPQs mean leadership improvement is in the cards. In: *Schools Week* [online]. https://schoolsweek.co.uk/new-npqs-mean-leadership-improvement-is-in-the-cards/

Inzer, L. D., & Crawford, C. B. (2005). A review of formal and informal mentoring: Processes, problems, and design. *Journal of Leadership Education*, 4(1), 31–50.

Jackson, J. F. L., & Lor, N. (2018). *Annual report, data brief*. Wisconsin's Equity and Inclusion Laboratory. NSF INCLUDES: Consortium of minority doctoral scholars.

Knight, J. (2007). *Instructional coaching: A partnership approach to improving instruction*. Corwin.

Knight, J., & van Nieuwerburgh, C. (2012). Instructional coaching: A focus on practice. *Coaching: An International Journal of Theory, Research and Practice*, 5(2), 100–112.

National Academies of Sciences, Engineering, and Medicine (2019). *The science of effective mentorship in STEMM*. The National Academies Press. https://doi.org/10.17226/25568.

Ofsted (2021). *Research and analysis, Research review series: Languages* [online] https://www.gov.uk/government/publications/curriculum-research-review-series-languages/curriculum-research-review-series-languages

Palombo, M., & Daly, C. (2022). Educative mentoring: A key to professional learning for geography teachers and mentors. In G. Healy, L. Hammond, S. Puttick, & N. Walshe (Eds.), *Mentoring geography teachers in the secondary school: A practical guide* (pp. 208–223). London.

Ryan, R. M., & Deci, E. L. (2000). Self-determination theory and the facilitation of intrinsic motivation, social development, and well-being. *American Psychologist*, 55(1), 68–78.

Sims, S. (2019). Four reasons instructional coaching is currently the best-evidenced form of CPD [online]. https://samsims.education/2019/02/19/247/

Stanulis, R. N., Wexler, L. J., & White, K. (2019). Mentoring as more than "Cheerleading": Looking at educative mentoring practices through Mentors' eyes. *Journal of Teacher Education*, 70(5), 567–580.

The National Academies of Science, Engineering, Medicine (2019). The Science of Effective Mentoring in STEMM [online]. https://nap.nationalacademies.org/catalog/25568/the-science-of-effective-mentorship-in-stemm

Timperley, H., Wilson, A., Barrar, H., & Fung, I. (2007). *Teacher professional learning and development: Best evidence synthesis iteration*. Ministry of Education. http://www.educationcounts.govt.nz/publications/series/2515/15341

Tripp, D. (1993). *Critical incidents in teaching: Developing professional judgement*. Routledge.

White, E. & Mackintosh, J. (2022). Educative mentoring versus instructional coaching: What approaches enables mentors to support student-teacher learning, 6(1). https://www.herts.ac.uk/link/volume-6,-issue-1,-april-2022/educative-mentoring-versus-instructional-coaching-what-approach-enables-mentors-to-support-student-teacher-learning

# APPENDIX 1: MODERN LANGUAGES LESSON OBSERVATION SCHEDULES

The Modern Languages classroom is a highly complex environment which can be difficult to make sense of.

To assist with this, we have created 10 structured lesson observation schedules, together with questions that you could ask the teachers about their practice. We see these observation schedules as valuable tools to help you understand what is going on in the classroom. Observations using these should begin early, rather than spending time engaged in "general observation" without a specific focus – which can be an overwhelming and unproductive experience.

## Lesson outlines

Every lesson has some kind of overall plan, outline, or sequence. A frequent example might involve the following (depending on the length of the lesson):

- an introduction to new language using the interactive whiteboard
- a question-and-answer session
- pair work by pupils
- pupils note down the new language
- the setting of a homework in which pupils will use the new language in written exercises

### *For you to do*

Choose a number of lessons from those you have observed (you will need at least 4) and write out their outlines (see Example 1 below) and sequences of activities, noting the approximate allocation of time to each of the main parts of the lesson. What language skills were involved and in what proportion? If the outlines or sequences were different, can you think of a reason for this? What activities do you think the next lesson might include? What activities might the previous lesson have included? For at least one lesson, make a detailed timeline (see Example 2 below) for the different activities, including the time taken for giving procedural instructions (i.e. explaining to the pupils what they will need to do). Note also what teachers do in order make instructions clear to the pupils (for example, modelling, providing examples, repeating and paraphrasing, and code-switching).

*Example 1*

| Class | Activity | Skills developed | Comments |
|---|---|---|---|
| Year 10 | Oral presentation of a topic 15 minutes | Memorisation; speaking | Pupils lacked confidence; pronunciation OK |
| | Listening to audio file 6 minutes | Listening - ability to pick out certain key phrases | Teacher stopped tape after every question |
| | etc... | | |

*Example 2*

| Time | Activity | Comments |
|---|---|---|
| 9.00 | Class enters, books distributed, lesson objectives | All routine instructions in the target language. Objectives in English. |
| 9.05 | Questions on weekend activities | Teacher nominated pupils, does not wait for hands up. Appears to be a revision of work previously done. |
| 9.10 | Writing activity - matching questions to answers etc... | Pupils working in pairs - allowed to talk quietly. |

## Starting, finishing, and linking the segments

Crucial parts of the lesson are the start of the lesson, the end of the lesson and any point where the nature and focus of the activity changes. Effective management of these parts of a lesson is essential to the smooth-running of the lesson.

*For you to do*

Select two or three different lessons and make notes of the following:

- How does the class enter? How does the teacher deal with latecomers?
- How does the teacher get the attention of the class initially?
- Are the first few minutes of the lesson conducted in the target language?
- If the lesson has a number of distinctive parts, how does the teacher get the class to stop an activity and go on to another ("linking the segments")? Go into detail here - exact words, gestures, tone of voice. Does s/he treat any pupils differently?
- What else is the teacher doing whilst s/he is "linking the segments"? How does this affect the "momentum" of the lesson?
- Are the "working conditions" different for each activity? If so why?
- How is the lesson concluded?

## Detailed observation suggestions

One possible way of collecting evidence:

|  | Examples of words used by teacher | Other things teacher does | Working conditions |
|---|---|---|---|
| Introduction | Bon, aujourd'hui... | Turns on projector, logs on to computer and loads ppt | Pupils silent |
| Link | Maintenant prÈparez le dialogue | Points to board where the parts are exemplified | Pupils mostly silent, a few exchanging a few words |
| Activity | Talking in pairs | Monitors talk but also arranges materials (next activity?) | Orderly rumble of talk |
| Link | etc... | | |
| Activity | | | |
| Link | | | |

## Oral interaction: teacher talk/pupil talk

What, roughly, is the proportion of teacher talk to pupil talk? What sorts of things do teachers and pupils actually say? In many lessons pupils are involved in talking to each other in the target language. To what extent are pair- and groupwork effective teaching strategies?

### For you to do

Ask the teacher permission for you to do these things in advance of the lesson.

- In the 1:30 situation (whole class, teacher up front), estimate the amount of time pupil(s) actually spend talking in the second language (L2). What are the functions of the classroom discourse? Specifically:
    - what sort of talk/language does the L2 teacher talk consist of - e.g. information/explanation/procedural instructions/questioning? What is the proportion roughly of each?
    - what sort of talk/language does the L2 pupil talk consist of - e.g. information, questions, requests, spontaneous remarks? Do learners ever initiate an exchange? What types of mistakes do they make?
    - what is the topic of the discourse?
    - is there any deviation from the intended topic? Why (not)?
- When the class begins to work in pairs or groups try to stand/sit close enough to one or more groups in order to hear what they are saying. Specifically:
    - are they speaking in the L2?
    - are they "on task"?
    - are some pupils dominating others?
    - how structured is the interaction?
    - are the activities differentiated in any way?

- what support is there to enable pupils to remain in the L2?
- what types of mistakes do pupils make?
- what do pupils do in order to "compensate" for language they don't know?
- how are the pupils assessed in relation to their competence in L2 speaking?

### *Detailed observation suggestions*

As well as the above you could:

- Ask two different teachers if you can record them during a lesson each. It would be preferable if these classes were in the same year group.
- Listen to the recordings and every 10 seconds or so try to work out who is speaking (teacher or pupil) and in which language (target language, English, or other)
- Or try to work out the proportions of different "functions of talk": for example, the amount of procedural instructions, grammatical/lexical explanation, questioning, etc.

## Oral interaction: procedural instructions (for setting up activities)

The efficient organisation of activities plays an important part in lessons running smoothly. Clear procedural instructions are vital to ensure that pupils know what they have to do. But are these given in the target language, and if so, how?

### *For you to do*

- What language are the instructions given in? Is there any "code-switching" (changes from one language to another)? If so, what is its nature, how often does it happen, and for what purpose?
- How does the teacher give instructions (e.g. all in one go, in short burst followed by a pupil activity, using body language or mime, accompanied by writing on the board)?
- How does the teacher check that all pupils have understood? Does the teacher treat any pupils differently?
- If the teacher is setting up an oral activity, pretend you are one of the pupils. Are you able to determine precisely what you have to say/do?
- Does the teacher reduce the content of the instructions in any way? Does s/he avoid them altogether? If so how?
- What is the "language content" of these procedural instructions? How is it different from the language associated with the "topic content"? (Think about verbs, nouns, adjectives).

### *Detailed observation suggestions*

Ask a teacher if you can record (at least three) bits of his/her lesson(s) when s/he is providing procedural instructions in the target language. Transcribe these instructions and try to answer some of the above questions in more detail and with firmer evidence.

## Oral interaction: questions and answers

Question and answer in the target language is a technique that many languages teachers employ at some time during most lessons. It is important to develop the very difficult skills which ensure that all pupils are given opportunities to answer without causing embarrassment to more reticent pupils.

### For you to do

You will need to compare at least four different question-and-answer segments in order to be able to answer the following questions.

- Are the teacher's questions closed, limited or open-ended?
- Does the teacher vary the questions according to the pupil s/he is asking?
- How long does the teacher wait for an answer?
- Roughly how long is the average "pupil turn"?
- Are the questions directed at a particular pupil by name or open to the class?
- Are pupils allowed to call out answers?
- For how long (how many times) does the teacher ask the same question?
- How does the teacher deal with different kinds of responses (correct, semi-correct and incorrect)?
- What is the purpose of the teacher's feedback in IRF (Initiation – Response – Feedback) exchanges?
- Are any groups or individuals asked questions more or less frequently than others? If so, why?

### Detailed observation suggestions

This is quite demanding in terms of time but very worthwhile.

- Ask two different teachers if you can record them during two (each) question-and-answer sessions. It would be preferable if these classes were in the same year group – and even better if they were being taught the same topic. However, these are not essential.
- Transcribe the question-and-answer sessions. Then add up the total number of verbs, nouns and adjectives used by the two teachers as opposed to the verbs, nouns and adjectives used by the pupils.
- With a stopwatch try to calculate the average length of a "pupil turn" compared to the average length of a "teacher turn". How many turns are there in all? What is the proportion of teacher turns to pupil turns?

## Oral interaction: classroom language

We define classroom language as "the types of utterances normally only found in the classroom". If pupils are taught to understand and produce such utterances in the target language and are encouraged to use them on a regular basis, this can be one step towards making the classroom a place of genuine, spontaneous oral interaction in the L2.

***For you to do***

Try to observe two or more lessons each with three classes in different year groups. Address the following questions:

- How is classroom language taught? (e.g. when the need arises/posters on walls/simple translation...)
- Does the teacher insist on use of classroom language once it has been taught?
- Does the insistence on its use vary from year to year, from teacher to teacher, from day to day?
- In what (if any) ways is classroom language different from "topic language"?
- Do pupils use classroom language (i.e. interact) with each other? What do they say in the TL?
- What feedback do pupils receive in relation to the classroom language that they use?

***Detailed observation suggestions***

As well as the above:

Make a note of all classroom language used by pupils and teachers over a series of lessons. Try to work out whether, and if so how, pupils are making progress with it. Think about: pronunciation; fluency/confidence/accuracy; the extent to which they are using classroom language to interact in pairs.

## Approaches to reading

Most secondary school pupils are able to draw on their existing (L1) literacy skills to support their learning of the L2, potentially making it much more efficient. For example, reading can be an important vehicle for introducing new language, reinforcing familiar language, and demonstrating language use in context. It can also provide a window into the target language culture and can facilitate access to many other exciting resources (e.g., web pages). However, none of this will be very effective if pupils are not able to "retune" their literacy skills to the second language. For example, they might not be able to "decode" from print to sound very effectively.

***For you to do***

Choose reading tasks used with different year groups (preferably at least one from each of Years 7, 8, 9, and 10). Address the following questions:

- What sorts of texts are pupils asked to read (narrative/informative; single words/longer texts; in book format/online; simplified material/authentic resources)?
- When do the pupils read (is it systematic/integrated, separate scheme, time filler, only from the board, for homework)?
- What is the source of the text (custom-written by the teacher/from a textbook/semi-authentic text/authentic text)?

- Can pupils take reading materials home?
- What are they expected to understand from their reading – and how do they demonstrate this?
- What cultural information are they getting from the texts?
- Do they work alone or in groups? Are the texts or tasks different for different groups or individuals?
- In what ways are the texts "mediated" (made more accessible) by the teacher?
- What strategies are they given for coping with a text on their own?
- What obstacles to reading might the learners be encountering?
- How is the pupil's competence in relation to L2 reading assessed?
- What is the nature of any feedback given (either to individuals or to the class as a whole)?
- How accurately are pupils able to read aloud in the foreign language?

### *Detailed observation suggestions*

As well as the above:

Choose two pupils from one class (preferably Year 9 or 10), based on the reading scores from their teacher's mark book (i.e. one high, one low). Ask them if they would agree to take part in a think-aloud task on a written text (which you should select after consulting the teacher). Ask your tutor how to go about doing a think-aloud task with a pupil. (This will also be covered in the curriculum sessions on reading). Ideally you should audio-record the pupils, which may require parental permission (check this with your mentor). Analyse the thought processes that they report in terms of some of the questions above: for example, what strategies do they use to cope with unfamiliar language? How accurately are they able to read the printed words aloud?

## Approaches to listening (to audio and video material)

Listening is often considered a difficult skill to develop, because of the fleeting nature of the spoken word. Most teachers expose learners to quite a lot of listening texts, but it is often claimed that these are used mainly to assess pupils' listening proficiency, rather than to help them develop their listening proficiency.

### *For you to do*

Choose several listening tasks from different year groups (preferably at least one from each of Years 7, 8, 9, and 10).

- Where in the sequence of activities does the listening task take place?
- Does the teacher involve the learners in any "pre-listening" activities or discussions?
- How is the text presented the first time – all at once or broken up? Why?
- How many times does the teacher play the audio file?
- Do the learners have any say in the number of repetitions or in when the audio file is paused?

- Are pupils allowed to interrupt if they have not understood?
- What do the learners actually have to do whilst they are listening?
- Do you notice any pupils getting frustrated and/or giving up?
- How is the pupil's competence in relation to reading skills assessed?
- What is the nature of any feedback given (either to individuals or to the class as a whole)?
- To what extent does the listening task help to develop pupils listening proficiency? In what ways?
- How "authentic" is the listening text?
- Is listening ever set for homework?

### Detailed observation suggestions

As well as the above:

Interview all the teachers in the department about their approaches to listening (e.g. using modified versions of some of the questions above or using additional questions of your own devising). Try to get them to make explicit their thinking behind why they favour one approach over another. Compare the teachers' answers to what you observe in their lessons.

    and/or

Make a detailed study of two or three Y11 or sixth form pupils and the ways they approach listening. Provide them with a suitable listening task (or use one which the teacher has given them). Tell them that they can pause and rewind the recording at any point and as often as they wish. Observe the way they go about the task: for example, do they keep stopping at every word they don't understand? Do they listen all the way through first? Do they/can they use a dictionary? You could also get them to do the task in pairs and listen to their discussions as they try to comprehend the text.

## Pupil writing

Written work is often used as a way of recording new language and of practising language that has just been introduced in controlled ways, with an emphasis on accuracy. But how often do pupils have the opportunity to undertake more creative, "free writing" tasks in which the emphasis is on expressing themselves? To what extent do the writing tasks they are set help them to develop their proficiency in l2 writing?

### For you to do

- Make a note of what teachers ask pupils in different year groups to write: for example, vocabulary lists; grammar notes; examples of particular constructions; responses to listening and reading comprehension tasks; drill-type exercises; authentic communicative activities.
- To what extent are pupils free to write what they want?
- Are the writing tasks differentiated in any way?
- Is everything in the notebooks or folders in the target language or is English allowed?
- Do pupils have rough books or scrap paper? If so for what activities?

- Where else is there evidence of pupil writing (e.g., vocabulary books, grammar books)?
- Is the teacher making pupils aware of the correspondences between letters and sounds in the L2? If so, how? If not, why not?
- What kinds of mistakes do pupils make?
- How do teachers react to mistakes when marking pupils' written work? Are all mistakes identified or only some? Does s/he provide the correct form or merely underline?
- What is the purpose of the teacher's feedback?
- What are pupils expected to do with the mistakes they have made?
- To what extent are pupils helped to develop their ability to express themselves creatively in the L2 (for example, by using strategies to cope with unknown language)?

### *Detailed observation suggestions*

As well as the above:

Select nine pupils from a class (preferably Year 8 or 9) who have quite a bit of writing in their books from last year. In consultation with the teacher, identify three more successful L2 writers, three who are less successful and three in the middle. Try to determine how, through the evidence of their writing, they are progressing. For example, is there any increase in accuracy and/or complexity? What mistakes which they were making early on have now disappeared? What evidence is there of dictionary use? Are they translating word for word? What evidence is there that they have internalised aspects of the rule system? How does the teacher provide feedback on their progress and (how) do they respond to this? Is there evidence of improvement in the areas on which the teacher has focussed in her/his feedback?

## Homework

Two or three hours a week in class is very little time in which to learn a language! Homework provides an opportunity for learners to extend their language learning outside the classroom. The internet now provides unprecedented opportunities to practise the language and to encounter authentic L2 resources at home. However, the teacher needs to think carefully about how to set up homework tasks, to ensure that learners are able to access them and get the most out of them in the absence of support from the teacher.

### *For you to do*

Examine as many different types of homework as you can in as many different year groups as you can.

- What type of homework is given mostly? Is it speaking, listening, reading, writing, vocabulary learning?
- How long (on average) should the homework take to do in each year? In your view, is this the right amount, or too much/too little? Why do you think this?
- Does the homework follow on from the lesson or is there a separate programme?
- How are instructions given for homework and in what language?

- In what way are learners encouraged to be (and feel) autonomous when they do their homework?
- How is the homework followed up? How is the homework product recorded?
- How do learners react to the homework? To what extent do they feel that homework tasks are accessible and valuable for their language learning? What barriers do they report when completing the homework tasks?
- To what extent do learners actually complete the homework set? What sanctions are imposed if they do not?

### *Detailed observation suggestions*

As well as the above:

Compare, if you can, the homework diaries of three different classes with regard to MFL. What is the "diet" of homework that they receive? What is the balance between the four skills? What evidence is there that they have understood what they were expected to do? What is the quality of the work produced for homework and how does it relate to the work produced in class by the same pupils?

*and/or*

Identify a sample of pupils containing a mixture of high, low, and middle attainers. Talk to them (individually or in small groups) about their experiences of recent homework tasks in MFL. What did they see as the purposes of the homework tasks? To what extent did they find them valuable for language learning? What barriers (if any) did they experience when completing the tasks? What sources of support did they draw on (e.g., websites, on-line dictionaries, parents, siblings ...)?

# APPENDIX 2: PROFORMA STRUCTURE FOR INTERACTIONS

1. Reflection Before Action

    - Email/discuss with ECT the focus for the upcoming meeting. Consider:
        - Identifying where the identified focus links with **SCRIPTS**. Aim to ensure that the focus remains languages-specific. There might be a pastoral issue to discuss and unpick as well: be guided by your ECT but remember you are likely the only source of subject specific formalised support.
        - Linking the focus with the relevant framework (e.g. ECF) *now* to avoid lengthy and panicked cross-referencing of the portfolio at the end of the year.
        - Suggesting some academic/published reading/articles/practitioner blogs to develop their understanding of the theory behind the focus.
        - Asking the ECT to choose a recent linked 'critical incident' in their classroom which they would like to explore further.
        - Asking the ECT to articulate their answers to the 'preparation' element of the reflective model.

2. Reflection In Action

    - 10 minutes or so looking at one specific 'critical incident' through the lens of the reflective model:
        - What happened in the moment?
        - How did you react?
        - What other things need to be considered?
        - How does your experience compare with your reading?

3. Reflection On Action

    - Spend longer here exploring themes and applying them to the ECT's next steps. Think about the specific 'critical incident' through a practitioner lens. Future application is key to this section.
        - Why did it happen like that?
        - What does your description (In Action) demonstrate about your feelings/role?
        - Which elements of **SCRIPTS** does this relate to and how?

- What does this mean for the future? If you could repeat this situation, where would you want to have more confidence?
- How would you compare this reflection on your experience to your wider reading?
- What more general themes have emerged from this incident? Again, use **SCRIPTS** to inform your discussion.
- What strengths and improvements can be celebrated? What needs further work?
- Which concrete, measurable steps could be taken? (e.g. further reading/CPD/informal chat/external support, etc.) Aim to make these targets SMART (Specific, Measurable, Achievable, Relevant, Timely).
- Have you cross-referenced these experiences with the ECF for consistency evidence?
- How does this fit with the ECT's broader career development aspirations?

# APPENDIX 3: POSSIBLE RESPONSES TO SCENARIOS IN TASK 17.5

| Scenario | Response as mentor | Response as coach | Response as critical friend |
|---|---|---|---|
| 1. Reluctance to create resources for sharing. | Add a discussion of wider roles and responsibilities as an agenda item to your regular meeting. | Initiate a conversation to find out reasons for reluctance. | Share an example of similar work you and your colleagues have done and emphasise its value. |
| 2. Use of Target Language becoming a barrier. | Arrange observations with a selection of colleagues, focusing on their use of TL. | Encourage the use of a "script" to promote familiar phrases and avoid overloading pupils. | Invite ECT to plan a lesson jointly, including planning for TL use. |
| 3. Over ambitious plans for a trip. | Insist on a change in timescale so that the trip will run in the following academic year. | Work together to create a list of "jobs" which will need to be done and by what date. | Introduce the ECT to longer standing members of the school staff who have run trips in the past and can advise. |
| 4. Working in isolation. | Give an overt invitation to the ECT to spend more time in the department office. | Initiate a conversation to establish which areas of professional life the ECT is finding challenging. Discuss strategies and decide when you are going to review effectiveness. | Suggest identifying one day a week as a "plate sharing" lunchtime where colleagues can swap ideas – for food and for teaching! |

# INDEX

*Note*: **Bold** indicates tables and *italics* indicates figures in the text and page numbers followed by "n" refer to endnotes.

accountability 19, 22, 103, 137, 145, 203, 208, 211–214, 218
adult learning theory 142–144
advice monster concept 148
Ager, E. O. 129
andragogy 142–143
areas of research 187, *188*
Association for Language Learning (ALL) 58, 69–72
Association of Coaching (AC) 139

Bandura, A. 230
Beauchamp, C. 103
Beckett, H. 129
Beck, J. S. 107
beginning teachers 45, 101; actions and behaviours 131; critical reasoning 105–106; development 102–105, 110–111, *111*, 132; experts setting 84–85; importance and challenges of 78–79; inquiry-based approach 110; lesson observation schedules 80–83; mentoring strategies 101–102, **102**; observation success 79–80; planning process 89; post-observation questioning 83–84; sources of knowledge 106–109; targeted support 109; *see also* observation and feedback to beginning teacher
behaviour management 201
Berne, E. 140
Best Evidence Synthesis (BES) Iteration 228
Black, L. 202
Blair, T. 203–204

Borg, S. 17–19, 48
Bown, R. 196–206
Broom, K. 167–177
Bruner, J. S., Spiral Curriculum 56
Buck, A. 127, 131–132
Buehl, M. M. 107
Bullock, S. M. 78
Byram, M. 61

career development 215–216
Chartered Management Institute (CMI) 226–227
checklists and mentoring standards 35–36
Clarke, D. 11
Claro, J. 155–165, 167–177
classroom language 243–244
classroom practice: barriers 182–183; engagement facilitation 183–193; research knowledge 181–182
Claxton, G., *What's the Point of School?* 198
clinical reasoning 4, 33, 104–105
Clutterbuck, D. 126
coaching: adult learning theories 142–144; applications and techniques 147–148; challenges and solutions 144–145; mentoring relationship 145–147; mentorship 141–142; mindsets 138–139; in modern languages mentoring relationships 140–141
Cochran-Smith, M. 33
Cohen, S. 77–85
collaborative lesson observation schedule (CLOSCH) 234–235
collaborative self-development 7–8, 23, 32

communities of practices (CoPs) 69-71
Conlon, C. 53-61, 225-236
contact parents/carer 199-200
content knowledge 55
contextual factors 19
contingency knowledge 103
contract/contracting 140
Cordingley, P. 12
core content framework (CCF) 14, 125, 182-183, 185
craft knowledge 9, 108
Crawford, C. B. 231
Crutcher, P. A. 24
Cundick, E. 208-223
curriculum knowledge 55
Curtis, E. 8

Dawes, L. 35
Deci, E. L., *Self-Determination Theory* 37
Decolonising Secondary Languages 70
deliberate botheredness concept 201
Department for Education (DfE) 225-226
destination 58
developed mentoring 34, 40, 103
developmental model (DM) 116, **116**
Dewey, J. 103
disciplined empirical/philosophical enquiry 56
Dixon, L. 125-134
Dix, P. 201

early career framework (ECF) 138, 210-211, 217, 220-221
early career teachers (ECTs) 46, 208, **209**; accountability 211-214; adaptive feedbacks 210-211; career aspirations of 215-216; potential pressures 212, *212*; professional challenges 213, **213**; reflective model 218-222; scenarios 221-222, 251; SCRIPTS framework 217-218, 222; work/life balance 214
Education Endowment Foundation (EEF) 186, 225, 227
Eisenhower Matrix 214, *215*
emerging teachers, principled practice for 56-60
England, policies for mentoring 13-14
English-as-a-foreign-language (EFL) 188
English Department for Education's (2024) framework 20

epistemological beliefs and values 55-56
evaluation model (EM) 116, **116**
evidence-informed approach 59
experienced teachers: golden thread theory 226-229; peer mentoring model 229-232; professional knowledge 232-235; professional learning and system-leadership 225-226
explicit knowledge 219

feedforward 210, **210**
Fisher, A. 208-223
Fraser, P. 157

Gallwey, W. T. 144-145, 149
Gardner, R. 30
general pedagogical knowledge 55
golden thread theory 226-229
Gordon, A. L. 3-14, 58, 155-165
Gosling, D. 116, **116**, 117
Graham, S. 181-193
Graydin approach 138
Gregory, K. 45-51

Hagger, H. 9, 40, 108
Hamilton, L. 125-134
Harrison, J. 83
Hascher, T. 115
Hazell, C. 64-72
Heen, S. 146
Hickman, D. 196, 198
Hobson, A. J. 20, 36, 50, 115
Hodkinson, H. 25
Hodkinson, P. 25
Hollingsworth, H. 11
Holmes, B. 53-61, 225-236
homework 82-83, 247-248
hooks, bell, power of definitions 57
Howard, K. B. 198
Hudson, P. 198, 201, 203-204
human mentoring, principles for 38

individual identity 107
induction frameworks 138-139
initial teacher education (ITE) 8, 34-35, 37, 41n1, 46-47, 49-50, 78, 89, 91, 95, 105, 107-108, 121, 155-158, 161-164, 176, 182, 185, 191, 193, 208, 218

initial teacher training (ITT) 41n1, 45, 66, 102, 115, 125–126
Initial Teacher Training and Early Career Framework (ITTECF) 14, 53–54, 138
Initial Teacher Training (ITT) Mentor Standard 45
inquiry-based approach 110
instructional coaching (IC) 9–10, 138, 232–233
interaction structure 249–250
International Coaching Federation (ICF) 139

Jaspers, W. M. 22
Javaid, C. 137–149
job motivation 20–21
Jones, M. 21
judgementoring 20, 36

Karpman's drama triangle 139
Kelchtermans, G. 19–21
Kemmis, S. 7, 24, 32
Kennedy, M. 65
Knight, F. 114–122
Knight, J. 9–10, 233
Knight's Instructional Coaching 138
knowledge: of educational aims, purposes, and values 55; of educational contexts 55; knowledge-*for*-practice 33; knowledge-*in*-practice 33; knowledge-*of*-practice 33; of learners and their characteristics 55
Knowles, M. S. 142–143
Koglbauer, R. 69, 71–72
Krashen, S. 25
Kriewaldt, J. 33, 104

Lamb, A. 167–177
Lamb, T. 69
Language Show online seminar 162
languages teaching, distinctiveness of 29–30
language teacher cognition model 17–19
Latimer, T. 140
Lave, J. 69
learning in partnership model 34
lesson plan proforma **93**, 93–94
listening approach 82, 245–246
Lock, R. 117
Lortie, D. 170
Lytle, S. L. 33

Macaro, E. 190
MacDonald, M. 183
Mackintosh, J. 233
Madden, L. 125–134
Malderez, A. 20, 36, 50
Mann, S. 110
Marland, M., *How to be a successful form tutor* 201–202
McIntyre, D. 8–9, 40, 104, 108
McNamara, O. 23
medium-term planning 95, **95**
meeting: first 47–48; needs and support 48–49
Menter, I. 182
mentor/mentoring/coaching: concept 6–7; contexts 33–35; relationship 145–147; role of 31–33; scenarios 30–31; styles 23–24; types of 32, **32**
Mezirow, J. 142–143
Michel Thomas Method 146
minimal mentoring 40
ML teachers 78
Modern Foreign Languages Pedagogy Review 56–57, 66–67
Molway, L. 3–14, 59
moral/ethical reasoning 60
Munro, C. 137
Murphy, V. 185–186
Murray, J. 23
Murtagh, L. 35
Mutton, T. 29–40, 101–112

Naseem, S. 24
NASEM Consensus Report 230–231
National Consortium for Languages Education (NCLE) 71, 234
National Mentoring Standards 125
National Professional Qualifications (NPQs) 225–227
National Standards for school-based initial teacher training mentors **13**
New Zealand study 228, 233
Niemiec, C. P. 37
no blame culture 50
non-judgemental questioning 83

Oancea, A. 101
observation and feedback to beginning teacher 114–117; Gosling's models 116, **116**, 117; practical

advice 117-118; value of 115; written feedback 118-122, **121**
Office for Standards in Education, Children's Services and Skills (OFSTED) 163, 199, 201
ONSIDE mentoring framework 50
oral interaction 81-82
Orchard, J. 101
Organisation for Economic Co-operation and Development (OECD) 197
Orland-Barak, L. 33

Panford, L. 167-177
pedagogical content knowledge (PCK) 55
peer and near-peer mentoring 232-233
peer mentoring model 229-232
peer review model (PRM) 116, **116**
peer-to-peer mentoring 229-230, 232-236
Peiser, G. 17-25
personality 23-24
personal, social, health, and economic (PSHE) 202
Pinnick, S. 50-51
planning process 87-89; beginning teachers to 89; challenges and purpose 90-92; lesson plan proforma **93**, 93-94; medium term 95, **95**; in modern languages 89-90; plan cycle 96, 96-97
Porto, Melina 61
positive relationships 168-169
post-observation questioning 83-84
practical experience 60
practical theorising 8, 104
pre- and post-lesson discussions 126-129, **128**, *130*, 133; questions and comments **133-134**
preparation period 46-47
principles-based approach 38-39
procedural instructions 242
professional coursework 18
Professional Development Consortium 183-184, 190
professional knowledge 33
professional learning: opportunities 58-59, **59**; and system-leadership 225-226
professional/professionalism 196-197; behaviour management 201; contacting home 199-200; languages teachers' roles 197-198; mentoring program survey 204-205; personal and professional conduct 205; relationships 202-204; resilience-building 204; standard English 198-199; tutor role 201-202; UK education system 197; wider life and ethos of school 199
pupil writing 82, 246-247
Puttick, S. 118, 122

qualified teacher status (QTS) 208
Quiney, A. 139

reading approach 82, 244-245
Reeves, D. 96
reflective practitioner 103
resilience-building 204
Rifeser, J. 53-61, 225-236
Roberts-Crystal, S. 167-177
Rogers, R., *How to be a successful form tutor* 201-202
Rowland, T. 103
Ryan, R. M., *Self-Determination Theory* 37

scenarios, range of: overconfidence 173-174; poor organisation 172-173; positive relationships 168-169; school adjustment 169-171; subject knowledge 175-177; UK education system 171-172
Schön, D. A., reflective model 103, *218*, 219-220, *220*, 223
school adjustment 169-171
school-centred initial teacher training (SCITT) 159
schooling concept 18
SCRIPTS framework 208, 217-218, 221-222, 249-250
Secondary Teachers of ALL (STALL) 70
second/foreign language (L2) 3, 5n1
second language acquisition (SLA) 106-107
second order knowledge 23-24
self-efficacy 58, 184, 186-187, *187*, 191, 193, 230
self-image 20
self-regulated learning 144
self-understanding 20-21
Shulman, L. S., *Those who understand* 55-56, 60
Shute, V. 116, 119
Smalley, P. 202-203
SMART (specific, measurable, achievable, realistic, and timed) 160
Social Cognitive Career Theory (SCCT) 230

social cognitive theory 230
special educational needs and disability (SEND) team 160, 199
Stanier, M. B. 147-148
Starr, J., *The mentoring manual* 144-145
STEMM (Science, Technology, Engineering, Maths, and Medicine) 229-230
Stone, D. 146
subjective educational theory 21
subject knowledge 67, 175-177
supervision 8-9, 23, 32
support, mentor 7, 23, 32
Sweller, J. 65

tacit knowledge 219-220
task perception 21
teacher knowledge(s) 53-55, **54**
teacher learning, stages of 11-12
Teachers' Standards 35, 156, 196, 205
teacher talk/pupil talk 241-242
teacher well-being 156-158; additional support 164; administrative management 163-164; challenges and protective factors 158-159; components of 157; defined 155; experienced mentor 159; lesson planning 161-162; marking and feedback 163; reflective and pro-active approach 157; responsibility of mentor 160-161; workload management 161
teaching as reflective practice model 34
theoretical knowledge 106-107
third space 24-25

Thompson, S. 156
Thornton, E. 208-223
three-point communication 129
traditional model 34
transformational learning model 143
transformative learning theory 142
Trevethan, H. 34
Turnidge, D. 33, 104
tutor role 201-202

UK education system 171-172, 197

van Nieuwerburgh, C. 9, 233
Vauzour, S. 87-98
Viac, C. 157

Walsh, S. 110
Wang, H. 164
Waret, M. 167-177
ways of working 174, **175**
Wenger, E. 69
West, C. 139
White, E. 233
Winch, C. 101
Woore, R. 29-40
written feedback 118-122, **121**
Wyatt, M. 129
Wynn, J. 118, 122

Zimmerman, B. J. 142, 144

For Product Safety Concerns and Information please contact our EU
representative GPSR@taylorandfrancis.com
Taylor & Francis Verlag GmbH, Kaufingerstraße 24, 80331 München, Germany

www.ingramcontent.com/pod-product-compliance
Lightning Source LLC
Chambersburg PA
CBHW080612230426
43664CB00019B/2866